SATAN SUPERSTAR

The Reprobate presents
SATAN SUPERSTAR

First edition - April 2018.

The Reprobate Press
http://reprobatemagazine.uk
Email: reprobatemagazine@gmail.com

Twitter: reprobatemag
Facebook: reprobatemagazine
Instagram: reprobatemagazine

Edited and designed by David Flint.

Satan Superstar: A Personal View compiled and edited by Billy Chainsaw.

Front cover: The Witch. Photo: Ilya Falchevsky. Model Sammm Agnew
Back Cover / Frontispiece: Satan by Billy Chainsaw

ISBN: 978-0-9955719-2-1 (print edition)
ISBN: 978-0-9955719-3-8 (digital edition)

Limited edition of 666 physical copies.

* = satanic panic relevant

CONTENTS

COME TO THE SABBAT

AN INTRODUCTION TO SATAN SUPERSTAR

DAVID FLINT

I was born into the age of Satan. Just four months before I emerged from the womb, Anton LaVey spawned the Church of Satan, and more than any generation before – or possibly since – I was surrounded by the occult, black magic, Satanism and witchcraft growing up. Not, of course, in the literal sense – I wasn't one of the mythical children caught in mythical Ritual Satanic Abuse rings. My mother was a typical Church of England type, not a church goer but determined that I should have the religious upbringing of a CoE school (which meant Bible stories in the morning, dinosaur stories in the afternoon and no explanation of the discrepancies therein). My father was a lapsed Catholic – something that I only discovered in my thirties, and which suddenly made sense of an elderly relative's trips to see the Pope. Until then, I'd just assumed that she just went on holiday to Rome and that the Pope was simply another tourist attraction.

As a pre-teen, I was tricked into joining the cub scouts, which meant more tedious trips to church than my religious school ever required (and, more importantly, forced me to miss the Christopher Lee **Fu Manchu** films on TV, which proved to be the final straw for my membership of that dreadful organisation), and for reasons unknown, my mother once took me to a Sunday School class – my determination to hate every second of it enough to cause a family row and ensure that I was never taken again. But that was the extent of our family's religious observance. In general, the Christian religion in my upbringing was of a rather woolly, non-committal style that never really impacted on my life.

But if Christ was a distant figure generally restricted – even in school – to religious education classes and morning prayers that made little sense to a young boy, then Satan was *everywhere* in the 1970s, and to a kid obsessed with horror films and comic books, he loomed large in my consciousness. Tales of the fires and brimstones of Hell meant little to me beyond the exciting imagery of the horror movie, and the Satan of the 1970s always seemed a rather avuncular, dapper chap who was much more fun that his opponents. While religious people were dull, worthy, angry and moralising, Satan seemed much more open to a good time. If I learned anything from the covers of Dennis Wheatley novels, 'non-fiction' books about witchcraft, surreptitiously read newspaper stories and horror comics, it was that Satanists and witches – an interchangeable bunch according to popular culture and the tabloid press even now – were into dancing naked, holding wild orgies and being granted their every desire. They probably wouldn't have a problem with me reading **Monster Mag** (with its pesky 'adults only' proviso on the front cover after an early run-in with the authorities) or Marvel comics or watching Hammer films on TV. They seemed urbane, cultured, charming and laid back, and their parties looked fantastic. The Christians I encountered, either directly or through the media, were none of those things. They were stuffy, judgemental and old-fashioned. The sort of people who would cane kids who stepped out of line and ran their primary school classes like it was still the Victorian age, who appeared on TV railing against everything modern and progressive (even as a pre-teen, I had an awareness that 'the permissive society' that Mary Whitehouse and her morally upstanding Festival of Light chums like Lord Longford, Cliff Richard and Jimmy Savile raged about probably included all the things I loved) and who seemed like the very worst sort of authority figure.

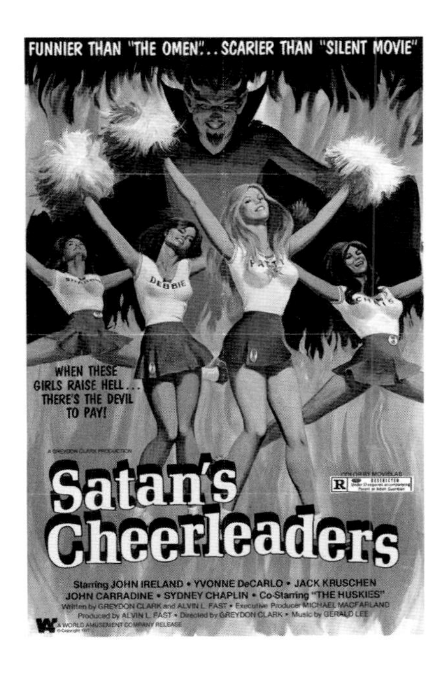

My cultural references were awash with the occult. The British censors, who had kept a firm eye on references to black magic and the like until the late 1960s, had loosened up just in time for films like **Rosemary's Baby**, **The Exorcist** and **The Omen** to usher in a decade of occult cinema, and while I was too young to see most of these films, it was impossible to avoid them. I have vivid memories of being thrilled by the teasing advertising for **The Omen** in local cinemas, and reading hysterical media reports about the malign influence of **The Exorcist**. In a decade when books and magazines seemed to be sold everywhere - from WH Smiths to Boots to local newsagents and seaside resort novelty shops - the work of Wheatley and magazines about witchcraft and occultism sat side by side with imported monster magazines and sexy cartoon mag **Funny Half Hour**, often in those revolving racks that always had the promise of something very exciting just one turn away. Typically, these books and magazines would feature topless women and salacious situations, guaranteed to grab the attention of any adolescent. Similarly, tabloid newspapers, keen for any excuse to show bare flesh and still twenty years away from the Satanic Panic, ran salacious features on witch cults and devil worshippers like Anton La Vey and Alex Sanders, who always seemed to be surrounded by naked women. Kids who might not have given a hoot about black magic or the serious nature of witchcraft and paganism were invariably pulled in by the bare breasts and the sense of the forbidden. Certainly, growing up, the occult was inextricably linked with sex in my mind. The religion we were force-fed in school, on the other hand, preached nothing but shame and punishment, from Adam and Eve to Noah's Ark. In a world where naked women appeared on the covers of books, magazines and records – not to mention in advertising and inside every tabloid – this prudish attitude to the human body seemed very old fashioned. The Satanists seemed a lot more with it.

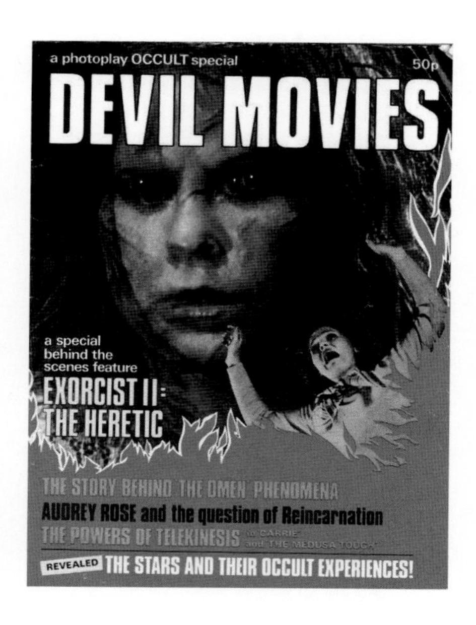

And when the Devil wasn't stirring the loins, he was tickling the funny bone. **Casper the Friendly Ghost**'s slightly naughtier pal **Hot Stuff** was a trident-wielding, horned Little Devil from 1957 onwards, while comical demonic characters regularly popped up in kids' TV shows and comic books. By the end of the 1980s, the Satanic influence of children's entertainment was being discussed in earnest documentaries and best selling books, but for now, the occult was often seen as a harmless diversion for kids.

As I got older, horror films on TV began to feature Satanism and occultism more explicitly as a subject matter (I was banned from seeing the TV broadcast of **Rosemary's Baby**, though less because of the occult content than the fact that my mother had decided that Roman Polanski was not the sort of person who's work she approved of), and once I discovered the joys of rock music, the Satanic was never far away. Be it those 'Knights in Satan's Service' complete with a fire breathing, blood spitting demon, Iron Maiden and the **Number of the Beast**, Black Sabbath selling their soul for rock 'n' roll or assorted emerging acts and also rans, from Venom to Witchfinder General – a band notable mainly for causing

tabloid and feminist outrage with their album cover shoot that featured Page 3 girl Joanne Latham posing topless and blood-stained in a church graveyard – you could hardly be a metal fan in the early 1980s without being immersed in Satanic imagery and lyrics. Home video opened up a world of films that were unlikely to turn up on TV – from **The Exorcist** and assorted Italian copycat films to more lurid fare like Jess Franco's sexy witchfinder film **The Demons**.

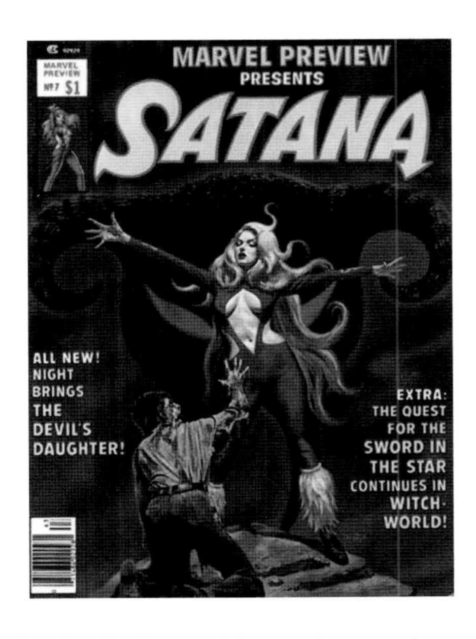

But this was the time when a new Christian fundamentalism was emerging into the mainstream of politics and culture, and the happy-go-lucky world of Satanic pop culture was about to come crashing to a halt. The fretting about backwards masking on records, **Dungeons and Dragons**, Video Nasties, Satanic Saturday morning cartoons and youth cults – be they metallers, goths or punks – who dressed in black and looked a bit sinister paved the way for the Satanic Panic that took hold during the 1980s, as culture in general became more censorial and more fearful. Satan was no longer a fun kinda guy – now, we were entering a nightmare world of Satanic Ritual Abuse, with its brood mares, baby murder, cannibalism, child rape and underground rings of satanic worshippers who could be anyone – the more powerful and respectable the better.

This hysteria was part of a growing moral backlash that also saw fears about Video Nasties, pornography and the dangers of nonconformity spreading across the political divide - in the 1980s, as now, the left and the right might have seemed a universe apart from each other, but both sides of the political divide like to think that they know what is best for us - and that is rarely free expression, sexual liberation, erotic entertainment, violent cinema or the occult. We go to press at a time when individual freedom is under threat as never before from fundamentalists of all stripes, and the spectre of Satanic Ritual Abuse - far from being banished by the wealth of evidence proving it to be a myth - is still believed in by the more fanatical extremes to be found lurking on the internet, where false accusations are thrown out with abandon, and where accusation all too often equals guilt in the eyes of social media followers.

But social media has also allowed the Satanists, the witches and the followers of more esoteric religions to have a more public face than ever before, and to fight back against the accusations and misbelief that have dogged them for years. The Church of Satan's Twitter feed is a joyful stream of put-downs, corrections and snarky replies to Christian critics. The Satanic Temple's attention-grabbing lawsuits and religious equality battles

have forced Satanism into the public eye like never before. With their battles for abortion rights, the Temple has had the sort of positive press that might have been unimaginable twenty years ago. The Satanists were actually being seen as the good guys in a religious battle. Whoever would've expected *that*?

There is, of course, still controversy among Satanic groups over who is or isn't the authentic voice of Satanism. I should say, here and now, that we're not taking sides in this book. There are representatives from various groups included here, as well as former Satanists, occult agnostics and outside observers who find the whole thing rather silly. None of the **Reprobate** editorial team are members of any Satanic group, though we sympathise with and relate to many of their (sometimes disparate) beliefs. We're not here to suggest that Satanism, witchcraft or occultism are either positive or negative forces – we assume that you are smart enough to make your own minds up. But we are unapologetic for pointing out persecution, hysteria and malicious behaviour by religious groups and individuals -which doesn't mean that we're setting out to offend anyone – we acknowledge that all religions are broad churches, with both the good and the bad within. Bearing that in mind, we've also covered the darker side of occultism, which has certainly had its share of bad eggs.

But we have to say that in the production of this book, we've met some genuinely lovely people who are following the (ahem) 'left hand path'. And I very much doubt that we are done with this subject – there is still so much that we haven't been able to cover, and as the Reprobate Library grows, we hope that we can return to this subject again. Nevertheless, though, we hope that you'll find **Satan Superstar** an entertaining snapshot of pop occulture, past and present, and – be you a hardened expert or a curious dabbler – find things here that are new and exciting.

David Flint
March 2018

WITCHCRAFT

The shocking truth!
The weird world of
UNSPEAKABLE CULTS
OBSCENE RITUALS
EROTIC RITES
as it exists today in cities and suburbs of our civilized world!

SEE: Actual Human Sacrifice on The Bloodstained Altar of Baal!

SEE: Weird Demonic Rites of the Cult of Kali!

SEE: Erotic Prayers to the Goddess of the Cloven Hoof!

SEE: Macabre Orgies of a Secret Sect of Evil!

SEE: The Church of Satan celebrate its infamous Black Mass!

SEE: Occult Manifestations in The Coven of the Dead!

SEE: The Sensual Ecstasies of Hippie "Families"!

EXPOSED thru the eye of the HIDDEN CAMERA!

A **P.A.C.-CARAVEL** PRODUCTION

Witchcraft '70

COLOR BY MOVIELAB

DIRECTED BY LUIGI SCATTINI • ADDITIONAL SEQUENCES PHOTOGRAPHED and DIRECTED BY R.L. FROST • A TRANS AMERICAN RELEASE

70/144

SATAN CALLING...

NIGEL WINGROVE

The Sixties and Seventies are synonymous with Peace and Love, hippies, miniskirts, protest, punk and excess, as well as - more recently - the perverse antics of lecherous bygone celebrities. Yet at the centre of this volatile cauldron was the great Satan, whose devilish machinations can be found influencing everything from wife-swapping suburban couples in Sussex to the flower children of San Francisco.

As the angry young men of the 1950s mellowed and began giving way to the radical rage and creative chaos of the 1960s and 1970s, it started a process that would change everything from the length of women's skirts and men's hair, to the way we lived, who we slept with, the laws that governed us, and the religions and beliefs many of us chose to follow. Nothing, in fact, would ever be the same again.

In just a few years, values and rules that had held sway for centuries were suddenly challenged, or attacked, or mocked, and in turn those being attacked and challenged fought back. The established order - from the Monarchy, Parliament and the Church down - at first reeled, and then struck back and in doing so unleashed a counter-revolution and counterculture that embraced everything from 'free love' to revolution. This desire for radicalism in turn created in many a seething hatred of the 'Establishment' - in particular, the Christian church, which for many represented, in the UK the Tory party at prayer and in the US, the Bible belt and the forces of reaction, racism and resistance to change. As such Christianity was anathema and represented not goodness and tolerance, but intolerance and bigotry.

As a consequence, the counterculture sought out alternative Gods, and new or older ways of making peace with ourselves and the wider world. Some found their answers in Buddhism; some in the Age of Aquarius inspired beliefs of New Agism; some in Paganism and Wicca. Some spurned religion altogether and looked to politics, nature and themselves for salvation. Others, though, spurned the niceties of these newly embraced beliefs and turned instead not to the light but to the darkness and embraced not God, but Satan...

There was now a huge upsurge in interest both in the occult as a lifestyle pursuit, and in the absorption of the occult, witchcraft, and Satanism into mainstream society. Driving this infatuation with the Devil was a mixture of influential individuals, writers, artists and bands within both the counterculture and mainstream commercial media.

By the mid-Sixties, the English occultist and Wiccan High Priest, Alex Sanders, claimed to have initiated some 1600 hundred witches across 100 covens and was proclaimed 'King of the Witches'. Sanders' habit of throwing wild parties and of being photographed at rituals wearing nothing but robes and a loin cloth while surrounded by naked women may also have contributed to the growing popularity of forming covens in suburbia. Certainly colourful occult practitioners like Sanders gave the tabloid press plenty of material and this culminated in the publication of **King of the Witches** (1969) and the film, **Legend of the Witches** (1970) both of which not only furthered a growing interest in witchcraft, but an association of witchcraft with sex, and often sex without restraint or the need for relationships which was perfect for the emerging free love generation.

The occult was now seen as creative, cool and sexy. New TV shows like **Bewitched** had softened the notion of witchcraft and rebranded it as an aid to domestic bliss, while cinema was unleashing one devilish epic after another and publishing was unleashing a whole slew of occult related books onto a seemingly insatiable public. It was fitting then that in 1966, in San Francisco, at that time the epitome of radical chic, that a struggling musician, former circus performer, and party organiser with an interest in the occult and rituals, called Anton Szandor LaVey, should on the 30th April, Walpurgis Night, found the official Church of Satan.

Satan now had his own champion and, like the Catholic church, his own (anti) Pope and his own place of worship, a small, completely black building in San Francisco - known appropriately enough as The

Black House - that would house the Church of Satan until 1997, the year LaVey died. The arrival of the colourful LaVey in San Francisco at a time when the city, and the wider world seemed on the verge of sliding into chaos, acted almost like a catalyst with the Black Pope metaphorically flinging open the gates of Hell.

The next few years were to unleash a cornucopia of occult and satanic material onto a world ravaged by war, protest, murderous cults, heavy rock, drugs and an unprecedented sexual revolution. From the Rolling Stones' definitive album **Their Satanic Majesties Request**, to Hammer's **The Devil Rides Out** (1967), Hell's Angels, **Rosemary's Baby** (1968), and umpteen publications covered in pictures of naked women disporting themselves before demons and devils, it was as if the world was being bombarded in a what would now be regarded as a Satanic marketing campaign of massive proportions.The Devil's disciples may have chosen to wear flowers in their hair, but in reality the flower children should have swamped their petals for horns and their petunia oil for sulphur...

New bands like Coven, Black Sabbath and Black Widow were also forming. They were not only open about their occult influences but championed them as well. The Rolling Stones track **Sympathy for the Devil** became an anthem to Lucifer and numerous people began embracing and championing a 'Satanic' lifestyle defined by many as *"Do What Thou Wilt"*, as espoused by Aleister Crowley's theorised concept of 'True Will' where a person follows their true needs and calling. This Satanic mania culminated in the very unsatanic accolade of being the **Time** magazine cover feature for June 1972, which declared *"The Occult Revival - Satan Returns"*. Satan was now mainstream and in danger of almost becoming Establishment.

Probably the Devil's popularity would have continued unabated were it not for a series of unfortunate events that began to slowly undermine brand Satan. The Sixties, the decade of peace and love, had drawn to a close not with hugs and kisses, but with stabbings

and brutal killings as witnessed by the murder of Sharon Tate and others by the fanatical followers of Charles Manson. At the same time, at the Altamont music festival, a man was stabbed to death by members of the Hell's Angels while their Satanic Majesties, the Rolling Stones, were on stage. While there was no direct link to the occult in either of these events, publications like **Esquire** magazine made the link anyway with articles like **Evil Lurks in California**, which linked the counterculture's interest in the occult to Charles Manson and the Tate-La Bianca murders.

As the Seventies progressed, the free-love, anything goes counter-culture saw the beginnings of a reaction against pornography, sexism, and the 'exploitation' that often underlined much of that era's attitude to women and sex. There was also a realisation that not everything represented by the old Establishment was bad, just as not everything espoused by the revolutionaries of hippiedom was good, and Satan and the occult no longer seemed quite as cool.

This move away from the occult, and Satanism in particular, gathered momentum during the late 1970s and by the beginnings of the 1980s was dealt a virtual exorcism by the arrival of a moral panic in the form of something called Satanic Ritual Abuse or SRA for short. This was the claim, mainly via therapists dealing with people who claimed to have been sexually abused, that people were being physically and sexually abused in the context of occult or satanic rituals, and that children were being abducted or bred for ritualistic sacrifice.

This theory and belief that groups of Satanists were using the practising of rituals for the abuse of children and other vulnerable people spread from the US, to the UK and to most countries in the West. It created a kind of hysteria that gripped communities and destroyed families and ripped communities apart. For a decade accusations and counter-accusations against individuals and officials were traded in courts and in the media until eventually it was admitted that no one had actually been found to have been abused in a Satanic ritual or indeed that any had ever taken place. Case dismissed.

Now completely discredited and compared to similar moral panics like the antisemitic blood-libel of the middle ages, witchhunts and the anti communism of McCarthyism, the Satanic abuse hysteria of the 1980s however ensured that Satan, was for a time at least, decidedly uncool and very, very unwelcome. That changed of course as Black Metal emerged in the nineties and popularised Satan again - but Black Metal's practitioners unfortunate habit of killing each other ensured that Satan still had limited appeal.

In turn the counterculture of the 1960s and 1970s reinvented itself as Alternative culture and repackaged witchcraft without the naked glamour models and sex orgies, Yet somehow a tamed, politically correct Satan, with his hoofs and horns shorn and his male and female disciples clad in matching asexual outfits is akin to Satan and all the damned souls wearing high-vis jackets and hard hats and somehow doesn't crack it. Perhaps it is time for Satan to put some flowers in his hair again ...

HYMN OF THE SATANIC EMPIRE
THE CHURCH OF SATAN
DAVID FLINT

The Church of Satan is the longest-established Satanist organisation in the world. Formed in 1966 by showman, carny and visionary Anton Szandor LaVey, the Church established itself with **The Satanic Bible** – a book of rules, philosophies and ideas that set out the idea of an atheistic Satanism, rather than one rooted in Christian ideas. To the surprise of many, The Church of Satan does not actually believe in a literal Satan, just as they don't believe in God; rather, Satan is a symbol of pride, individualism and enlightenment – taking the idea of Satan as adversary to be a questioning, indulgent and libertarian (in the old-school, non-political meaning of the word) counterpoint to a world swamped with religious repression.

The Nine Satanic Statements first published in **The Satanic Bible** set out the philosophical beliefs of the Church:

Satan represents indulgence instead of abstinence.
Satan represents vital existence instead of spiritual pipe dreams.
Satan represents undefiled wisdom instead of hypocritical self-deceit.
Satan represents kindness to those who deserve it, instead of love wasted on ingrates.
Satan represents vengeance instead of turning the other cheek.
Satan represents responsibility to the responsible instead of concern for psychic vampires.
Satan represents man as just another animal who, because of his "divine spiritual and intellectual development", has become the most vicious animal of all.
Satan represents all of the so-called sins, as they all lead to physical, mental, or emotional gratification.
Satan has been the best friend the Church has ever had, as he has kept it in business all these years.

As important as these in representing the Church of Satan's philosophy are the *Eleven Rules of the Earth:*

Do not give opinions or advice unless you are asked.
Do not tell your troubles to others unless you are sure they want to hear them.
When in another's lair, show them respect or else do not go there.
If a guest in your lair annoys you, treat them cruelly and without mercy.
Do not make sexual advances unless you are given the mating signal.
Do not take that which does not belong to you unless it is a burden to the other person and they cry out to be relieved.
Acknowledge the power of magic if you have employed it successfully to obtain your desires. If you deny the power of magic after having called upon it with success, you will lose all you have obtained.

Do not complain about anything to which you need not subject yourself.
Do not harm little children.
Do not kill non-human animals unless you are attacked or for your food.
When walking in open territory, bother no one. If someone bothers you, ask them to stop. If they do not stop, destroy them.

Over the years, the Church of Satan has survived the highs of pop culture acceptance – when celebrities, musicians and sensation-seekers would make their way to the 'Black House' headquarters in San Francisco to take part in theatrical and erotic rituals, and when LaVey was the go-to expert in all things occult for the media and filmmakers alike – to the lows of the Satanic Panic, when the Church was dragged into unfounded and sensationalist claims. These days, after LaVey's death in 1997, the Church is not only still going, but is more active – if less publicity hungry – than it ever was.

We met up with Church of Satan spokesman Reverend Raul Antony, to talk about the history, philosophy and beliefs of - and misconceptions about – 'the world's most notorious religion.'

Let's start at the beginning. Tell us how the Church of Satan was first formed.

Well, the Church of Satan was started by Anton LaVey in 1966. At the time, he was holding occult and black magic classes in his home, and after a little bit of time he developed a network of people in the area, and so he decided he could start a church, The Church of Satan, to develop the philosophy of Satanism as a formalised religion. He was the first to really establish it as a religion. Prior to him, there hadn't been an actual formalised definition for Satanism – it meant anything from paganism to general occultism. There are some instances that researchers now have found of some people trying to define Satanism, but they never succeeded, it never took hold and had very few followers. So LaVey decided to do it himself, and it has been successful.

How did he succeed where others had failed?

I think the time was right for that – it was the revolutionary time of the mid-Sixties. And he was a showman – he had a knack for the theatrical, and he knew how to get attention and hold it. And at the same time, he was a smart, self-taught person. He developed a very concrete philosophy based on Nietzsche, Ayn Rand, Mark Twain and the history of secular American rebelliousness. So he had both the theatrics and the underlying philosophy behind it to keep it going, and once the theatrics ended – in the early Seventies he stopped with the big media presentations and focused on the philosophy and publishing articles in his magazines like **The Cloven Hoof** and such – he was able to maintain a core group of members. He wanted the Church of Satan to be seen more like a think tank, and not just a place where people get together and party, which was becoming the image – that this was just one big sex group. That perception worked for a while, and it garnered a lot of attention, but he thought it was time to take it more seriously. And there was some fallout from that – Sammy Davis Jr said something like he removed his red nail polish (he had one red fingernail symbolizing his allegiance to Satanism) when he realised it wasn't just all partying. When it got serious, he backed away from it. But that was part of LaVey's plan, he knew the need for shock and media attention, but he also had a vision of Satanism as a real religion that lasted a long time, not just a quick fad.

So it was like he was weeding out the people who weren't serious.

Yeah, it was exactly that. It was also because of the situation with the Temple of Set…

Can you tell us a little about that split, and how the Temple of Set differed from the Church of Satan?

The split with Michael Aquino and his followers was something that was happening in the background for some time. As I said, the media attention brought in a lot of people who were into the theatrics of Satanism, who didn't read **The Satanic Bible** – or if they did, they read more into it than was really there. LaVey was optimistic, and thought OK, if you don't get it completely, you're still on board – you'll learn over time. And as the focus came to the philosophy of Satanism, that's when things started to get a little shaky with people like Aquino and some of his friends in the organisation; they thought of the Church of Satan as an organisation dedicated to the occult, black magic, and theistic

ideas. They thought that because of the media, LaVey had to hide his true feelings, he had to play up the atheism a little bit, but he didn't really mean it... that behind closed doors, in the ritual chamber, LaVey actually believed in a real Devil. And Aquino was starting to write material in the newsletter, **The Cloven Hoof**, that led in that direction, that started to talk about Satan as a real being and an actual deity. LaVey then fought back, and there are letters – some of which Aquino published in his Church of Satan book – where he says he was not happy about this, and essentially says *"that's not the case at all. In the ritual chamber, I am talking about Satan as an externalisation of myself – I'm not talking about a literal Satan".* This is detailed in his open letter titled **Hoisted by His Own Patois** and you can find a video interview from that time in which he explicitly rejects theism.

Another problem was that Aquino heard that LaVey was handing out memberships to celebrities and some people who were giving him gifts. Aquino thought how can you be giving away a Reverend title to anybody who just has money? They don't know the material, they haven't studied, they haven't gone through all the steps. LaVey's response to that was to remind him that his philosophy is about material success in the here and now. LaVey preferred to spend time with actors, artists or businessmen than occultists who memorise rituals and can do the black mass backwards but are losers otherwise. That drove Aquino crazy. Aquino comes from a military, very professional, structured background. He likes to have things orderly, going through the examinations and the certifications and the levels to achieve rankings. And this was great for him, he has had a lot of success with that in his career, it gave him plenty of medals and pieces of paper to hang on his wall. But that wasn't LaVey, that wasn't his philosophy. He was more impressed by real world accomplishments than test scores.

So Aquino eventually had enough and said that LaVey had tarnished his infernal mandate and betrayed Satan by selling titles and not giving him his real due as the Prince of Darkness – that Satan in the form of Set has come to him in a vision and revealed him to be the next representation of his mandate on Earth. LaVey was was bewildered, he never claimed to have some 'divine right' or any such nonsense,, but there were a handful of people who believed Aquino because that's what they *wanted* the Church of Satan to be. So he took a couple of dozen people with him and formed the Temple of Set. Ever since then, they've done their own thing. There was a little back and forth between the Church of Satan and the Temple of Set for many years after that, but in the late Nineties, early 2000s, when Stephen Flowers and Don Webb became more

Church of Satan witches - from Daikaiju book launch. Photo: HOWL Books

involved with the Temple, they were ready to acknowledge *"we're Setiens, not Satanists"*. From time to time, some things will flare up – usually through fans of one or the other sniping across, but I think generally right now, we're happy to each do our own thing.

Obviously, the Church of Satan has a very defined idea of what Satan represents, and what Satanism is. How do you feel about the way that Satanism, as a word, is used by people outside the Church, who might have a different take on it than you do?

The concern that I have is that Satanism will revert to being a loose term. Prior to 1966, Satanism was a term that was applied by anybody to demonise 'the other', whether it's a Christian calling a Jew Satanist, or calling Islam Satanic, pagans Satanic – anything that was deemed blasphemous or dark was considered Satanism. It didn't have a concrete definition, so it could always be conveniently attached to something you wanted to scapegoat. Part of the reason why LaVey formulated Satanism and created the Church of Satan – and the reason why it continues today – is because we want a strict definition of what it is and isn't, but for it to still be flexible enough to be applied in different ways. So I see Satanism as like an open source philosophy – you have the fundamentals, the framework, but you can apply it in different ways. How I apply Satanism might be very different from the way another Satanist applies it, based on our aesthetics, our backgrounds, our histories, our points of view. We may disagree, we may even not like each other, but if the fundamentals are there, we can work with that. Some people want to change the fundamentals of Satanism to fit something else – to reach a greater audience, to be more edgy, more dangerous or because they want Satanism to be something that makes people afraid of them - thus compensating for some lack of confidence, like the Norwegian Black Metal scene in the Nineties; they thought LaVey was too soft, they thought Satanism *should* be about human sacrifice and Devil worship and all that – you should be killing people and burning churches. And the other end of that are the social justice types today who want us to be more friendly and open – let's do away with the elitism and the social Darwinism, that's outdated, nobody thinks like that anymore, they say. That completely ignores what Satanism is: it's not a different application of the framework, it's a completely different framework. To me, Satanism should always be an outsider philosophy – it should always be challenging to the mainstream. LaVey's ideas of social Darwinism were not popular in the late Sixties. He started Satanism as a reaction against the peacenik, hippy movement. We're seeing a little bit of that coming back today, and people are saying that we should embrace and work with it. But the whole point was to react against it – in a sensible way, not to be a caricature. Being mindlessly rebellious is pointless, especially when your 'rebellion' is in fact the mainstream position. But being a rational counter-balance is important.

It's interesting that you have a great Twitter presence that counters some of the more ludicrous ideas about Satanism in general and the Church of Satan in particular. But as we've seen recently, you'll get that social media backlash as soon as you say things that fit into the established philosophy of the Church that people don't like.

(laughs) The whole gun control thing?

Yeah. How do you deal with the people who want you to take a political stance, to become a reflection of their own beliefs? To essentially become what they THINK you are, rather than what you actually are?

I think it's a delicate balance, and there's even some disagreement between Satanists – different opinions about the way we apply the philosophy. I think we have very good leadership in Peter Gilmore – he's got a long term approach to things, and he knows

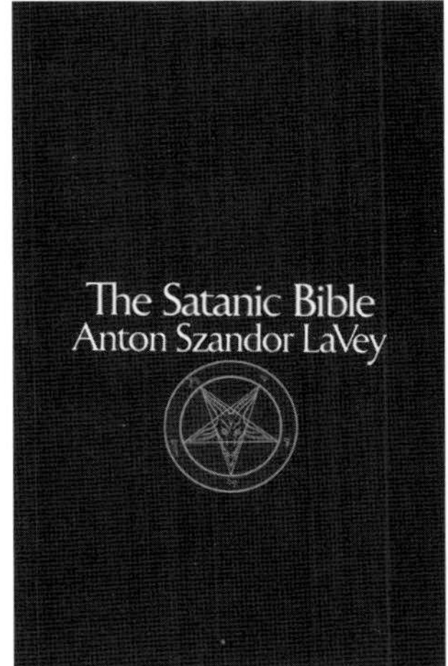

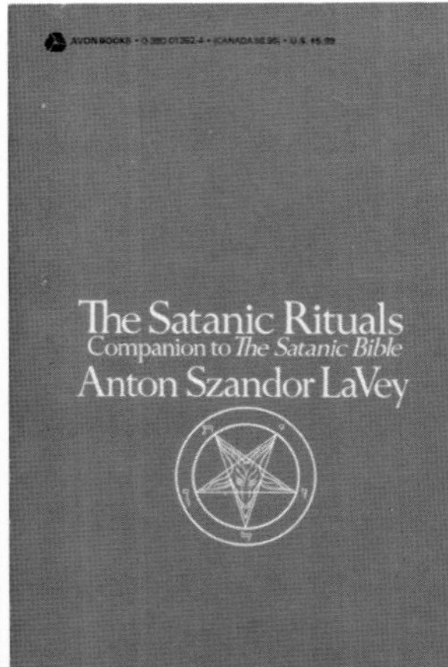

that we *should* use some form of lesser magic to navigate the social environment we're in, but at the same time stay true to the principles of Satanism. We'd never want to whitewash anything, but sometimes we want to focus on *these* elements rather than *those* elements. But that's the Church of Satan as an organisation, which is different than the Church of Satan members. Individuals are free to express their Satanism however they want. We're not going to say *"hey, you're being too extreme, tone that down"*. You can be as extreme as you want, as long as you're accurate to the philosophy. If you want to be on the extreme left or right in your views, your art, however you want to apply it, that's on you. You're responsible for that. But as an organisation, we have to think long term. Pragmatic, that's the key word. LaVey liked to say that Satanism is nine parts social acceptability, one part social outrage.

How has the Church of Satan changed in the years since LaVey? Assuming that it has.

I think that it's bound to change. Peter Gilmore's not Anton LaVey. They have different backgrounds, different interests, different temperaments. We never claim to be a cult of personality. We don't *want* another LaVey. The philosophy is applied by different people, and can vary from person to person. It *should* vary from person to person. Whoever is the leader of the Church of Satan should be consistent with the base philosophy but will have their own flavour. And if you look at it objectively, it is consistent throughout. For one, Peter Gilmore is more actively involved with the Church of Satan. If you look back through the history of LaVey, he was more hands off. He did his own thing in his home, and was very selective about who he allowed into his life. Especially towards the end of his life. He didn't do a lot of media representation or interviews, he cancelled a lot of things… he was a pretty misanthropic guy. He was very distrusting of the media, so he let other people handle things.

Anton LaVey and Jayne Mansfield - photographed by Walter Fischer. From the book California Infernal (Trapart Books)

One of the criticisms levelled against him is that he wasn't a visible presence during the Satanic Panic years.

That's absolutely right, he wasn't a visual presence. He let other people handle that, Magus Gilmore was all over the media at that time. But it's not that LaVey wasn't doing anything, he was. There are records – we've actually gotten hold of all the Church of Satan archives. All his letters, all his correspondence, we have them all. They were in storage for decades, but we've got access to them now. So we've

Peter H. Gilmore - High Priest of the Church of Satan. Photo: HOWL Books

got records of LaVey writing to lawyers, writing to journalists, writing to other members during the Satanic Panic, saying *"OK, this is how we should be doing things"*. He was contacting the publisher of **Michelle Remembers**, he was contacting journalists who were misrepresenting Satanism. So he was doing things in the background, but his face wasn't out there. Partly because he did not want to be the face of Satanism. People say LaVey was an egomaniac, a showman, carny, he just wanted fame and fortune. But he really *didn't* want to be the sole face of Satanism. He wanted other people to be out there representing The Church of Satan. He had feedback from people when they appeared on television – he was happy with some, unhappy with others. So he was certainly active. Peter Gilmore doing some of that right now, in that he's like the conductor, we call him the Maestro – he will organise individuals to appear where they would be the best fit, and focus on strategy and logistics. But when he has the time and the opportunity to make an impact, he'll make the appearance himself.

The metrics speak for themselves.I think anyone who looks at the number of books published, media appearances, podcasts, videos, interviews, articles, art exhibits, performances - the Church of Satan is exponentially more active after LaVey than before LaVey. Part of that is technology. LaVey passed just as the internet was growing. Would things have been just as active if LaVey was around? I don't know. But if you look at it objectively, his death didn't put an end to anything, and it's fairly obvious that the Church of Satan is more active now than it's ever been.

The early days of the Church and the Hollywood era seems a pretty popular subject for documentarians right now.

Yeah, I actually watched **Mansfield 66/67** last night.

What did you think?

It was a fun film about Jayne Mansfield. They brushed over the LaVey parts a bit. There was some commentary on LaVey, but towards the end, I was annoyed by the comment that "*the Church of Satan died with LaVey*". That's obviously not true at all. Even Kenneth Anger, their one connection to Satanism, said *"is the house still around? I don't know"*, so even he's not not really all there. So it slides into questionable, ignorant territory, I think. And also – they didn't have any Satanists, anybody who knew anything about Satanism. Their Satan scholar was a random artist who I've never heard of and has no credentials other than having an Instagram page. So I think it was a missed opportunity. They could've had someone from the Church of Satan on. They could've had Carl Abrahamsson or any of the many scholars of Satanism and Jayne Mansfield, even if not from the Church of Satan – if you want to keep it objective, that's fine. But they could've had someone who knows the philosophy and the history to talk about it more than just dismissing it as a publicity stunt. I think there was more to their relationship than that.

There's a pretty eccentric selection of talking heads in the film.

Yeah, they had a drag queen, a queer feminist, a black lesbian… a whole collection of interesting ideas, which is great. They're all good perspectives. But they never got a Satanic perspective on it, and that was strange.

Why do you think a lot of people don't realise that the Church of Satan is still around?

I think it's because people are attached to LaVey. They're not interested in Satanism, but they love LaVey. That's cool – he was a fascinating individual. They look back and think *"oh, LaVey, he was such a media darling"* – but that was not even ten years. After that, he was in the shadows.

But you do still have your finger on the pop culture pulse to a large degree.

If you look at our Twitter feed, you can see we're mingling with celebrities and pop culture people. And we have members who are well known people. But we're not the Church of Scientology, we're not naming names to help prop up our numbers. I'm sure it would be great, I'm sure people would want to join up because they want to be in the same group as so and so, but that's not what we're interested in. I think it'd almost be to our detriment in some ways, because celebrities for the most part are fickle. We had a situation with the guys from The Alkaline Trio – one of them was a member of the Church of Satan, and then had to tone it down because his record label had a deal with Disney. So he put out an interview saying *"I did it as a gag, I wasn't really serious"*. But we have his letters, we have his correspondence, and he was pretty on board. So those things happen. There's still a situation where people have an idea of Satanism being tied to things like child abuse, and even if they can prove it to be not true, the cost of going through all that is not worth it for them.

I guess that's the mark of a genuine outsider religion. You can't be a respected member of society and work in certain industries while being an out and proud Satanist.

There's also a legitimate danger to Satanism. Not because it's supporting any kind of child abuse or crime or anything like that. But Satanism does advocate elitism, it does go against egalitarianism. It believes that some people are better than other people, that we're not equal to each other. That can be a very unpopular opinion. As you saw with the gun control post – it was a very general post saying that we would not support any gun control measures that would limit responsible ownership. LaVey was very smart in the way he worded things – that statement supported independence and freedom and liberty, but also put in that qualifier about 'responsible persons', and most people don't see that. Most people immediately see *"we do not support legislation"* and boom, they go off. The one sentence that's presented in front of them, they don't see.

Now, I can understand that it was a little too soon (*after the Florida high school shooting*), maybe a little insensitive. Personally, I think Satanism *should* be a little insensitive here and there – being out of harmony with the mainstream is good. But, who wins? Do we gain? That's always the question we have to ask ourselves. A large part of Satanism is politically incorrect today, as it was in the Sixties. So I can imagine some celebrity getting into Satanism and saying *"yeah, I love Satan as a rebel, and carnal lust"*, and then someone picks over a Church of Satan article and says *"oh, wait, you support this idea?"*, and then all of a sudden they're backtracking. That's not beneficial to us. If you want to be out as a Satanist, do it. If it's not worth it to you, then don't. I will say this as a criticism of LaVey. I have a lot of respect for him, he was a huge influence on me. But I do not worship LaVey. I think he was a little loose on giving out memberships to people that were interesting and fun, and kind of got the idea. Unfortunately after he died they then get the courage to backpedal and start recanting. But he also drafted some high quality people, so you win some, you lose some. It happens.

I think LaVey had this idea of water seeks its own level. The Church of Satan should sink or swim based on its member as a representation of Satanism in the real world – not on activism. He explicitly said that Satanism should not be a political or theological organisation. The Church of Satan should be an organisation focused on material pursuits and accomplishments in the real world – a showcase of its members. Beyond that, it becomes too much of a typical organisation or collective, and that's a criticism I hear – the Church of Satan is not a real organisation, because they do this or that thing to benefit 'the common good'. But the whole point was to be unlike any other organisation, unlike a religion. It's a paradox in some ways, but that has always been a big part of Satanism – the carnal religion, the church without a church, Satan without God. It's always been about finding a third way. Something altogether separate.

Satanic art: Derek Noble. From The Devils Reign 3: Daikaiju. Courtesy HOWL Books.

There's something reassuring about an organisation that doesn't follow trends. It shows that you are sticking to what you believe, regardless of how inconvenient it might be.

I think that can be frustrating for some people who want it to be that – to be in the news constantly, talking about this or that issue. Within the Church of Satan, you'll have members with different opinions on things. Because we're not a collective. I follow the Church of Satan Twitter account and see people trying get some statement on whatever the trending topic is, and the response is *"this is our policy: think for yourself"*. That level of consistency is reassuring.

What's the most oft-expressed misconception about the Church of Satan?

It goes both ways. There's one misconception that we're devil worshippers and that we kill babies and animals. Obviously, that's not true. We see Satan as a symbol, and we value life, children and animals, so we would never do such a thing. That's something that goes back to the Satanic Panic. On the other hand, there's this misconception that we're just atheist pranksters, that we're not serious about Satanism. That we're just trying to annoy Christians. And that's not true either. We are atheistic, but we do have a shared aesthetic, culture and philosophy that we apply to our lives. The Church of Satan is an organisation that showcases that. That's what it's for – to showcase the application of Satanism through its membership. It's not a traditional church, but it still represents a philosophy and it's not just to piss off Christians. Christians aren't even our biggest concern. LaVey thought Eastern mysticism was more offensive to the Satanist than Christianity. I'm more often annoyed by pearl clutching secular moralists than most Christians, some of whom might have more Satanism to them than they'd like to admit.

How do you counter the mad accusations of devil worship, child-eating etc.?

You counter it with the evidence. The FBI did a thorough investigation of the Church of Satan during the Satanic Panic, and cleared it of any kind of wrongdoing. There's an article out there that says *"FBI investigates Church of Satan and finds out they just have a spooky house"*, and that was essentially it. Since then, the Church has actually worked with the authorities on cases of ritual killings – Peter H. Gilmore has appeared as a court expert witness on such cases. There have been situations where people have contacted us saying that they plan to do some crime in the name of Satan and we can forward that information to the authorities, because we have contacts with those authorities. We will not tolerate anything like that.

I guess you also get the other negative backlash, with people who come to you with their ideas of what Satanism is, and you have to disabuse them of those ideas. Can you guide those people to a better path?

Yeah. These people are raised in churches where they're told what horrible things Satanists do, so when they want to rebel, that's what they go with. When they want to act out against whatever repressive religious upbringing they had, they'll act in the way that they've been told Satanists behave. But some will contact us or they read our materials, and see that Satanism can be a positive thing, an empowering philosophy, and that can move them away from those kind of actions. But of course, there are also people like the Black Metal scene who don't think that we are evil enough – they *want* to be evil, and they think we're just posers.

You must be a disappointment to them.

Yeah, but that's not who we are. If you're looking for that, there's a whole history of Christian heresy that they can latch on to. Sometimes it's insincere too. A lot of these people are kids, or adult losers. NEETs who want you to be just as disenfranchised and powerless as they are. There's an art to being subversive without being a caricature, that's Satanic.

Magus Gilmore celebrating The Satanic High Mass on 6/6/06 at the Center For Inquiry West. Image copyright Church of Satan

So how would you describe the structure of the modern day Church of Satan?

I would say it's very similar to the way it first started. Actually, I was talking to Blanche Barton about this recently, and she was really happy with what the Church is doing right now, and talked about how it's very similar to the early days – it's a collection of individuals from a vast range of professions and creative endeavours. It's not an organisation that meets together all the time – it's not a traditional church like that. It's a loose network. People join the organisation, they network with other people who have similar interests, they collaborate on projects and draw inspiration from each other. And there are members who keep to themselves. They join because they want to pay respect to LaVey, to the organisation and the philosophy, and then they go about their lives. So the way I see it, it's like a clearing house – a network of individuals who might collaborate from time to time. Also, the Church of Satan showcases the activities of Satanism, the application of Satanism. So we have our newsfeed – news.churchofsatan.com – and that's updated almost daily with all the things our members are doing, be it concerts, publishing books, art exhibits… trying to show the public this is what Satanists do, and that there are verified, valid Satanists out there in the world. We occasionally have get-togethers. We had two large conclaves recently to celebrate Year 50 and the fiftieth anniversary. But that's very rare – the last one similar to that was on 6/6/6.

We talked about the Temple of Set earlier. But what's the Church of Satan's relationship with other organisations?

We don't affiliate with any other organisations. Our focus is being consistent with our definition of Satanism. We see other groups that repackage LaVey's ideas and throw in some more occultism or actual Devil worship, and those things don't have any real followings. Academics have actually studied this and many of these other organisations are just websites, web forums – they don't have any concrete literature of their own. Some other neo-Satanic groups that have sprung up recently are activists and pranksters, and are self-identified as that – they're in it to make a political point. And that's fine, but it serves to dilute what Satanism actually means and tries to turn it into another collectivist slave morality.

So just one final thing to clear up… is Chelsea Clinton a Satanist?

(laughs) No, she is not a Satanist. She is a Methodist. That does not end. That is everyday, ever since she said *"Happy New Year"*. People say *"oh, she said it's been a long time – does she mean she's been in the organisation a long time?"* No! She was talking about it being a year since we were put into threads together by the conspiracy theorists. That ended that! That was the implication that some people took. But you get a lot of agitators on Twitter, and some people who profit off that – which I guess is Satanic is some ways. I've seen this before – even when they know it's not true, they'll continue saying it because it helps their cause. LaVey actually talked about this – the idea of the invisible war, where in the future – which is now – warfare is not going to be armed conflict necessarily. It'll be about ideas, demoralising and panicking people…

Fake news.

Yeah. Exactly. That's part of information warfare right now. As Satanists, we have to be aware, and we have to be able to spot it, work around it… maybe even use it. Satanism is not a good guy philosophy, and some Satanists are scoundrels. We're not trying to be a saviour for anybody.

DOG-FEARING

THE RISE AND FALL OF ST GUINEFORT

DAZ LAWRENCE

As we all make haste towards Armageddon, it's worth the risk of obtaining salvation the traditional way - by kneeling and begging. For the sake of a few moments of discomfort and indignity, all this woe and pestilence will have been worth it to recline for eternity in the clouds – for all Hell's attractions, it's never been portrayed as comfy.

We admit that we're a little late to this party and there doesn't seem time to make a truly scientific choice of being, which by any analysis is nothing to do with science or reason, so we've gone on instinct. Saints seem a fairly decent bet - what with their flying exploits and healing ways, there's something for everyone, as their adverts probably say. Not for us the flag-waving, chest-beating saints of countries, nor the tunnel-visioned do-gooding of antics of attention-seekers. We want our saint to be bold; to be loyal; to cause a fuss. We want our saint to have a wet nose.

In the mid-13th Century, near the nun-speckled hamlets of Dombes near Lyon, a faithful hound, a greyhound to be specific, was left in charge of looking after the recently-born baby of the household, whilst the lord of the castle went hunting. With his ladyship and nanny also absent, br'er snake saw his opportunity and made legless speed towards the cradle. With resolute canine bravery and sense, the dog (his original name is lost to the ages) at once leaped at the reptile, sending the cradle flying and child arse over tit but still tearing the snake into more manageable, dead morsels. Good boy.

Upon their return, the nanny was greeted by a tail-wagging familiar doggy that now sported a face and lolling tongue drenched in blood. Eyes, flicking to the upturned crib, she let out a scream, alerting her master to the tragedy - putting deux and deux together and getting fünf, he ran through the dog with his sword, certain it had eaten his own flesh and blood. One can only imagine the bollocking he got from his wife when the obviously live child started crying.

In an attempt to make amends for their idiocy, they laid their dead pet in a well and capped the memorial with stones, planting trees around it in memory of the animal that had saved their child's life. The castle was destroyed by divine hand and the lands around turned to desert, with only the grave site spared. The locals, hearing of the tale (of The Tail), soon came to venerate the grave and, as happens in these situations, miraculous healings were soon attributed to the dog, now referred to as St. Guinefort. Guinefort is said to have been an even earlier saint, about who very little is known, other than he didn't fare too well against a shower of arrows.

Women in particular took the saving of the infant as a sign of the dog's ability to cure children of illnesses and would visit the site to lay offerings (salt not schmackos, oddly) and would hang their children's clothes from the branches of the nearby trees so that St. Guinefort's mystical powers might imbue the garments with something stronger than Vick's.

By the time of the first written reports of these events only a few years later by the Dominican inquisitor, Etienne de Bourbon, suspicion had been cast upon the activities at St. Guinefort's grave:

"When preaching there against sorcery and hearing confessions, I heard many women confess that they had carried their children to St. Guinefort. I thought he was some saint. I made inquiries and at last heard that he was a certain greyhound..."

"(They) began to visit the place and honour the dog as a martyr in quest of help for their sicknesses and other needs. They were seduced and often cheated by the Devil so that he might in this way lead men into error. Women especially, with sick or poorly children, carried them to the place, and went off a league to another nearby castle where an old woman could teach them a ritual for making offerings and invocations to the demons and lead them to the right spot...

"They then put the naked baby through the opening between the trunks of two trees, the mother standing on one side and throwing her child nine times to the old woman on the other side, while invoking the demons to adjure the fauns in the wood of 'Rimite' to take the sick and failing child which they said belonged to them (the fauns) and return to them their own child big, plump, live and healthy. Once this was done, the killer mothers took the baby and placed it naked at the foot of the tree on the straws of a cradle, lit at both ends two candles a thumbs-breadth thick with fire they had brought with them and fastened them on the trunk above. Then, while the candles were consumed, they went far enough away that they could neither hear nor see the child. In this way the burning candles burned up and killed a number of babies, as we have heard from others in the same place".

Assembling the locals, de Bourbon fervently preached the word of God and rejected all claims as to St. Guinefort's powers, going as far as to disinter the dog's bones and burn them, along with the trees that had previously been decorated with tiny clothes. Suspicions of sorcery and paganism were dealt with swiftly and the alliance of women, animals and nature was as clear a sign as the church needed – in 1262, it was decreed that any visitors to the site were to have their worldly goods taken from them and sold. Regardless, St. Guinefort was still worshipped by pockets of followers throughout France, only slowing when the emerging Protestant church held up Guinefort as an example of Catholic folly, three hundred years later. Oddly, this still wasn't the end – in 1879, a local historian found a wood named after the beast – stranger still, evidence was found of St. Guinefort cults as late as the 1930s.

2018 is a time for rational thought; a time to reflect and a time to devote oneself to the important things in life. We see no finer character to lead this charge into the light than St. Guinefort, a magical animal who ate snakes and upset Catholics. All praise.

THE BLACK VELVET UNDERGROUND

SATANISM AND THE OCCULT IN 1970S MADE-FOR-TV MOVIES

BEN SPURLING

In his microscopically brief essay, **The Devil Reassured** (from **A Short History of Decay**, Arcade Publishing, 2012), Emil Cioran, the world's foremost humourist and all around cutup, asked *"Why is God so dull, so feeble, so inadequately picturesque? Why does He lack interest, vigour, actuality and resemble us so little?"* In the U.S., after the assassination of JFK in 1963, the rise of the inclement and demagogic Weather Underground in 1969, and the Tate-LaBianca murders that same year, Americans were beginning to ask the same questions; similarly, the Brits were beginning to follow Cioran's wayward train of thought, although with more restraint in terms of overt violence, after the Notting Hill Riots of 1958, the Profumo Affair in 1963, the earth-shaking release of **Sgt. Pepper's Lonely Hearts Club Band** in 1967, and the legalisation of abortion in that same year. As Grady Hendrix points out in his **Paperbacks from Hell** (Quirk Books, 2017), 1967 was also a watershed year for fictionalised diabolism; with the publication of Ira Levin's **Rosemary's Baby**, horror turned from a sordid pastime for the vaguely suspect to a felicitous matter for the modishly inquisitive. The release, one year later, of Roman Polanski's film adaptation of Levin's novel opened the floodgates even further, pointing the way for a subconsciously profligate public to baptise itself in the blood of a thousand venereal sins.

As an inevitable result, pop culture of the Seventies indirectly, and rabidly, embraced those exact same recalcitrant doubts which Cioran espoused, probably nowhere more surreptitiously than in the made-for-TV movies of that era. In February of 1970, the decade's mating dance with the occult opened auspiciously with NBC's **Ritual of Evil**, sequel to the same network's slightly more efficacious **Fear no Evil** (1969), both starring Louis Jourdan as Dr. David Sorrell, a suave psychiatrist turned suave paranormal investigator. While lacking the feverish Dutch-angled scenes, creepy cinematography, and phantasmal script of Director Paul Wendkos' **Fear no Evil**, as well as the substantially sinister performance of Carroll O'Connor as Myles Donovan, Director Robert Day's **Ritual of Evil** still packs a punch, with Composer Billy Goldenberg's unearthly score and Anne Baxter's eccentric channeling of Phyllis Diller in her portrayal of a stewed Jolene Wiley, mother to Loey Wiley (Belinda Montgomery) and Aline Wiley (Carla Borelli). Its plot of

occult detective battling a woozy jumble of sinister forces at the root of multiple deaths is typical of American TV horror film production of the time, and appropriately so, considering the silly ballyhoo of marketing mountebanks like Anton LaVey, Carlos Castaneda, and Timothy Leary; with them, witchcraft mingles with Satanism which, in turn, becomes indistinguishable from ESP, reincarnation, ghostly communications, and paganism.

The main thrust, if you will, of **Ritual of Evil** is that a coven of Satanic witches is performing sacrifices to Priapus, an ancient Greek fertility god who would normally be depicted with an enormously erect phallus, but in this case is limited to representation by a vaguely sensual and smoulderingly malevolent Satyrish statue which could easily be passed off as one half of a set of macabre book ends. The sterilisation, of course, was due to the Federal Communications Commission's regulation and definition of obscene content at the time, which has fluctuated along with common opinion since its inception. According to **Bold! Daring! Shocking! True!** (Duke University, 1999), Eric Schaefer's meticulous examination of exploitation film history, restrictions for television have only been tighter than that for theatrical films since the late 1950s when lawsuits such as Burstyn vs. Wilson helped undermine the relevance of state film censorship boards; this, along with the gradual diluting of the Production Code, aided by the antitrust Paramount decision in the late 1930s, ultimately helped prep the American public for what became the corroded and overripe moral jitters of the 1970s, which led directly to the laughable extremities of William Friedkin's **The Exorcist** (1973). The same occurred in the UK, but with less giggling and in a slightly different fashion; in 1957, when Hammer Films chose to release **The Curse of Frankenstein** while proudly touting its dreaded X-Certificate, the success of the film in Britain drastically reduced the negative potency of the rating and encouraged independent exploitation producers to up the ante; money cures all malignities, it appears. John Hamilton, in his **X-Cert: The British Independent Horror Film: 1951-1970** (Hemlock Books Limited, 2012), also suggests that the loosening up of British television standards began with the establishing of the Independent Television Network by a 1954 act of Parliament which broke the monopoly of the increasingly stodgy BBC; after this, themes over time became a bit more dynamic and darkly primeval, and old goat in UK made-for-TV horror films, despite being fewer and farther between than their American counterparts and, as pointed out by Lorna Jowett and Stacey Abbott in **TV Horror** (I. B. Tauris & Co. Ltd, 2013), focused less on commercial concerns than public service.

A brilliant example from Britain is James MacTaggart's taut direction of John Bowen's astute and dexterous **Play for Today** script, **Robin Redbreast** (BBC, 1970), a stunning mixture of 'problem play' and rural gothic horror. Arriving in December, ten months after **Ritual of Evil**, this intricate and dryly minacious tale cautioning against cheeky modernity is a masterly lesson in less-is-more, and less-is-frequently-more-unsettling.

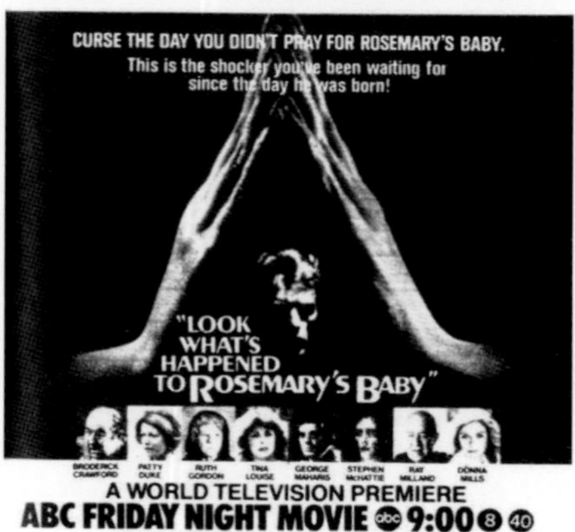

Cinematographer Brian Tufano keeps things stark and cold without losing the faint hint of blood-rich ferment at the bottom of old-country customs; all the actors deliver, with Bernard Hepton particularly compelling as Fisher, the frigidly opaque village observer watching over a drawn-out fertility ceremony possibly dating back to a very crimson pre-history. Surprisingly, while the plot sounds remarkably like that of British Lion Film's classic, **The Wicker Man** (1973), John Bowen's filmed script predates Director Robin Hardy's movie by three years.

In November, a few weeks before the appearance of **Robin Redbreast**, ABC introduced its entry into the rural occult corpus: **Crowhaven Farm** (1970). Following **Ritual of Evil**'s tangled lead, this is an eerily drawn depiction of reincarnation, Satanic Pilgrim witchery, and a creepy kid with traces of paedophilic seduction on her mind; for good measure, a brief touch of fecund ritual is tossed in, as well. Walter Grauman's direction is solid, providing ample disquiet through seemingly innocuous moments; Cinematographer Fleet Southcott's use of soft filters reinforces the otherworldly focus of the plot; and the majority of the cast delivers appropriately heated performances, keeping things energetic, nicely countering John Carradine's gift for simmering cloudiness.

One month previous to this, in late October, ABC took a step back from the seedy and aired an old-fashioned ghost story with twentieth-century occult trappings when it premiered the Barbara Stanwyck vehicle, **The House That Would Not Die**, another tale of haunted early American colonials - but this time cloaked in the black velvet of séances, possession, hidden rooms, and constant wind. Television horror maestro, John Llewellyn Moxey (who, back in 1960, had helmed the impressive New England witchcraft shocker **The City of the Dead**), directs with his typically expert skill from Henry Farrell's script; based on Barbara Michaels' **Ammie, Come Home**, the film, having moved the action from the novel's location of Washington, D.C.'s Georgetown neighbourhood to Amish country, is a perfect example of the modern rural gothic, or - as outlined in **Paperbacks from Hell** - women in nightgowns running from houses. While the denouement might seem a bit soft for modern viewers, it does fit nicely with the occult gothic, old-fashioned ghost story vibe, making this a solid and worthy production.

By the mid-seventies, after the alluring exhibitionism of Piers Haggard's **The Blood on Satan's Claw** in 1971 and the grisly spectacle of **The Exorcist** in 1973, there was really nowhere else for TV to go but toward a daffy sincerity that could help in releasing the pressure. **Look What's Happened to Rosemary's Baby** (ABC, 1976), plopped onto the scene in late October like an absurd blob of melted Halloween candy. Coming off as little more than a forward-looking quickie rip on **The Omen**, which had been released four months previously in June, the TV movie is at turns wild, disturbing, laughable, incomprehensible, and ludicrously fun. Ruth Gordon as Minnie Castevet staggers through her part, seemingly unconcerned that she's on camera, while Ray Milland as her husband, Roman, tries to grouse and grumble her back into the scenes. Stephen McHattie as Adrian/Andrew, Rosemary's matured titular baby, delivers an over-the-top method performance which is uncomfortably out of sync with all the other cast members, except Gordon.

Stepping back three years and into the soon-to-be hoary terrain concerning Satan's offspring, **The Devil's Daughter** (ABC, 1973) dishes out the same hokum as the aforementioned **Look What's Happened to Rosemary's Baby**, but this time the he is a she, and the production is far more durable and poised, while never laughing off the risible mumbo jumbo at its core. Director Jeannot Szwarc takes the sweltering script by writing team Colin Higgins and Phill Norman and constructs a visually poetic lesson in tension-building by making well over half of his shots either Dutch-angled, low-angled or high-angled, subtly and aggressively, depending on the stress desired; J.J. Jones' expressive cinematography incorporates elegantly soft filters, turning both exterior and interior lighting velvety smooth while shifting colours toward the warm end of the spectrum. The acting is appropriate for this sort of thing and accommodates the premise, but it's the skilled artists behind the camera that put a frightening itch in the viewer's mind.

Satan's School for Girls

Penda's Fen

While **Look What's Happened to Rosemary's Baby** offered up absurd delivery, **Devil Dog – The Hound of Hell** (CBS, 1978), three years later presented a deliriously rendered nemesis -Satan's pup who's in need of adoption - that's immunised by extremely competent production values. A solid script, with an admittedly ridiculous concept, from Steven and Elinor Karpf, superior direction from Curtis Harrington, and fine acting from Richard Crenna and Yvette Mimieux somehow all add up to a wicked little potboiler that works well but shouldn't.

Satan's School for Girls (ABC, 1973), Directed by David Lowell Rich, is an early example of the kitschy titling that would later bring us the likes of **Satan's Cheerleaders**, and is one of the few TV movies to have been remade (in 2000, with Shannen Doherty in the lead role). The original stars Pamela Franklin as Elizabeth Sayers, a woman whose sister committed suicide under mysterious circumstances while attending Salem's School for Girls. Suspicious of her sister's death, Elizabeth enrols at the school in order to investigate and soon, with the occurrence of another suicide, she finds herself caught in an increasingly complex web of dark and anomalous happenings. Odd behaviour abounds: the headmistress, played astutely by acting maven Jo Van Fleet, is at first stiffly composed almost to the point of repressiveness, projecting an aura of smothered perplexity; Roy Thinnes is impeccably smooth as Mr. Clampett, the hip art teacher professing mind-expanding theories of perception bordering on the delirious in order to get his students to reach a deeper level of creativity; and Lloyd Bochner gives a typically vigorous performance as Mr. Delacroix, the brittle and unsettled psychology instructor fixated on the breaking of wills; Kate Jackson's Roberta, on the other hand, is one of the few characters to come off relatively stable, adding a poised buoyancy to the otherwise increasingly thick atmosphere.

Murrain

Notwithstanding the death which opens the story, the first half of the film is brightly lit, with frequent outdoor scenes counterbalancing tense indoor moments; the second half, on the other hand, bubbles with a deepening dread accentuated by Cinematographer Tim Southcott's murky lighting and judicious framing as characters weave in and out of adumbral hallways, bosky night time locales, and a shadowy basement that anyone in his right mind would avoid. Director Rich, whose career capably spanned many genres, here delivers fitting, if not scintillating, imagery while seemingly allowing actors to pull out their own performances, not always to good effect; Debbie's (Jamie Smith-Jackson) neurasthenic hallway crackup approximately twenty-one minutes into the film makes the viewer shriek from laughter rather than unease, and Cheryl Ladd is merely present for most of the film, with only a hasty moment of well-done classroom befuddlement before fading back into the scenery. Arthur Ross' script is strictly a journeyman's effort, competent but unremarkable; everything follows logically from everything else, all the right notes are played, tensions gradually build through a sound three-act format, and the conclusion is vaguely haunting without being too convincing. As is so common from the era, Ross as the scripter obviously knows very little about the occult, and therefore, wisely avoids delving too deeply into details, which helps keep the whole thing from tumbling into catastrophic silliness; unfortunately he, like most tradesman writers of the time, mistakenly conflate witchcraft with Satanism, melding the two most prominent bogeymen of a casually dabbling viewership into one, giant, shuddersome, cloven-footed fiend. It works, if you put your mind on hold and don't sweat the shorthand. The truly weak spot in the film, though, is the naked foreshadowing of every vital plot point, a safe telegraphing which was expected at the time but has since fallen out of favour, leaving the modern viewer feeling slightly cheated.

In 1974, the BBC tried its own hand at occult burlesque with the **Play for Today** airing of **Penda's Fen**, an over-blown, meandering slog through an adolescent's hallucinatory coming of age and sexual awakening. Though it provides intriguing Satanic, pagan, and general occult imagery, it's a tough go and obscenely pompous with an enfeebled sophisticate's taste for the decadently obscure; even the Director, Alan Clarke (better known for his grimly social realist dramas), has said he doesn't really know what's going on with a lot of it. A bad sign for anyone wanting to be horrified - in a good way. **Penda's Fen** feels more like a self-absorbed, turgid, and juvenile slap in the face for populist broadcasting than any kind of progress, and very much of the 'worthy' side of the BBC's output, where public service and the assumed public good overrode commercial concerns. The BBC in particular has long been squeamish about admitting that it produced 'horror' – even the increasingly bleak 2000's series **Being Human** was

Quatermass

referred to as a 'comedy-drama' throughout its entire run – and the obtuse nature of Clarke's film doubtless helped legitimise it for both broadcaster and critics.

One year later, Nigel Kneale's **Murrain** crept onto the scene as an instalment of ATV's **Against the Crowd**. Directed acutely by John Cooper, with bleakly vicious production design by Michael Eve, a typically perspicacious script from Kneale, delicate sound design by Roger Knight, and sagacious acting from all - especially that of Bernard Lee as Beeley - the movie concerns itself with the mean superstitions of an insular village and the shut-off woman they believe to be a witch. Returning to the same type of agrarian environs as **Robin Redbreast**, the countryside here feels even more primordial and the people aggressively resolute but irreparably worn. The rural gothic of John Bowen's story is distilled down to a viscous pitch in Kneale's **Murrain**, a quicksand of lurking despair which feels very palpable and quite ready to smother if one's guard is dropped for even the briefest of moments. A true classic of its kind.

Although sharing the same theme of possession with **The House That Would Not Die**, NBC's **The Possessed** (1977) has an entirely different pedigree of occupancy; for the former, the possession is by rapt human spirits fixated by a residual earthly passion; for the latter, it's the result of a demon with ill intent. Is there any other kind? A hesitant and vacillating priest, played sensitively by James Farentino, comes back from the dead as an exorcist; he's to redeem himself by opposing a demon whose ironic proclivity for causing death by fire at a girl's school has become a bit too flagrant. Though a possession story, the arson element dominates, causing the film to bear a more than passing resemblance to Stephen King's **Firestarter**, though the movie predates King's novel by three years. If it has to be considered, consider it an inspiration. Leonard Rosenman's score wonderfully reinforces a mounting unnerving tension, and John Sacret Young's writing is strong, with some very clever dialogue; the acting by most is of high quality, but impeccably so by Harrison Ford; it makes one wish he were in more of the film, if not the entirety of it. **The Possessed** is highly compelling up to the final encounter, but then becomes a watered-down and unconvincing riff on **The Exorcist** and unfortunately fizzles to some degree.

A year later, the UK issued a stunning movie not necessarily about possession, but something close to it. Shot for the BBC in Cornwall, **Tarry-Dan, Tarry-Dan, Scary Old Spooky Man** involves an inherited curse, an ominous tramp, and historical details clouded in a coastal community's dubious past. A dark film, touching on the rural occult gothic, that could have come off as a fine but creaky old ghost story, instead here becomes a baleful tale reminiscent of the 13th Century folklore revolving around the myth of **The Wandering Jew**, thanks to a brilliant script by Peter McDougall, strenuous direction from John Reardon, resonant cinematography by Peter Bartlett, a shuddery score by Jeremy Barlow, spectral sound design by Tony Miller and Ian Sansam, and an exquisitely sepulchral performance from Paul Curran as Tarry-Dan The Spooky Man. It doesn't get much more agonising than this.

By 1979, horror was once again beginning to mingle intimately with science fiction in the form of films like Ridley Scott's **Alien** and George Miller's post-apocalyptic nightmare **Mad Max**, both released that year. With that becoming a trend, British TV jumped horns-first into the fray with the character that helped solidify the merger in the first place, Nigel Kneale's Bernard Quatermass. Migrating from the BBC, **Quatermass** (ITV, 1979) is a sign of the waning of made-for-TV occult-focused horror films; more would follow but to a lesser extent and usually of a lesser quality. Ironically, it's also the concluding film in a series that goes back to the earliest days of televised horror in the UK, starting with the BBC's broadcast of **The Quatermass Experiment** in 1953. In this final entry, Kneale has the prescience to bond the modern taste for dystopian fantasy with the aforementioned rural occult gothic by placing Quatermass in a now crumbling and debased civilisation steadily nipped at by new age, Stonehenge-worshipping neo-pagans, led by Kickalong (Ralph Arliss), a character Kneale claimed to have based on Charles Manson; though not as impactful as the previous films in the series, it does deliver not necessarily horror, but a sense of impending doom, thanks in part to the performance by John Mills as Quatermass, who portrays the character's flagging hope perfectly, reflecting real-world sentiments of the time; sentiments of a people, at this point, without a compass but overflowing with copious amounts of acedia.

In his essay, **The Devil Reassured**, Emil Cioran answered his own question of why God lacks interest, vigour, actuality and why he resembles us so little. Because we've invested our best qualities not in God, he says, but in the Devil: our wickedness, our friskiness, spite, irony, despair and our pettiness, in effect, all of our dominant qualities we've shrouded in black velvet and given them the solidifying name of Satan. We sardonically recognise ourselves in the Devil; our worst natures usually win in 1970s TV occult horror. It mirrors the best parts of our self-loathing dissipation. We enjoy the stuff because it allows us to exorcise ourselves while simultaneously wallowing in our own obscenities. It's a Hell of a way to be.

GERALD GARDNER: THE FIRST NAKED WITCH?

DAVID MCGILLIVRAY

Well, no, he wasn't. And nor did he invent Wicca, "the only fully-formed religion that England has ever given the world." But Gerald Gardner, Britain's first celebrity witch, certainly had a big influence on the way we regard modern witchcraft. It's time to separate fact from fiction in Gardner's life.

As with strawberries and black pepper, Leopold Stokowski and Mickey Mouse, witchcraft and naturism is a combination that shouldn't work. But it does. So much so that, for those who grew up in the sexploitation years, roughly the 1950s to the 1970s, it's hard to imagine a witchcraft initiation ritual without the participation of at least one gorgeous, blonde, naked woman. The connection lingers on to the present day.

It's probable that one man is mainly responsible for our perception of modern witchcraft, now called Wicca. He is Gerald Gardner, who in the 1930s was a naturist in the New Forest before he happened upon a local witches' coven. He became a leading light in the secretive world of paganism. (It was inadvisable to use the word 'witchcraft' while the practice remained a criminal offence in Britain). But soon after the Witchcraft Act was repealed in 1951 Gardner came out as a witch. His revelations about the craft, for example *"To work magic you must be naked"*, excited the media at a time when nudity in popular culture – glamour magazines, strip clubs and nudie movies – was new and different. In the public eye witchcraft and nudity became synonymous.

Gardner didn't just put the sauce into sorcery. Remarkably many of the trappings of sexploitation movie witchcraft – the pentagram, the circle and the high priestess – were also popularised by him. But although he was for a time its leading exponent, Gardner didn't invent Wicca. How could he have done when he admitted that he was initiated into a cult that already was well established? What is now apparent is that his brand of Wicca was British paganism mixed with many other influences, among them Freemasonry, spiritualism, Malayan folklore, neo-Druidism and Aleister Crowley's 'magick.'

If we now hear the word witchcraft and imagine women dancing naked in a forest, that's because of a succession of fateful encounters in the interwar years. For the naturist Gardner, one of the most appealing aspects of his initiation into witchcraft in 1939 was that he was required to strip naked. In interviews – and as a relatively well-known author he was on BBC television as early as 1951 – Gardner made no secret of the fact that witches were sometimes naked. The tabloid press took the next step, implying (as it had done with naturism itself) that groups of naked people hidden far from prying eyes were in fact indulging in sex orgies.

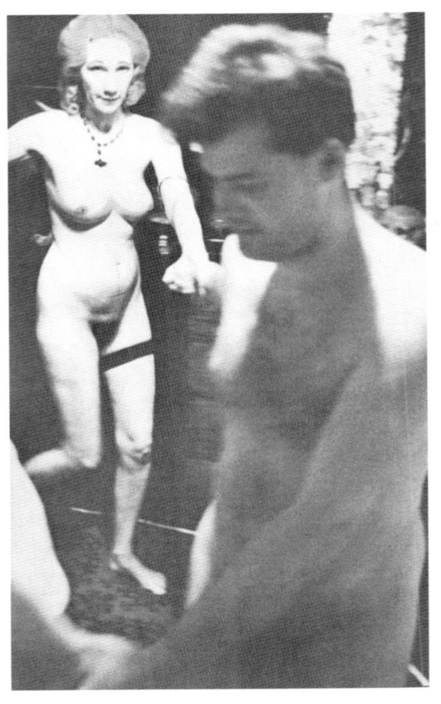

Probably this was nonsense. *"I have never heard of sexual orgies within such covens,"* wrote one of Gardner's high priestesses Lois Bourne in her book **Conversations with a Witch**. *"Most members are married couples and it seems rather pointless to gather in a circle for magical and religious rituals and then waste time and energy on an orgy."* Witches work naked, Bourne explained somewhat prosaically, *"because they feel comfortable that way."*

There have been representations of naked witches for hundreds of years but for most of that time they were not the kind of naked witches portrayed by dolly birds in soft porn. In art (solely the work of men responding to the perceived wisdom of witch hunts) the intention was almost invariably to show the monstrosity of female old age. When medieval witchcraft is discussed today the picture most often shown is Dűrer's engraving, circa 1500, of an old hag with flabby belly and misshapen breasts, riding backwards on a goat. An exception is the most famous of Goya's witch paintings, **Vuelo de Brujas** (1798), in which three ghouls, seemingly sucking blood from their naked victim, are young and well-built. The presence of a donkey and what may be dunces' caps suggests that the artist considered credence in witchcraft mythology stupid.

In the 19th century belief in superstition waned. Specifically people began to question why only sexually frustrated spinsters should possess magical powers. In art a new type of alluring young witch emerged. Luis Ricardo Falero (1851-1896) painted all kinds of sexy enchantresses but is particularly well-known for his **Witches on the Sabbath** (1878) in which hideous demons, bats and a goat cavort for no apparent reason with the type of shapely nude female model that was by now appearing live on stage in London in so-called *poses plastiques*.

The use of French was a deliberate reference to the fact that, to British minds, every imaginable carnal desire could be indulged openly in Paris. Nude revue (the Folies Bergère opened in 1871) was but the tip of the iceberg. Joris-Karl Huysmans' scandalous novel **Là-Bas** (1891) dealt with Satanism, and the City of Light was later to host black masses and all kinds of other debauchery. Maria de Naglowska (1883-1936) preached *"The Mystery of Hanging"*; and when the first English translation of her book **Advanced Sex Magic** was published in 2011, it was prefaced by a health warning. *"The Mystery of Hanging"* was none other than auto-erotic asphyxiation.

The movement that led directly to the modern cult of naked witchcraft, however, was Freikörperkultur, literally Free Body Culture, which developed in Germany at the turn of the 20th century. Germans who threw off their clothes were of course not the world's first nudists; but they were the first in modern Europe to espouse a worship of nature that included shameless nakedness. A comeback for full-fledged paganism was not far off.

Called the father of British naturism, Harold Clare Booth (1875-1943) first wrote about German naturism in the magazine **Physical Culture** in 1913. He founded the first British naturist group, usually called the English Gymnosophist Society, in 1922, and opened the first British nudist colony, near Wickford in Essex, in 1923. In 1927 this moved to Bricket

Wood, Hertfordshire, as Five Acres. Within a few years more nudist camps, notably Spielplatz, opened in the same area. The scene was then set for the arrival of Gerald Gardner.

Haxan

Born into money in Blundellsands, Lancashire, in 1884, Gardner became a world traveller, working first as a tea and rubber planter, then as a customs officer. He later claimed to have picked up at least two doctorates; but in fact he had almost no formal education. By the time he returned to the UK around 1935, Gardner had been exposed to most of the influences that would shape his life. He was a Freemason; he had observed magic rituals in Malaya; and he had married Donna Rosedale, a spiritualist medium. In London Gardner joined his first nudist colony, the Lotus League in Finchley and, after he and Donna retired to Highcliffe, a village on the edge of the New Forest, they became members of Five Acres. The couple also hosted naked parties in the high-walled garden of their house.

Thanks to the research of several scholarly authors, particularly Philip Heselton, who wrote the book **Gerald Gardner and the Cauldron of Inspiration** (2003), we know how Gardner became a witch. The Highcliffe area was a hotbed of witchcraft, although the term was taboo. ('Wica', an Old English word for witch, had been re-introduced in the early 1920s. Gardner heard it at his initiation). Highcliffe witches were male and female, but the women were predominant, another aspect that appealed to Gardner.

Rosamund Sabine (1865-1948) was connected with the Hermetic Order of the Golden Dawn, a Victorian occult organisation whose membership also included W.B. Yeats, Aleister Crowley, horror writer Arthur Machen, and Charles Rosher. Rosher joined a splinter group, the Ancient Druid Order, and performed magic here. (As soon as rituals were reinstated at Stonehenge in 1946, Gardner attended). Katherine Oldmeadow (1878-1963) was a children's author who delighted in pools of water-pixies and *"fairy loveliness."* Daringly she wrote about a white witch in 1926. But the women who were the greatest influence on Gardner were Edith Woodford-Grimes (1887-1975) and Dorothy St Quintin-Fordham (1880-1951). They may have been at Gardner's initiation into the New Forest coven at Quintin-Fordham's home, Chewton Mill House, in 1939.

Of the male witches in Gardner's circle, two had a particular interest in naturism. Harry (later Dion) Byngham (1896-1990) and his girlfriend danced naked on the South Downs in honour of the sun god in 1925. It was he who taught Gardner that *"the feminine aspect of divinity was important."* At Spielplatz, Gardner met poet Ross Nichols (1902-1975), who had drawn a pentagram under a rug in his chalet.

Secret Rites

Soon after his initiation in 1939 Gardner published his first novel, **A Goddess Arrives**, a quasi-historical romance that touches on witchcraft. In 1946 he became the co-owner of Five Acres, which for Professor Ronald Hutton is *"the birthplace of modern pagan witchcraft."* The following year Gardner met Aleister Crowley (1875-1947), formerly the self-styled prophet of Thelema, the religion that gave the world '"sex magick', but by this time a destitute heroin addict.

Gardner and Crowley didn't really see eye to eye. Gardner wrote of The Great Beast, *"He approved of being nude in a dirty way, but highly disapproved of it in a clean and healthful way."* On his part, male chauvinist Crowley dismissed Wicca as *"a woman's cult."* He hoped nevertheless that Gardner would become a torch-bearer for Crowley's secret society, Ordo Templi Orientis. Some commentators detect elements of magick rituals in Gardnerian Wicca.

Gardner's second and last novel, **High Magic's Aid** (1949), was another historical romance but this time Gardner incorporated much of what he had learned about modern witchcraft into the fictitious story. It was the last time that he was required to pretend that 'the old religion' no longer existed. Only two years later he was able to tell the Sunday Pictorial, *"Of course I'm a witch. And I get great fun out of it."* Gardner was about to open the Folklore Centre of Superstition and Witchcraft in Castletown on the Isle of Man. Witchcraft was no longer a crime. In 1954 Gardner wrote *Witchcraft Today*, the book that made his name.

By 1964, the year of Gardner's death, Wicca had travelled almost as far as Gardner himself. It is acclaimed by Professor Hutton as *"the only fully-formed religion that England has ever given the world."* In his entertaining 2013 TV documentary **A Very British Witchcraft** Hutton also alleged that Wicca is *"one of the fastest-growing religions*

Above: Virgin Witch
Below: Satan's Slave

in the world." If this is true, then the time has come to attribute no small part of its rapid growth to popular culture. As Gardner was becoming a celebrity witch, almost the only stage productions that were pulling in the crowds around the country were those starring naked women such as Phyllis Dixey and Christabel Leighton-Porter. Soon the producer of many of these 'tat shows', Paul Raymond, would open a striptease club in London, while other fast buck merchants would succeed in putting naked women on British cinema screens.

The new exploitation film industry thrived on four things it was hard to find on TV – sex, nudity, violence and horror. Modern British witchcraft, which was under discussion in the **News of the World** and on **Panorama** (John Freeman: *"Is it not a fact that these meetings are really very largely sexual orgies?"* Gardner: *"They're not"*) seemed as though it might provide all four. Aspects of Gardnerian Wicca were the focus of such shockers as **Night of the Demon** (1957), **The City of the Dead** (1960) and naturally **Witchcraft** (1963) and **The Witches** (1966).

Wicca also appealed to film makers in the lower depths of the American exploitation business. Two of America's most renowned bad directors – Larry Buchanan and Andy Milligan – both made films called **The Naked Witch**. Buchanan's 1960 effort kicks off with a **Häxan**-like history of witchcraft and then gets down to business with footage evidently too hot for its time. The DVD now in circulation has black bars covering the witch's nakedness. Milligan's 1967 movie must for the time being remain a mystery. It's reputedly a lost film.

A possible turning point in the UK came in 1968 with the long-delayed release of the 1922 Danish film **Häxan**. The rights had been acquired by sexploitation bad boy Antony Balch, who went on to direct **Secrets of Sex** (1969) and **Horror Hospital** (1973). Balch cut the two hour film to a more manageable 77 minutes and got his mate William

Burroughs to intone the commentary. But its main point of appeal was naked witches. Burroughs reminds us that *"It was a general belief that the witch was naked when, at night during the so-called Witch Sabbath, she danced with the devil."* The film's most memorable production still was of a demonic claw prodding a naked woman's body.

The success of the film produced more witchcraft documentaries. The ponderous **Legend of the Witches** (1969) was followed by a 1970 episode of the BBC series **24 Hours** in which Bernard Falk cast a cynical eye over the activities of self-styled King of the Witches Alex Sanders (1926-1988). They included plenty of full frontal nude dancing. This inspired sleazebag Derek Ford to feature Sanders in **Secret Rites** (1971), which opens with a group grope that was very much Ford's stock in trade.

Made in 1970 but long delayed by censorship problems, **Virgin Witch** is an archetypal sexy witch movie. Ann Michelle is naked in every other scene and the coven into which she's initiated doesn't seem to do anything except have sex. One of the films that inspired Nigel Wingrove to launch a succession of video labels specialising in Eurotrash, it also inspired sex-and-horror director Norman J. Warren to make two witchy films – **Satan's Slave** (1976) and **Terror** (1978) –in the house used for **Virgin Witch**.

The knock-on effect of all this naked necromancy is evident in the mainstream films of the period. In Polanski's **Macbeth** (1971) not only are the three weird sisters naked, so is their entire coven. And without Wicca would there ever have been **The Wicker Man** (1973)? It's unlikely. Lord Summerisle's paganism is very much the dark side of Gardner's. That's why naughty Britt Ekland and her body double strip naked in a magical attempt to seduce virginal Edward Woodward.

Without Gerald Gardner it's probable that the connection between witchcraft and nudity would have been all but forgotten. Writing of Gardner's naked initiation, Philip Heselton proposes, *"I suspect that he liked this because it fitted in with naturism and [he] may then have introduced it for all the rituals."* This has also proved to be a heady brew for non-pagans and our taste for it has not gone away. In 2016 at least three films fantasised about Gardner's preoccupations.

In **A Dark Song** two occultists perform a ritual in which the woman strips and the man masturbates. Anna Biller's **The Love Witch**, in which a woman's love potions get her into terrible trouble, was one of the biggest cult successes of the year. And in **The Ghoul** an occultist/psychotherapist takes his client to a forest he claims is *"the centre of the magical world"* and then invokes not only William Blake and John Dee but Gerald Gardner himself. In the New Forest in 1940, the shrink recalls, Gardner and his coven performed a ritual to stop Hitler invading. *"They stripped naked, danced and chanted,"* he declares.

Not everything we read about Gerald Gardner is true. But this is.

SIGIL MAGICK

K.K. EYE

The word 'sigil' comes from the Latin for 'little sign'. Speaking for myself, a woman with an RSI from masturbation, I refer to them as 'little deaths.' 'Sigil' is basically a synonym for 'wanking over a bit of paper with a squiggle drawn on it.' You create a sigil from a combination of letters, then charge it magically by coming while looking at it. I can't tell you the number of times I've had to squeak *"leave me alone, I'm charging a sigil!"* in the direction of an ominously opening bedroom door.

Sigils are most often used by practitioners of chaos magick. Chaos magick has only been in existence for a few decades, and while it doesn't really have any rules, one of its basic guiding principles is to use what works. Chaos magick is results based. If it doesn't work, it's not magick. Many chaotes record rituals in an attempt to define what can truly create change in the world around them. Paradigm shifting and an allergy to dogma are also a couple of important factors in chaos magick. It tends to get a bad name at times for its use of belief shifting. A chaote can shift beliefs from day to day in accordance with whatever rituals they are doing. One day you might be using your belief to create a manifestation using sigils, the next day, you're using hoodoo. It's all done in service of attaining your goal. The only thing I can say with any certainty is that every chaote follows a different path through the deep dark of the magickal forest.

The type of sigils that chaos magicians use were jettisoned into the world by the Grand High Dad of Sigils, one Austin Osman Spare (1886-1956). Spare was a truly talented and extremely precocious artist. At the age of only seventeen, his first painting was exhibited at the Royal Academy. His work is characterised by the exemplary clarity of his line, while the images themselves are at turns decorative, grotesque and technically brilliant. Though his art remains fascinating, his most famous creation of all is the sigil. You'll find them referenced in comic books, on album covers, the subject of endless bitching arguments in Facebook groups that end in gif dissing matches. Spare himself would refer to them as *"monograms of thought."* Think of a finished sigil as a logo for your desire.

Images have obviously had magickal qualities since humans first made cave paintings of slain bison to guarantee a successful hunt. Pictures seem to be easier than words for the subconscious mind to process. Therefore, an image or visualisation, when fixed within the subconscious mind, has the power to change the world around you. Think of the influence of art down the ages, used by the church, the state or by companies using advertising and logos to get you to think or act a certain way, or buy buy buy. Sigil magick is a way of influencing your own life and its outcomes by using a symbolism you create yourself from language.

Here is my 'How 2' for sigil creation. Imagine I'm Carol Vorderman and you just sat through that Gareth guy teaching you how to make slime.

Step One: Ask yourself what you want to bring into your reality and decide behind all doubt that it is your true desire. Magick that works has no room for your conflicting emotions. If you're the kind of person who eats Neapolitan ice cream, go away and choose strawberry and stop being indecisive. The universe is not your therapist, you'll only get confused results if your emotions are conflicting.

Step Two: Write down this desire as though it has already happened or is happening in the present. Spare, however, constructed sentences such as *"This my wish to obtain the strength of a tiger."* It can work this way. However, you may also end up simply wanting or wishing forever for what you ask for. *"I want an artisanal crystal dildo made by the fair hand of Richard O'Brien"* may result in a heart-wrenching, unending search for one. And a restraining order from Riff Raff. This is because all you did was tell yourself you want it. *"I will Richard to send me a crystal dildo"* is a bit more likely to happen, but still doesn't describe the end result. Visualise your end result. *"I am masturbating feverishly with a handmade crystal pump stick"* has a better ring to it, no? Or even *"I put my crystal dildo in its display case this morning."* (Mum asked me what it was, I said it was a a posh lemon squeezer).

Step Three: Write out your phrase in capital letters. Here are some more examples:

I AM A SUCCESSFUL AUTHOR. MY BOOK IS A BESTSELLER. MY HEALTH HAS IMPROVED SO MUCH RECENTLY. MY BOYFRIEND IS GORGEOUS. MY BOYFRIEND IS NOT THREATENED BY MY GIGANTIC CRYSTAL DILDO.

The example I have used in the accompanying photo is I AM IN A ROMANTIC RELATIONSHIP. It's not just any old relationship, like the one you have with your mum, or the postman, or with alcohol. As I said, phrasing is key.

Step Four: Cross out all the vowels and repeated letters and write out what you are left with. MY BOOK IS A BESTSELLER becomes MYBKSTLR. MY BOYFRIEND IS GORGEOUS becomes

MYBFRNDSG. I AM IN A ROMANTIC RELATIONSHIP becomes MNRTCLSHP.

Step Five: Use this skeleton of letters to make create the sigil. Join them together, hiding the lines and curves inside each other. It will begin to look like something occult, the kind of thing you'd find carved onto a tree trunk in a haunted wood, or on an old goth's t-shirt. Your will has become an image rather than a sentence, the meaning locked inside it, ready to be opened by your subconscious mind when you activate it.

Step Six: Refine your sigil into something simple and aesthetically pleasing. It helps for the sigil to be as simple as possible so that your subconscious mind can recognise it. Think of the McDonald's M. Imagine if veganism had a logo half as memorable.

Step Seven: Draw your finished sigil in thick black pen and put a circle around it to seal the magick within. If you want to use a colour like blue for your sigil, so that it glows orange on your eyelids when you activate it, go ahead. You can make this as beautiful or as colourful as you like. Personally, I'm a goth forever. A little black sigil is classy, sexy, chic and might well get you banged by the person of your choice.

Step Eight: This step either begins with you putting the sigil away for a time until you can't remember what you made it for, or activating it and forgetting it afterwards. Sigil Alzheimer's: the struggle is real. The reason for forgetting your sigil is that magick often works well when you do not have 'lust for result.' Forget your ritual, carry on your life as though you never did any magick, and only remember it when your outcome occurs. That, my friends, is where sigil magick is a bit of an assfucker. Forgetting is not always so easy, so it can help to make up a few sigils ahead of time and activate them at random.

So, how do you activate them? To activate your sigil you need to go into a state called gnosis. Gnosis is a way of shutting your conscious mind down so that your unconscious mind can turn up to take your sigil and activate it, bringing your desire into manifestation in the world around you. Wanking is one way to do this. Simply stare at your sigil as you orgasm, the second your conscious brain turns itself off.

If your wanks are too precious to waste on sigils, I recommend meditation. Staring fixedly at a candle flame for a time until you zone out can be an effective way to go into a trance. Then look at your sigil. You will notice the longer you stare, the more the lines seem to burn with an iridescent light. If you close your eyes, it is likely you will see your sigil imprinted on your lids. It means it is making the crossing towards your unconscious.

This is why different coloured inks can be useful, as the sigil will burn more intensely against your eyelids when you close them.

Other methods of activation include spinning until you're really dizzy, extreme fear and exhaustion. Anything that shuts down the conscious mind so that the unconscious takes over, will work. Another method of activation used by many chaos magicians is Spare's 'Death Posture', which basically involves a lot of hyperventilating - so if I were you I'd have a wank instead. (If you ever want to ask yourself *"what would KK do?"* the answer is *"have a wank instead"*). Whatever you choose to do, zoooooooone oooooouuuuuut.

Step Nine: After activation some people like to wipe some sexual fluids on the sigil. Go ahead if you have some left. Now, you can dispose of it. Simply throw it in the bin if you like. Or maybe you'd like to burn it and watch the flames consume it, muttering *"does not matter, need not be"* as you do so. The disposal is part of the way to neutralise your lust for result and forget the request. Remember: care less, manifest more. You can also throw it in running water (some people just flush it down the toilet). I've heard of people drawing the sigil on the beach and letting the tide take it away. A sigil for love might well

be thrown into water. Something creative could be consumed in fire. Whatever feels right, will be right.

There is also another way, and this involves not disposing of it at all. Put the sigil somewhere you will see it but see it so often you simply forget about it. The idea here is that it will enter your subconscious as it hangs around innocuously in the background like that stoned teenager eating Oreos and drinking Five Alive on the sofa. It's doing something naughty but you don't notice. I myself have also photoshopped sigils onto profile pictures, Instagram posts and YouTube thumbnails to get a bit of a boost from unsuspecting viewers. Evil, maybe. But I'm a chaos magician, what did you expect?

You can also influence people by leaving sigils lying around where they'll see them. You'll suddenly find him desperate to wear a ball gag where he had previously refused, or take you roughly on that M&S fleece beside a roaring fire. Whatever pervery you're into. A suggestion for those of you who might have a sex-crush on a close friend: ask if you can swap sigils to charge them for each other. Whether they like it or not they'll be thinking about you when they're wanking. Win-win!

Another quick tip is to experiment. This is about magick that gives you results so try out different methods and phrases to find what works best. Activate several at once. Just try not get too chafed in the 'activation process'. If you charge sigils too often it'll cost you a fortune in Vagisil.

Now just follow the synchronicities that your magick has produced. Sometimes these will seem really normal and not magickal at all. Then one day, you'll realise that you are on a path towards your desire.

Sometimes what you asked for will occur and you'll remember a sigil you made for it and forgot about.

Sometimes your desire will manifest into reality in a way that feels so utterly beautiful, you know it could only have done so with the power of magick itself.

Happy sigil charging! (At least you know with this method there'll always be one happy ending).

Suggested reading:
Phil Baker, ***Austin Osman Spare, The Life and Legend of London's Lost Artist****, Strange Attractor Press, 2011.*
Frater U. D, ***Practical Sigil Magic, Creating Personal Symbols for Success****, Llewellyn Publications, 2012.*
Gordon White, ***The Chaos Protocols, Magical Techniques for Navigating the New Economic Reality****, Llewellyn Publications, 2016.*
Anything by the original chaos magicians Peter J Carroll, Ray Sherwin and Phil Hine.
runesoup.com

SATAN SUPERSTAR - A PERSONAL VIEW

A.D. HITCHIN

68% of our universe is dark energy, an unknown (or occult) form tending to accelerate expansion. Dark matter, a non-luminous material, comprises 27%. The rest, including everything on earth ever observed with all instruments, accounts for just 5%. 'One does not become enlightened by imagining figures of light but by making the darkness conscious.' (Carl Jung) Stars are born, destined for death. Darkness is unborn, never-ending.

2 Corinthians 11:14 tells us that 'Satan disguises himself as an angel of light', but Christianity itself represents an inversion of values; a slave morality originating in the weak. Jehovah was the demiurge, a mundane bully; Satan, the serpent liberator, kundalini, caduceus, whispering rebirth and regeneration. 'I teach you the overman. Man is something that shall be overcome.' (Nietzsche) When the deluge came, the Nephilim escaped, and to this very day their descendents walk the earth...

The primordial horned god, union of divine and animal; sum total of Baphomet, Goat of Mendes. Recognition and acceptance of nature as she is – stratified, unequal; acceptance of man as he is – diverse, differentiated. The holding of power according to merit. Fools made to suffer, not be suffered with.

And the light shone in the darkness and the darkness swallowed it.

DELECTABLE MISDEEDS

THE SCANDALOUS MADAME CHANTELOUVE AND 'THE DAMNED'

'KERI O'SHEA

France has a long and illustrious history of fraternising with the Devil, and centuries of subverting the important, and usually solemn ritual of Mass for this purpose. Mass itself, to an outsider, is a peculiarity at best: as we've simultaneously inherited and (for most of us) shelved the practice, we may have forgotten how strange the consumption of the transubstantiated blood and flesh of a religious leader really is. Our ancestors, for whom Catholicism was a far more potent, immediate force, didn't have the luxury of forgetting; the reverse side of this coin was that, over the centuries, worshippers often experimented with the ritual, subverting it for their own purposes, or simply mocking the rite for all it was worth. It's perhaps the spiritual equivalent of laughing at the back of class, or of passing notes: it may be based on the lesson, but the parody feels far more fun and profitable. The practice of the Low Mass was probably one of the tamest examples of this kind of subversion, being as it was the practice of hired hands performing bespoke masses for the particular needs of parishioners. There are also examples of harmless, but irreverent spoofs, such as drinkers' and gamblers' masses - based on the Catholic rites, but making fun of the decidedly ungodly clergy who were rather too fond of their wine and their dice.

RAISING HELL...

But go back far enough - as far as the Templars, if you wish - and you begin to see there are more sinister versions of the Mass, in which it is not the simplistic worldly pursuits of gambling or taverns that feature. The term 'Black Mass' has never simply meant one thing to any one group of people, and written accounts of the alleged practice have always been scant - but certainly, most people understand what the term signifies: a corruption of the Christian rite and a re-dedication of the mass to the Old Adversary, taking the form and routine of the Catholic Mass in some way (whilst absorbing elements of the older, pagan 'sabbats'). Tantalising snippets on the subject have made it down through the years to us, though as cloaked in intrigue, half-truths, exaggerations and outright lies as they no doubt were even when they were contemporary.

15th Century nobleman Gilles de Rais - whom we will come back to later - was beyond doubt a child murderer, but also spoke at his trial of attempts to raise demons, sometimes using murdered children for this purpose. Then, there's the Mass of the Severed Head, rumoured to have taken place in France in the 16th Century at the behest of the then Queen Mother, Catherine de' Medici. The story goes that, to glean the fate of the vulnerable young monarch Charles IX, the Queen Mother held a mass, which culminated in the murder by decapitation of a Jewish child. As the account goes, the trembling Charles IX was commanded to weave his way to the black-draped altar with its black candles to question the severed head about his future; whatever was said, the young king went mad, screaming to be released before dying in his bed a few short days later. But in perhaps the most scandalous chapter of them all, at the court of Louis XIV the 'Affair of the Poisons' saw largely women vying for influence at court with a combination of worldly means (abortifacients, aphrodisiacs, arsenic and other improvements) and spiritual ones - using black masses to further their aims, rites that they procured by fraternising with cunning layfolk like Catherine Monvoisin, or 'La Voisin', a clever businesswoman whose reach extended to Satanism whenever the need arose. Even the King's favourite mistress, Madame de Montespan, was implicated in the subsequent investigations that rocked the court; she was rumoured to have served naked as the altar for some of these rites, desperate to maintain her position as the most powerful woman in France by blasphemous means, if necessary.

"A BOOK FULL OF WEIRD FANCIES AND CRUEL REALITIES"

But surely, by the 19th Century, France - rich or poor - would have no need for such devilish rituals? You'd be forgiven for thinking that the bright lights of modernity would certainly have swept away this kind of irrationalism; even the conventionally religious had new issues to face, as new information and the kindling understanding of the new age gave them altogether different questions to ponder. Well, this is, as it turns out, an oversimplification, and one which is considered at length in the extraordinary novel, **Là-Bas** (literally meaning the euphemistic *'Down There'*, but often translated as *'The Damned'*), written in 1891 by civil servant Joris-Karl Huysmans (and much of the novel was written on official headed paper, which is clearly use of work time to which we should all aspire.)

Certainly, modernity – and its so-called advancements - are interrogated at length in the book. The novel links modern-day France with medieval France throughout, as its main character, Durtal, is an author, researching the life of the debased Gilles de Rais in order to write his biography. Durtal's increasing fascination with his topic leads him towards the black magic for which de Rais sacrificed everything. Durtal begins to ponder: where are these rituals now? Do they still exist? Tantalising conversations with his peers lead him closer and closer to an answer, and he is able - by the end of both his biography, and

J.K. Huysmans

Huysmans' novel - to see for himself. Huysmans referred to **Là-Bas** as *"a book full of weird fancies and cruel realities"*, and it would make sense here to take a lightning tour around the 19th Century Paris in which both Huysmans and his semi-autobiographical character Durtal lived, in order to catch a glimpse of just some of those 'cruel realities'. For all of the bright lights and the dancing girls, the new science and the new buildings, there was always something of the Babylon about those Parisian streets. A programme of civic improvements had been undertaken in the decades prior to Huysmans' career as a writer, with old, winding warrens of streets and lanes being torn down to make way for leafy boulevards, shopping arcades and municipal edifices. But not all of these disappeared, and the inmates of Paris's poorest areas were not adequately accounted for in these projects. They crammed into neighbouring slums in the areas of the city they knew best (a case of 'better the devil you know') but couldn't afford to move elsewhere, anyway.

Overcrowding in the poorest areas accordingly worsened; diseases like cholera, syphilis and TB continued to haunt the city, and substance abuse in the form of alcohol, heroin and cocaine became endemic. Never too far from the electric lighting, the civic palaces and the modern improvements, the stink of the cesspool and the spectre of the absintheuse lurked, crossing into the light at intervals, an inconvenient miasma. In these years where Parisians could easily scoff at the idea of inevitable forwards progress – after everything, La Republique had turned virtually overnight back into a monarchy – indicators of backsliding, or simply of the march of modernity leaving people and things behind could be glimpsed everywhere. Parisian commentators debated these things at length in their salons, their coffee-houses, and of course their literature.

Parisian progress always seems to cast a noticeable shadow in this way. Although all cities have their alter egos, Paris has long made an art form out of its own. And, as the 19th Century drew towards its close, progress had taken another new face: newly scientific approaches to human behaviour became the talk of the town, with Jean-Martin Charcot's defining works on hysteria and neuroses transforming ideas of (usually, but not exclusively) feminine maladies and their treatments. Mysterious ailments that had historically been considered supernatural in origin were now being medicalised and pathologised – but, curiously, this did not seem to mean the demise of irrational beliefs and practices. Far from it. The *fin-de-siècle* was actually an era of renewed interest in the supernatural, with a new vogue for spiritualism, table-turning and séances, trends imported from America to Europe. Belief in Theosophy persisted; people turned towards exotic Eastern mysticism to augment their understanding of a changing world; astrologers and cabbalists still vied for trade. In fact, rather than shooing away the occult, the new science of mind seemed to invite direct parallels with it: after all, if the mysterious phenomenon of hypnosis could manifest results, then why not magic?

"FLOGGED INTO LIFE BY THE VOID..."

In this multifarious world, the lives of Parisian women (of at least modest means) had reached a zenith of opportunity and liberation, but – there's that Parisian shadow again – distaste and distrust were never far behind. Even respectable women going about their business were sometimes believed to be prostitutes, or at least on the cusp of prostitution, by virtue of their very natures – fallible, materialistic, carnal. How could an attractive, independent woman not be on the make, somehow? Attempts to curtail sex for sale in the previous decades had revealed a Parisian preoccupation with illicit sex, whether policing it or procuring it. Terror of disease meant that the government had demanded registration programmes and compulsory health checks, but simultaneously, civic improvements had torn down a lot of the brothels, driving working girls into the heart of Paris in unprecedented numbers: these women were not only a fact of life now, but they were up close and personal, which inevitably muddled the distinctions between good women and bad ones for years to come. Working girls were both tantalising and threatening, whilst visible like never before.

Still, as rife as prostitution might have been, there was far more than 'the oldest profession' at play for women at the time, and the rise of the 'New Woman' throughout Europe meant new freedoms and opportunities. Women could move around unchaperoned now in a way which was still difficult in many European cities, and vibrant city life afforded them the means to mingle with artists and writers, acting as their muses, models and collaborators. Women could also put themselves at the heart of fashionable debate and intellectualism by becoming hostesses, or *femmes de salon* – inviting the great and the good into their homes, both facilitating and participating in society.
Thus, the stage was set for **Là-Bas**. Huysmans' world – as a civil servant engrossed by ideas of spirituality and Satanism, with a narrator also looking to the past and comparing it to this brave new world – was in many ways the *fin de siècle* in microcosm. And as such, Huysmans encountered extraordinary women in his social life, something which he was able to use as inspiration for arguably the most delectable and debauched Satanist in literature – Hyacinthe Chantelouve. Could an infamous character like this really be based in any objective reality? In *fin de siècle* Paris, this turns out to have been eminently possible.

As much as Chantelouve is a chimera, and often referred to as such in the novel, Huysmans was inspired to create her after meeting the current mistress of his civil service colleague, Remy de Gourmont. Her name was Berthe de Courrière, and she was already a notorious figure in the Paris salons: a demimondaine, she was the former lover of the scandalous sculptor Auguste Clésinger, a man who immortalised several of the *grandes horizontales* of his day. Perhaps his most famous work, **Woman Bitten by a Snake**, was modelled on Charles Baudelaire's muse Apollonie Sabatier, and was believed by many to be a barely-veiled rendition of the female orgasm. Clésinger sculpted Berthe, too, and his work reveals a beautiful, if quite severe face: she was known to be affectionately teased on account of her statuesque figure. She and Huysmans became friends. More perilous rumours about her abounded, though. An intelligent, scandalous woman, Berthe was regarded as well-versed in occult knowledge, and Rachilde asserted that she fed stolen communion wafers to stray dogs, from a little pouch she carried just for the purpose.

As an aside, but one which is important here, as much as conventional Christianity was challenged during the century, anxieties over the potent ritual symbol of the communion wafer still beset modern society. This had a historical basis: going back to the Affair of the Poisons, the notorious Guiborg (alleged to have officiated at the Black Masses) was rumoured to have devised a 'Spermatic Mass', where the communion wafer was mixed with bodily fluids in what sounds an awful lot like an early version of sex magic. Heretical masses in the 1700s were gender-bending, and often based around aphrodisiacs: Durtal's great friend des Hermies talks at length about these practices in the novel. Yet even in the 19th Century, people fretted over what illicit uses there could be for stolen wafers, worried about where and how to store them, and agonised over what could happen if they were put to the 'wrong' use. There were even modern-day allegations of women retaining the hosts during conventional Masses by spitting out the wafers and keeping them, and of crooked priests (with their unparalleled access) blaspheming by feeding the wafers to animals. Given the pervasiveness of the rumours about Berthe, it would seem that feeding them to dogs figured reasonably high on that list, too. This issue would find its way into **Là-Bas**, too.

Berthe de Courrière appeared in other fiction before Huysmans' work, such as Gourmont's novel **The Phantom** (as a sexually voracious masochist, no less) but another piece of the puzzle was vital to her eventual appearance in **Là-Bas**. During her colourful life, she was linked to a notorious clergyman, at one time the incumbent of the Basilica of the Holy Blood in central Bruges, a man called Louis Van Haecke. I've been to this Basilica; perhaps it's just me, but a more sinister house of God I've never seen, which only makes the following part of the story that bit more salacious.

Around a year after beginning her friendship with Huysmans, Berthe was apparently in Bruges, as she was found there by policemen: she was shaking, terrified and hiding in the bushes at the side of the road in only her underwear. She told the police a curious tale about that so-called man of God Van Haecke, insisting that she had just narrowly escaped him. The subtext of this, considering her lack of attire, is that she had avoided being raped. Whether because her story concerned an influential figure in the city, or else because a nearly-naked woman telling tales wasn't exactly a credible source at the time, the policemen assisted Berthe… by dumping her in an asylum in the city, where eventually, some of her friends had to come and retrieve her. Did Huysmans believe her story? As he knew her as a woman who didn't scare easily, I'd put money on the fact that he did.

In any case, other strange rumours were already in circulation about this ostensibly pious priest, one of which was that he had crosses tattooed on the soles of his feet,

so that he could forever tread on the Christian symbol. Huysmans wasn't above spreading a few tales of his own, either, claiming at one time to have seen Van Haecke abroad in Paris, where he was involved in a Satanic ritual with other renegade priests. Van Haecke would go on to inspire the Satanic Cardinal Docre in Là-Bas, associate of Madame Chantelouve and master of ceremonies. If Van Haecke had terrified Berthe de Courrière in real life, then Huysmans put them on a par with one another in his novel, making them equals and instigators, which is a more fitting tribute to this extraordinary woman than to pass her down to posterity as some sort of vulnerable, cowering figure.

This brings us, then, to the extraordinary literary figure of Hyacinthe Chantelouve herself.

"I HAVE AN IRON WILL AND I BEND THE PEOPLE WHO LOVE ME TO IT"

During the early part of the novel, Durtal's immersion in the unseemly world of Gilles de Rais is interrupted by a series of strange, anonymous letters professing love for him. At first, he finds this an odd, unexpected distraction. As an old cynic who treats women as a perfunctory phenomenon – to be paid for only when the need arises – Durtal is surprised to quickly find himself rather flattered and interested, even feeling a few fleeting moments of a *joie de vivre* which he usually lacks. He decides to respond to the writer, imagining all manner of phantasmagorical figures as 'her', and he's genuinely curious as to who his mystery woman could be. She intermingles with his research and his fantasies, becoming a 'chimera', stimulating his imagination – even appearing as a contemporary of de Rais in his mind, merging fantasy and reality in a tantalising way.

A correspondence ensues. His mystery woman turns out, after all, to be a lady called Hyacinthe Chantelouve, the *"bizarre rather than beautiful"* wife of an acquaintance: he had attended their little salon gatherings previously, but never suspected the least attraction on her part, seeing her as a rather cold, detached figure who looked perennially bored. Not so: they begin a brief, passionate love affair, with him soon describing her as a *"spiritual nymphomaniac"*.

He admires her enigmatic eyes (*"like the distant reflection of a cemetery and a carnival"*) and supple figure, feeling that her interest in him is a great compliment. However, she is not content to demur, and Durtal reveals that he's rather conservative for a man making a cuckold out of a friend. The pace of the relationship displeases him. It is Hyacinthe who first comes to his home, alone, and it is also she who seduces him for the first time, in her husband's house. He quickly becomes horrified by her mixture of coyness and voraciousness, and how she can go from one state to the other, seemingly in seconds. Durtal moves from being entranced to being repulsed; he had assumed he would be calling the shots, perhaps, but it dawns on him that Hyacinthe may have done all of this before, and certainly doesn't lack confidence. Worst of all, he eventually says of their sexual relationship that *"she initiated him into obscenities whose existence he had never suspected"*: he is not so worldly nor debauched as he would wish to believe, perhaps, and he decides to shun his lover.

He might have persisted in this, if not for a series of conversations about Parisian Satanism with a group of friends. Considering the topic of his current book, Durtal keeps coming back to the idea of understanding blasphemy by really seeing it for himself. So, when he discovers that there have been rumours of the infamous Satanist, Cardinal Docre – an acquaintance of Madame Chantelouve – currently being abroad in Paris, Durtal develops a plan. He decides to turn his relationship with Madame Chantelouve to the purpose of an encounter with Docre, something which, after some resistance on her part, she agrees she will do. Hyacinthe tells Durtal that when the time is right, she will arrive by carriage to collect him. Bringing proceedings right up to date, she even makes him sign a disclaimer (!) dismissing as nonsense anything he will go on to see in her company. Curiosity calling the shots now, Durtal signs.

What follows is one of the most extraordinary scenes in literature: it blends historical rumours of the Black Mass with Huysmans' own formidable imagination, and places a strange, unique woman at the heart of the proceedings. It is, after all, through Hyacinthe Chantelouve that Durtal gains access to a bona fide Black Mass.

"I HAVE HAD MY FILL OF SUCH HORRORS!"

Madame Chantelouve collects him as promised, and takes him to a disused chapel on the outskirts of the city, where they gain admission – as she is clearly already known to the attendant. The scene inside the chapel is initially alarming, although dark and difficult to see. Christ on the cross has been defaced and sexualised, a smile etched on his face and a mock phallus attached to him, and a choking incense of henbane, nightshade and myrrh issues from the mock altar. An assembly of outcasts and debauchees are already seated, waiting. Durtal has at last found his way in, and the formidable, red-horned Canon Docre is about to begin the rite.

The impact of all of this on his sense of right and wrong is compounded by the very modern sermon which Docre gives: Satan, he declares, is the real master of *fin-de-siècle* France, and the true friend of the modern Parisian. In this respect, Huysmans' Black Mass reflects what it has always been rumoured to do – representing the real hopes and fears of the people, those who have been let down and ignored by traditional piety and religion. Docre rails against the 'mute God' who answers no prayers, and addresses the lives of the people in his absence: *"Thou are the favoured vassal of the banks and the financial institutions! Thou hast seen the weak crushed beneath the weight of capital; Thou hast heard the death rattle of the timid, weak with hunger, of women disembowelled for a crust of bread..."* Satan however is a realist, a *"God of logic and reason!"*

Interestingly, Docre also appeals to Satan as a means of dismissing the Biblical edict to 'Be fruitful and multiply'. Satan, he declares, presides over 'abortion', 'obstetrics' and the 'stillborn', as well as being guardian of *"our strident Neuroses [and] the Prison of our Hysteria"*. So if Satan is a realist, then he's a modernist, too: he helps those who helps themselves, locking up their secrets against the likes of Charcot and his new methods. Control, self-direction and equality; these are the things our *fin-de-siècle* Satanists espouse. Docre's sermon, as he stamps on the consecrated host, finally sends the women gathered into frenzy, and they writhe and contort on the chapel floor as the gathering becomes orgiastic. Durtal is appalled. He looks for his mistress, who has left his side, and eventually finds her. *"She was inhaling, with flared nostrils, the sexual perfume of the rutting couples. 'The smell of the sabbat!' she whispered to him between clenched teeth."*

Enraged, even intimidated by her behaviour, he demands that they leave. The entranced Hyacinthe agrees to follow him, but instead of hailing a cab (not in any case an easy thing to do in this deserted, rundown street) she takes him into a decrepit little wine shop near to the chapel. The people there seem to know her, and do not seem surprised when she takes Durtal into a private room. Although he tries to evade her, she is like a *"ghoulish fury"* and coaxes him into bed. Here, he later discovers that they have had sex on a bed littered with fragments of communion wafers. Even this lapsed Catholic is disgusted. Durtal has committed sacrilege, and it's the final outrage.

Given that Durtal (and Huysmans through him) would soon be on the path to re-embracing Catholicism, it seems that this was one move too many: Durtal flees, and refuses all further contact with the 'mad, morbific' Hyacinthe Chantelouve, a woman who, as it turns out, has been in control throughout, using Durtal for her own desires and controlling the progress of their affair. Going further than that, for all of his bluster, Durtal seems genuinely afraid of her now: she is part of a cabal of Satanists whose existence he thought may be a rumour, nothing more. Now not only did he have proof, but he has himself been initiated into appalling blasphemies. It's certainly more research for his biography than he was perhaps expecting, and he repels all further contact. Thus, our Madame Chantelouve goes back to her ordinary life, though we could guess that she will continue to supplement her existence in any way she sees fit.

Madame Chantelouve is such a fascinating figure because, in many ways, she is the ultimate modern woman. She is emancipated, outwardly respectable, educated, charming and every bit the society hostess, participating in social gatherings alongside her husband, where she is graciously accepted as an equal. This simply masks her other activities, however, and Durtal only slowly comes to this conclusion after seeing the worst of her excesses. It seems likely that he is not her first lover; she pursues him quite aggressively, and her protestations that she will break all contact with him seems to be part of a ruse: she approaches him, visiting late at night, and even invites him into the home she shares with her husband. Durtal always struggles with her single-mindedness, preferring his imagined version of her to the rather worldly woman he actually encounters.

But it's through her entirely other life as a Satanist that he is truly shocked by her. Her voraciousness, her appetites, and the fact that she tricks him into behaving in a way which offends his sensibilities is enough, ultimately, to make him leave her for good. He understands that this is the case, too. Comparing her to de Rais, a man who presented very different faces to the world at different times, he notes that she juggles being a society woman, a *"mud-spitting harlot"* and finally a *"thoroughgoing Satanist"*. This is ultimately too much, even for a man who can appreciate little good in the world, but both Huysmans and Durtal, two jaded aesthetes, would soon embrace Catholicism, moving away from the dangerous demi-monde and its antagonistic women altogether.

Critically, and inevitably, many readers were shocked by the novel. Originally serialised in **L'Écho de Paris** before being published in book form, several readers objected to the blasphemous and explicit scenes appearing in such a conservative paper. When it was published as a novel, its sale was banned from French railway stations, thus limiting its market quite substantially during a boom time for cheap paperbacks. However, for female readers of **Là-Bas**, this was a secondary concern: Madame Chantelouve, as it turns out, was someone to admire, even emulate. She had enough of the strange and enough of the aspirational to appeal to a range of New Women who were probably already fascinated with the new overtures of occult thinking in polite society. Critic Jean Lorrain notes, with disdain, that *"there was no brasserie in Montmartre, or studio in Montparnasse, where a little model, with eyes dilated by morphine and ether, did not rise, at the mere mention of Huysmans' name, to exclaim: 'His heroine, that's me!'"*

J.K. Huysmans

Madame Chantelouve's libidinous nature and bloody-minded pursuit of her own happiness seemed to chime with young women of the day, then, and they were not at all repulsed by her Satanism, seeing it instead as a facet of feminist emancipation; Chantelouve was a woman who had turned her back on a Church which had long served women peculiarly poorly, placing them at the root cause of man's Fall and then managing to go downhill from there. Chantelouve is highly-strung, but clever, respectable, but independent, au fait with the unwritten rules of her society, but unapologetically able to challenge them. Not only this, but she was inspired by at least one real woman who offered the same challenges to society, and as such she reflected changing times, non-conformity and liberty. This may be why establishment critics were less keen on the scandalous Madame Chantelouve than a rebellious female readership who saw something of themselves in her, giving rise to what Lorrain called *"a crowd of Madame Chantelouves on the market"*. These women knew, and enjoyed, Chantelouve's deliciously modern take on that old, special relationship between sinful women and the Devil.

WHEATLEY AND ALL HIS WORKS

THE CURIOUS CAREER OF BRITAIN'S MOST POPULAR OCCULT NOVELIST

DAVID FLINT

Ahh, Dennis Yeats Wheatley – probably the most famous author of occult fiction we've ever had. Born in 1897, he was also one of our most prolific writers, producing over sixty novels – plus papers, short stories, non-fiction and autobiographies, as well as inventing three board games – between 1933 and 1974. His work spanned the genres – while best known for his occult stories, he also wrote adventure and espionage novels (his Gregory Sallust series was an acknowledged influence on Ian Fleming when he was creating James Bond), science fiction, historical romances and more, often in series featuring recurring characters (Sallust, Duke de Richleau, Julian Day, Roger Brook) and frequently mixing his styles – his main characters would sometimes battle occult forces, other times enemy agents. Sometimes, both at the same time. As well as his own work, Wheatley also edited a series of occult books in the 1970s. He is one of the 20th century's best selling authors, selling a million books a year throughout the 1960s, but by the time that century came to a close, his work was - for the most part - out of print. Wheatley was a man of his time, and his time had been and gone.

For many years – throughout his whole writing career and beyond his death in 1977 – Wheatley's novels were continually in print, and were impossible not to be impressed by, at least on the surface level. For the well-off, or those wanting a serious looking library, there were the uniform hardcover editions of both Hutchinson and Heron Books. The editions that I recall seeing everywhere as a child – the mid-Seventies Arrow paperbacks – seemed the mainstay of the Satanic boom of the era, with their uniform covers that featured the same image of a topless woman surrounded by flames (a different colour for each book) with some arcane occult artefact in the foreground. With evocative titles like **The Satanist**, **The Devil Rides Out**, **The Ka of Gifford Hillary** and **Gateway to Hell**, these books promised to be the very height of black magic sensationalism, a veritable feast of salacious sex and supernatural horror. The fact that the books were more hefty in size than the works of Guy N. Smith and other pulp merchants of the time (**The Satanist** weighs in at 512 pages) simply suggested that they would be a more substantial read. And Wheatley, after all, was famed as a man who knew his stuff – no mere hack, he was a noted expert of black magic and its dangers. He'd even written a non-fiction, illustrated book – **The Devil and All His Works** – that was hyped as the last word on the subject (and this being a time when heavily illustrated, affordable hardbacks on witchcraft, occultism and Satanism were all the rage). Clearly, Wheatley's books were going to be a cut above everything else out there.

For reasons that the passing years have rendered mysterious, I didn't actually buy any of Wheatley's books when I was a nipper, despite gobbling up pulp fiction like it was going out of style (as, indeed, it was, though no one knew that at the time). Perhaps the sexy covers were just a bit too sexy to buy on shopping trips with my parents. Perhaps the books seemed too mature. Whatever the reason, Wheatley's work remained the forbidden fruit until the start of the 1980s, when they were reprinted – for what turned out to be the final time for decades – with new covers, again playing on the sexual (teasing nudity, cleavage-heavy gowns) and the horrific (giant floating skulls, unconvincing monsters). My choice in Wheatley books at this time was very much influenced by a love of Hammer Films, who had filmed two of Wheatley's black magic novels – **The Devil Rides Out** and **To the Devil – A Daughter** (as well as his adventure story **Uncharted Seas**, adapted as **The Lost Continent)**, and had planned to film **The Satanist** before a disgruntled Wheatley withdrew the rights to his work and Hammer went into terminal decline. It was these three black magic tales that I bought. And then didn't read. Or, more accurately, I began **The Devil Rides Out**, quickly realised my mistake and put it back on the shelf, to gather dust alongside the other two books for several years. Subsequent attempts to wade through the Wheatley oeuvre have been only slightly more successful - the books finished, but never really enjoyed. Reading Wheatley has often felt like a duty, rather than pleasure.

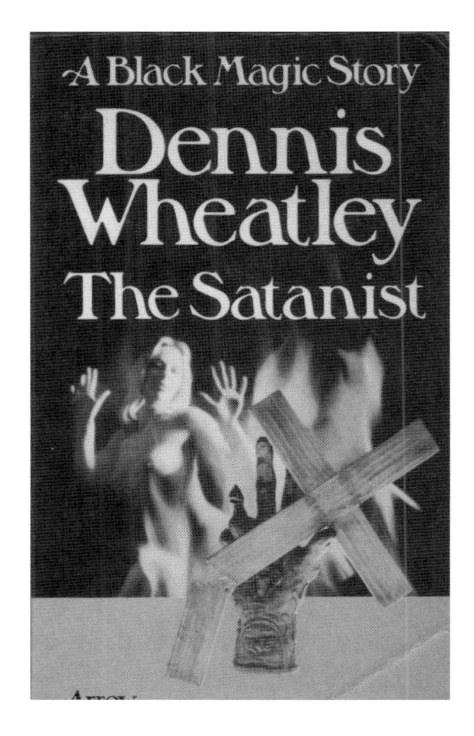

The problem with his work is that, while there is unquestioningly a cracking horror and adventure story at the heart of the novel, it is all too often buried within pages and pages of long-winded nonsense where the author indulges in his personal bugbears and attempts to display a lifestyle that he presumably believes to be relatable – or at least enviable – but which often seems

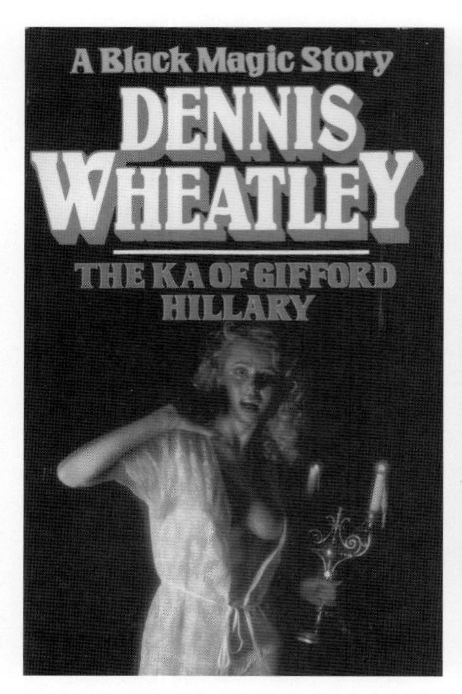

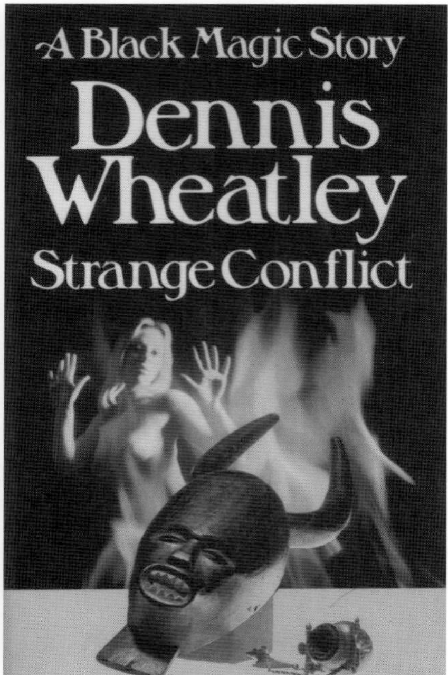

laughably indulgent. For instance, in **Gateway to Hell** (1970), he describes a meal that the heroes are sharing:

"The dinner had consisted of smoked cods' roes, beaten up with cream and served hot on toast, after being put under a grill, followed by a bisque d'Homard fortified with sherry, a partridge apiece, stuffed with foie-gras, and an iced orange salad laced with crème de menthe. With the roes they had a glass of very old Madeira, with the soup a Marco-brunner Kabinet '33, with the partridge a Chateau Latour '28 and with the orange salad a small cup of cold China tea. Now, having cleared their palates with the tea, and as they lit up the eight-inch long Hoyo de Monterreys that were the Duke's favourite cigars, Simon was giving them an Imperial Tokay of 1908."

All this is on the first page of the novel.

Wheatley was a man of convictions, and his convictions were that the lower orders should know their place, foreigners were generally untrustworthy, and the class system, monarchy and Empire were things to admire. While certainly not alone in those views amongst the literary establishment, Wheatley worries away at these obsessions throughout his work, often to the detriment of the story. Similarly, his undoubted knowledge of history, occultism and other subjects might have put him in good stead as a writer on those subjects if only he didn't feel the need to show off quite so much. In **The Devil Rides Out** (1934), several pages of the third chapter are given over to lengthy monologues about the true meaning of the Swastika and 'the Esoteric Doctrine', all of which might be interesting in a non-fiction story (though even then, only if less dryly written) but here manage to bring the story grinding to a halt before it even has a chance to get going. And that's overlooking the references to 'bad blacks' that can at least be seen as a reflection of racial attitudes of the day rather than a deliberate slur – though it's doubtful that Wheatley had much time for multiculturalism up until his death.

Shifty foreigners and the class system were not Wheatley's only obsessions, though both arguably come together in another recurring irritation for the author. To quote the back-cover blurb for **The Satanist** (1960):

"For years Colonel Verney had suspected a link between Devil-worship and the subversive influence of Soviet Russia."

Eh, what?

This belief that the atheistic USSR was a hive of Satanism is not simply a character trait of Verney, by the way. It's a theme that crops up in more than one of his books, including the non-fiction **The Devil and All His Works** (1971), as well as in his **A letter to Posterity**, written in 1947 and buried in his garden to be found by future generations (it was, in fact, unearthed in 1969, while Wheatley was very much still alive). Here, he paints an apocalyptic (or **Daily Mail**-flavoured) picture of a socialist Britain, in which the Monarchy has been abolished, feckless lower orders are pampered and the country is sliding into financial ruin. At one point, he even advocates armed resistance to this 'Dictatorship of the Proletariat' in a demented rant that is well

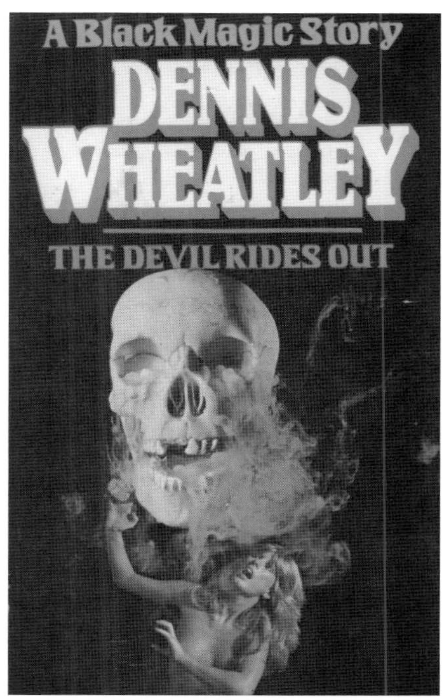

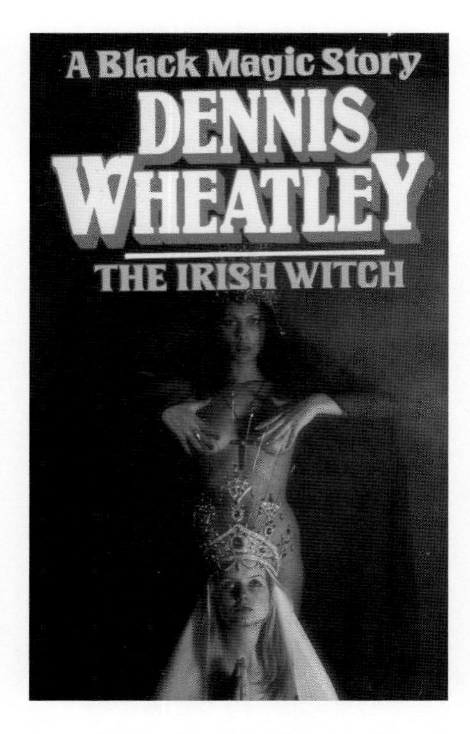

worth a read (it's available online, should you care to look).

But as dangerous as socialism seemed to Wheatley, it was perhaps secondary in his list of threats to society. The biggest danger was black magic.

Wheatley had a curious, some might even say hypocritical relationship with the occult. He seemed to genuinely believe that black magic was an authentic force, and a malignant one. It will come as no surprise – given his other beliefs – that he was a God-fearing Christian, and so perhaps his belief in the Devil as a very real entity is understandable. In **The Devil and All His Works**, Wheatley states that *"I am convinced (that) the opening of the minds of thousands of people to the influence of the Powers of Darkness… has formed a cancer in society"*, and posits the intriguing theory that many of the world's 'ills' – which he defines as including *"riots, wildcat strikes and anti-apartheid demonstrations"* - could be the result of Satanism. In interviews, Wheatley – much like his friend Christopher Lee – was quick to point out the very real, physical and moral dangers of black magic and occultism. Many of his occult books included the following disclaimer:

"I, personally, have never assisted at, or participated in, any ceremony associated with Magic – Black or White. Should any of my readers incline to a serious study of the subject and thus come into contact with a man or woman of Power, I feel that it is only right to urge them, most strongly, to refrain from being drawn into any practice of the Secret Art in any way. My own observations have led me to an absolute conviction that to do so would bring them into dangers of a very real and concrete nature."

And yet if anyone was responsible for the spread of interest in the subject, then surely it was Wheatley, with his overblown potboilers that not only traded off the forbidden lure of the occult but also made it oddly attractive. He seems to have wanted to have his cake and eat it – if he was genuinely concerned about this malign influence, then why continue to promote it with his work? His disclaimer has the ring of the carnival barker about it – promising the ultimate in horrors for those brave enough to enter within. I don't for a moment think that this was the intention – though Wheatley clearly knew that sensationalism sold – but his relationship with black magic seems to have been a touch ambiguous at times.

After all, not only did Wheatley promote black magic through his writing, but he also supervised **The Dennis Wheatley Library of the Occult**, a series of books published by Sphere in the 1970s. As well as horror fiction like **Dracula** and **The Werewolf of Paris**, this collection included works by Aleister Crowley and non-fiction occult volumes by H.P. Blavatsky, magician Isaac Bonewits and others. This seems a peculiar way of discouraging interest in the occult.

But Wheatley not only felt that occultism was dangerous, he actually wanted it outlawed. He bemoaned the 1951 legalisation of witchcraft in England, stating that it was *"a principal breeding ground for dope-addicts, anarchists and lawlessness"*, and demands that psychic investigation should only be carried out under licence.

In retrospect, it seems that it was not so much Satanism, witchcraft or even Communism that terrified Wheatley as much as the general decline of the old order and the rise of the permissive society that these 'dangers' represented. The world was changing around him, and he didn't like it one little bit. This perhaps explains his very different reactions to the two major Hammer films based on his black magic work.

The Devil Rides Out, made in 1968 is, if nothing else, evidence that beneath the waffle, Wheatley has the knack for a good story. Terence Fisher's film sticks pretty closely to the novel, but strips away the fat, allowing the dramatic action to shine in what is one of the best Hammer films from the 1960s. Wheatley loved it. He was considerably less happy with **To the Devil – A Daughter**, made in 1975 and based on the 1953 novel. This was the last Hammer Horror film for over thirty years, shot as the company struggled with changing tastes and a declining British film industry. Wheatley's novel was in many ways, a logical choice to film, given the continued popularity of his work; but Hammer clearly realised that the story, full of asides about socialists and dated moralising, was hardly going to fly in a post-**Exorcist** world. All but the basics of Wheatley's story were dumped by screenwriter Chris Wicking, with the story modernised and – to a degree – sensationalised, with some of the most outrageously lurid scenes that Hammer had ever sanctioned.

Wheatley relaxes on holiday in the 1960s

Wheatley, understandably, hated it – he found the film 'disgusting' and promptly refused to allow Hammer to film any more of his books (not that they were in a position to do so anyway). Plans to film **The Satanist** continued throughout the 1970s - the film at various times being planned by would-be Hammer rivals Tyburn and EMI - but ultimately came to naught. By the end of the decade,

Possibly one of the scenes in Hammer's To the Devil - A Daughter that Wheatley found 'disgusting'

Wheatley's class-ridden black magic seemed very much like your dad's horror in the face of **Halloween**, **Dawn of the Dead** and **Friday 13th.**

The only other notable Wheatley adaptation came three decades after his death – **The Haunted Airman**, made in 2006 by the BBC, takes even greater liberties with the source material, **The Haunting of Toby Jugg** (1948), essentially abandoning the supernatural aspects in favour of the psychological and – naturally – stripping out the jingoistic, hawkish approach of the original novel. It's unsurprisingly terrible.

Wheatley died in 1977, around the time that his books began to fall out of favour with readers looking for thrills and chills – a new generation of literary and high-profile horror authors like Stephen King would soon make his work redundant, an embarrassing hangover from the days of Empire. He is buried in Brockwood Cemetery, also known as the London Necropolis. Copyright issues hampered any efforts to bring back his books in later years, but in the late 2000s, several of his books appeared as part of the Wordsworth classic fiction collections – usually found in discount bookshops. More recently, Bloomsbury Reader have started to reprint his work, sometimes only in eBook format. Notably, these new editions have been both abridged and edited by his grandson, Dominic to remove the more awkward opinions and make the novels less cumbersome

– Wheatley's reactionary attitudes are no longer acceptable, it seems, even with the context of age.

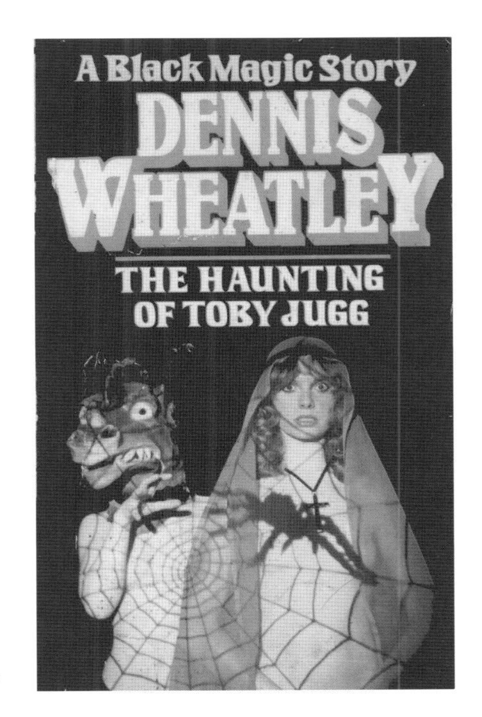

Yet for all the problems with his books – the bigotry, the elitism, the mad tangents, the hypocritical moralising and the aimless waffle that makes even the best of them feel like hard work – there is something about Wheatley's novels that remains oddly attractive. It's not just the lecherous covers of the paperbacks – though they certainly help. It's more the sense that these are a strange part of history that is now being buried.

No matter what their faults are, the fact remains that these books had a tremendous impact on a whole generation of horror fans and occultists alike – even if they never actually read them. The Dennis Wheatley collection is an important part of British literary history, and we should be treasuring these odd, eccentric tales of Satanism and snobbery.

THE WHEATLEY OCCULT WORKS:

The Devil Rides Out (1934 – Duke de Richleau series)
Strange Conflict (1941 – Duke de Richleau series)
The Haunting of Toby Jugg (1948)
To the Devil – A Daughter (1953)
The Ka of Gifford Hillary (1956)
The Satanist (1960)
They Used Dark Forces (1964 – Gregory Sallhurst series)
Unholy Crusade (1967)
The Witch Witch of the South Seas (1968 – Gregory Sallhurst series)
Gateway to Hell (1970 – Duke de Richleau series)
The Devil and All His Works (1971 – non-fiction)
The Irish Witch (1973 – Roger Brook series)

GOLDEN IDOL

HOW MY EXPERIENCES IN THE ORTHODOX CHURCH LED TO SELF-REVERENCE, SELF-DETERMINATION, AND SELF-EMANCIPATION

LOGOSPILGRIM

By the time I was in my mid-thirties, an ardent need to confront and at long last overcome the forces that kept me from attaining my life potential manifested itself in a most unusual way. At first glance, it would no doubt even seem like the path I took to achieve self-empowerment was self-defeating and the exact opposite of the steps one should take to reject all forms of invasive, despotic control.

Ultimately, however, this bold rejection is precisely what happened. But then, I've never been one to do anything the usual way. My essence is baroque.

To rid yourself of a foreign agent, it's sometimes necessary to absorb it. In my case, the foreign agent was the Judeo-Christian worldview, which carried within itself the vehicle of its destruction, namely mysticism.

This worldview was injected in my system when I was a young child, and it was mixed with other ingredients that made it extremely potent: emotional bonds, self-preservation, and as the years went by, the complications due to post-traumatic stress disorder.

In other words, the religion didn't come on its own. It was linked to a multitude of relational variables and problematic circumstances.

Fortunately, I had the sort of personality, the inner resilience, that enabled me quite early in life to distill benefit from what appeared, on the surface, to be wholly negative and harmful. I was a Satanic alchemist without knowing it. No matter how adverse my conditions were, I was at my core a survivor, a champion of my self.

Therefore, the final outcome of my experiment with Eastern Orthodoxy doesn't surprise me in the least.

I now fully celebrate myself. Shamelessly, gloriously, decadently, unabashedly. I achieved this through what I'll call a deliciously diabolical transmutation.

When I was younger, I knew Judeo-Christianity in its Roman Catholic, then Evangelical embodiments. The former was cold and remote, the second even more so—and insidious as well. For all its promises of unimpeded rapport with the so-called divine, Evangelicalism stripped human beings of their power with an even more total and brutal efficiency than Roman Catholicism did, while, ironically, making the divine more unreachable, remote, and inhuman than its despised Catholic opponent.

Regardless of its strict hierarchy, Roman Catholicism had one major quality going for it: the beauty of its churches. It was steeped in mystery. Theater. Art. Poetry. As such, it was far more human, despite its heavy legalism.

It's this search for the human in the divine that led me to the most theatrical embodiment of Judeo-Christianity: Eastern Orthodoxy.

I had first encountered Orthodoxy during my studies at university. Eastern Orthodoxy portrayed itself as the most ancient, the truest and most elemental Christianity. It was the very consequence of my character and upbringing, fierce endurance, that gave rise to my decision to pursue this final quest for something valuable in Judeo-Christianity.

Subconsciously, I was searching for the god I would only find inside my human self. The god that was my human self: my self as the sole supreme meaning of my life. My self as liberator.

The years I spent within the Orthodox Church were like sharp knives that sliced each cord, one after the other, entangling my emotions, my affections, my traumatic experiences, in the knot of nonsensical Judeo-Christian dogmas.

Key to this were icons and sacred objects.If you think that Roman Catholic masses are a feast for the senses, you haven't savoured the richness of Eastern Orthodox liturgy.

Many of my life experiences had driven me deep inside my mind, the one space where I enjoyed freedom. I was, in effect, detached from myself, from my body, from my humanity. Inside the Orthodox church, with its myriad lights and shimmering, golden walls, the mind and the body slowly became one again.

Let me set the scene for you. It's Holy Week, the most liturgically intense time of the year. We're venerating the cross. The silver Orthodox cross is anointed with fragrant rose oils and lying in a basket overflowing with fresh blooms. The air is thick with incense smoke, the scent of beeswax candles. The soft sound of chanting is omnipresent as you prostrate yourself before, then kiss the silver cross. The sweet perfume of roses fills your nostrils with sensual delight. All around you, from floor to ceiling, calm saints and deities gaze at you, and their clothes are adorned with gold, so much gold; there's gold everywhere. The doors that guard the altar are closed, hiding the holy place from view. You're encompassed by mystery made physical, tangible. You taste earthly ecstasy. Your humanity is elevated like the chalice in the priest's hands. How far you are from the atrocious, Calvinistic 'utter depravity'!

And when you touch the icons, when you kiss them, your physical self, your human self, is part of the mystery, the gods. These images remind you that you are in a synergetic union, that you are a Christ, a god. Juxtaposed to this are profoundly mystical notions of self-forgetfulness, so that you imitate the human Christ God who died to give life to the divine in you. There is a dissolution between here and There.

Little by little, I reintegrated my humanity. My own senses showed me the way out of the illusory Other that was nothing but a semblance of my power, the only true power in my life. The greater the dissolution between here and There, between I and the Other, the fainter the intangible, otherworldly windows become. As I said before, mysticism carries within it the elixir of a religion's evaporation, which is why religious institutions are wary of it and caution against it: mystical experiences are 'reserved for the saints' who are pure enough not to stray from the institution and its laws, its wise precepts.

I had come close to comprehending this power of mine in the past, when I was in my mid-twenties, but I wasn't ready then. I was in too much pain and couldn't pry myself from the grip of a nihilism that stemmed from depression and unaddressed rage. I hadn't come to the understanding that although life had no inherent meaning, it didn't make my life inherently meaningless.

I alone had that power: I gave my life the meaning I desired to give it.

When I emerged from the useless golden shell of Orthodoxy, an Orthodoxy that revealed the inner god and yet made certain to tame it, to confine it, to tie it to a non-existent Other and consequently to the Orthodox institution and its clergy, I progressively discovered that all my human desires and emotions were valid; along with this discovery, the ability to have these desires and emotions without being dominated by them or fearing them. What is permissible is normal, free of the pernicious compulsory urges and pathology that characterises the 'forbidden'.

At the same time, I was standing over a primal fear as one stands over a conquered foe. It was all coming together like the elements in an equation. I gave my life meaning because the malignant narcissist, the psychic vampire who attempted to rule my existence from the days of my childhood, who wanted to crush my identity, to silence my voice, to annihilate me as a person in my own right, had no power over me anymore. Neither the man, nor his dim echoes in fabricated Judeo-Christian deities under their assorted and wildly contrasting, duplicitous guises, with the same predatory *raison d'être*.

The post-traumatic stress disorder that had given me so many difficulties, and of which I'd been unaware for much of my life, had also nurtured this fearsome power in me, the power to erase those who would deny me my personhood, my godhood.

The formidable power to survive.

This power burst into flames inside of me. Lo, the Satanic alchemist drank the elixir of life, and the old griefs, the old guilts, turned to dust. And there were no futile regrets, no 'if onlys': as ever, I made the absolute best of what I had at hand. What's the alternative, save a foolish waste of precious time? This is what it means to turn lead into gold. I assumed myself as the master of my destiny.

There is no omniscience, no omnipotence, but there is the god self: the self as priority, as measure of one's life and world. This requires knowledge and a daring, independent mind.

I would eventually express this coming forth of my triumphant, radiant godhood by covering myself with vintage polyester and the golden shimmer of the disco era. I was the living, fleshly icon worthy of my self-veneration. A glittering disco ball.

The Seventies are my total environment of choice.The Me Decade.

As I cast away every fetter and rejected every false imperative, I reclaimed everything that had enabled me to survive, all that had filled me with joy and the strength to keep going. I decorated my personal space with objects, symbols, of the freedom and individuality no one and nothing had been able to quench.

A vintage Fisher-Price writing desk; a Sears Merry Mushroom cookie jar; a 1975 Eaton's Christmas catalog; a K-Tel Looney Tunes vinyl record: these and more joined modern collections, especially toys, and Eighties New Wave music, in a personally significant, nostalgic symbiosis that ignited pleasure within me and formed a temple dedicated to me, my life, my gratification.

I adorned myself with gold jewels, lay down on luxurious shag carpets, and took self-portraits. I thrust myself into the world in the manner of my own choosing, proudly displayed and yet inaccessible, because I only belong to me. I am mine, in a fascinating relationship with myself and whatever I cherish, whomever I love.

The outer world won't impose its prerogatives upon me.

To stand strong, you must be capable of standing alone. That, I learned early in life. Thankfully, I've always had a solitary temperament, as well as a willfulness that made me resistant to pressure, to sweeping currents. If some ridiculed me because of my interests, I loved what I loved regardless; if some spurned me because of my decisions, I persisted in my choices, I faced the repercussions with grit and tenacity. With belief in myself.

I've known pain, but the rewards have outweighed the losses by far. The losses have been as nothing to me in the end, because what was most important is what remained and was enhanced by the process: myself.

Perhaps this is why I find so many things interesting, why I love life as I do. Why I dance like a golden idol on the illuminated dance floor. I have prevailed. I am truly alive. I've breathed life into myself; I am my own creator. I shine. Do you?

HEAVEN SHALL BURN WHEN WE ARE GATHERED

BLACKHEARTS AND THE INTERNATIONAL BLACK METAL UNDERGROUND

C.J. LINES

"I remember that moment exactly," says Sina Winter, on the first time he heard Burzum's **Filosfem**. *"It was a Thursday night and I came back home. I'd just got the tape and I was suddenly listening to that album and everything was completely different, the sound, the atmosphere was all different, all unknown. It felt strange and mysterious and I couldn't understand it. I remember that I listened to it five or six times in a row that night. I just felt like the atmosphere was so close to my inner being. It's really hard to explain when you are talking about your emotions but there was something special about that. From that time, I couldn't listen to any other type of metal music for a long time. I was just searching to find more black metal albums. I didn't know much about it, I was trying to find more info and other bands and it was completely different. Like stepping into a new world for me."*

That may sound like a standard reaction for any metalhead exploring darker territories for the first time but for Sina, a metalhead growing up in Iran under the regime of Ayatollah Ali Khamenei, it was something far more important. This is a country where metal music of any kind is considered blasphemy - and blasphemy can be treated as a capital offence. Risking his freedom and his life, Sina not only listened to black metal but also recorded his own albums (first as Sorg Innkallese, then as From The Vastland) and, in 2013, made history by travelling to Norway to perform a live set at Inferno Fest.

The general consensus is that black metal has mellowed out since its heyday in the early Nineties. Back then, a group of young Norwegians shocked the world with their mysterious raw music, occult lyrics, incomprehensible band logos, church burnings and multiple murders. The horrors of this scene are well-documented, most famously in Michael Moynihan's **Lords Of Chaos** (1998) but, even by then, most of the major players had distanced themselves from the controversy. As the 2000s hit, black metal was commercially bigger than ever with bands like Dimmu Borgir and Emperor adding a keyboard-driven symphonic quality to their songs and reaching a wide audience. By 2017, for many original fans, 'true Norwegian black metal' had taken on something of a pantomime quality.

However, in other less obvious parts of the world, the genre thrived as it always had done – off the radar and underground – and remained as extreme as ever. Sina's story is part of **Blackhearts**, a documentary by Fredrik Horn Akselsen and Christian Falch that looks at modern black metal subculture and the effect it's had on the lives of three different musicians in countries not normally associated with the genre. It's a heartfelt, compelling and strange journey to the heart of what drives black metallers to such lengths and why the music means so much to them.

"I had a private moment of realisation when I understood this would be a good film," says director Falch. *"I'm married to a lady from Colombia and she's a black metal fan herself. She told me that when she was 15 years old her father threw her out of their apartment in Bogota. He said she had brought the devil to their home with her black metal albums so she would have to get rid of this music or she would have to go. So she went! A 15 year old girl in Bogota which, at the time, was one of the most dangerous cities in the world! And this fascinated me very much."*

When asked about exactly what it is about black metal that inspires such devotion, Falch replies *"I think it sparks some kind of religious feelings in people because it's more than just music. The black metal genre provides people with the full package - a way to dress, a way to look, a way to act, how to think, what to like, what not to like and, on top of this, comes very strong, great music. So I think it offers a way of life and an ideology and all these elements make it potent and powerful."*

In choosing the three subjects of his film – Sina, Hector from Luciferian (Colombia) and Kaiadas from Naer Mataron (Greece) – Falch spent over a year buried in research. *"I met a lot of interesting people that never made it to the film in the end but chose the ones you see because they have their own unique approach to the music and the ideology. They come from very different backgrounds and cultures but they share the same dream, which is going to Norway to play a gig in the country that they admired and heard so much about for many years."*

Luciferian are the band most in touch with the occult side of black metal and it's far from just posturing. Their Satanic lyrics reflect their lifestyle, which involves regular consultations with a sinister Colombian dark magician in a wheelchair who guides them down the left hand path. At one jaw-dropping point in the film, they hold a dramatic black mass involving naked women and blood sacrifice, a ritual designed to enlist Satan's help in securing travel visas for their Norwegian show.

"By that time I had been hanging out with these guys for more than two years so I felt pretty safe about who they are, but I never thought they would go that far!" admits Falch. *"Doing this ritual was not my idea. We just followed them in there and yeah, it was quite intense and lasted for more than two hours actually. I was positively shocked but, you know, I was making a film so I understood that it was going to look good and be one of the highlights!"*

But does he think the ritual actually worked? *"Well, I have to admit that I also made a couple of phonecalls to the Norwegian Embassy so maybe it was a combination of the ritual and my connections... But they are pretty convinced the ritual helped! I mean, having the visa is one thing but they did also experience a major success with their band afterwards. So if you ask me, I'm not quite sure about how it worked but, if you ask them, they are convinced that this ritual kickstarted their careers."*

Over in Greece, Falch spent time with Kaiadas, who plays bass in Naer Mataron, a black metal band with far-right political connections. Unexpectedly, Kaiadas was arrested half-way through filming Blackhearts for *"playing a pivotal role in a criminal organisation"*, the ultranationalist party Golden Dawn. *"I had mixed feelings on this"*, says Falch of the arrest. *"I mean, honestly, I didn't try to understand why they threw him in prison for something like this but again, as a filmmaker, we do like it when things change rapidly. Everyone was expecting his release to happen very quickly but he ended up in custody for 18 months, which is a very long time when you're making a film. We had to do some rethinking so started following his other band members instead. Him being arrested because of politics also underlines a little bit about the statement we want to make in the film about his story."*

It's not the only film Falch intends to make about Kaiadas either. *"I've used my access in Greece to make a film about the Golden Dawn Party. It's not about music at all, it's about extreme right-wing politics in Greece and it's gonna be a pretty heavy documentary... They have a zero media policy so that's why I just had to take the plunge on this unique access. We hope to release it this autumn. It's almost ready..."*

There's a surprisingly large 'National Socialist Black Metal' scene (as explored in the comprehensive **Wolves Among Sheep** book by Max Ribaric and Davide Maspero) and while Naer Mataron claim their politics are music are separate, it's interesting that so many bands link the two. *"I think it's about extremity,"* muses Falch. *"A lot of black metal fans tend to have some kind of magnetic energy that drives them towards all kind of extremes. The most extreme music, the most extreme political ideas, the most horrific jokes, they want to take it as far as possible. It's natural for them to seek the extremes."*

The irony that in one thread of **Blackhearts** we have Sina being persecuted by an oppressive regime and, in another, Kaiadas being part of one, is not lost on Falch. *"It just goes to show that this thing with black metal depends on each culture and it's interpreted very differently, depending on the religious backgrounds or the political situation in each country. I wanted to show in the film the diversity in opinion and interpretation of this music."*

It makes for an interesting contrast, but **Blackhearts** is a film full of them. In one scene, the local mayor appears onstage to kick off the Inferno Festival, remarking on how the sore throat she's suffering makes her sound more black metal. *"Yeah!"* says Falch, laughing. *"We chose to include it as an absurd moment in the film because this happened in the same city where they killed each other and burned down churches 20 years ago but now, these artists, you can see them on Friday night talk shows, they are everywhere just like pop musicians and everything that used to be scary or occult about these bands have been domesticated. We wanted to show them the contrast between how it's perceived in Norway compared with how it's perceived in Iran."*

Certainly, sending Sina back from Inferno Fest to Iran was a low point in the whole process for Falch. *"I was very sick,"* he says. *"I had sleepless nights because of this. One of the worst days in my life was saying goodbye to him at the airport in Oslo, seeing him board that plane. But I've been very open and very honest with Sina about this all along. I had to trust his judgement on everything and whenever a situation occurred where he said 'no, I can't do this', we respected it. He was in charge of his own destiny."*

Sina himself confirms this, recalling his initial conversations with Falch and the decision to be a part of **Blackhearts**. *"You know, first I said 'yes!' then I thought about the problems! Back then, all we could do was record our albums in our homes and release them outside the country and that was the max. We couldn't get a gig anywhere and I didn't have a band anyway. With From The Vastland I worked as the only band member.*

But I knew that this would bring me new chances. This is more than just music for me. This is my passion so I couldn't resist and I couldn't say no."

This passion, to some extent, is cemented by the adversity he faced and the efforts he had to go through just to be a black metal fan. *"There was no internet, no record shops, no label companies. It was banned. I had just two other friends who were fans of metal music and we were trading our tapes in secret. Someone would come into the country and bring in some tapes or you'd meet someone who already had some tapes you could borrow or copy. We were taking weeks and weeks just to find one new album and that was if we were very lucky."*

As a result, there wasn't much of a metal 'scene' in Iran. *"If you're a musician and you want to release your album, you need to get permits from the Ministry of Culture,"* Sina explains. *"That's what it says in law. But in reality it doesn't work like that. Those religious people who are in power, they don't allow this kind of music that comes from western culture. They call it Satanic and they call it blasphemy so you're not allowed to release or buy metal albums."*

From The Vastland's records take their influence from classic raw Norwegian black metal but with middle eastern motifs and lyrics deeply rooted in Zoroastrianism. *"I was always into history and mythology, not just my country but Norse, Egyptian, Mayan… but more and more I was reading about our own history, the epic stories, the Persian stories, all the myth and legend and the battle between darkness and light. It is proper for this kind of music."*

There's another irony to be found here in the fact that Sina's lyrics take their inspiration from his own cultural heritage and yet the Ministry of Culture has banned them. *"Yeah, that's like a paradox!"* He laughs. *"What I'm doing is talking about our history and I'm*

not saying anything against it but still I'm not allowed to it because they call this music Satanic and I can't understand it. Those people who are in charge of our country have no idea what black metal or metal is, they just call it all blasphemy.

"I was lucky because my family have always supported me - even now I get a phonecall from my parents and they ask how things are going with my music - but a lot of people don't know if what they're doing is the right thing or if it's what is called 'sin' and that's sad. People look at you, as a metal fan, like you are a criminal. There were a lot of cases during past years where other musicians tried to release an album or play a concert and the government makes problems for them. I don't know if you have heard of Confess?"

Confess were a nu-metal influenced band from Tehran whose members were incarcerated in 2015 and charged with several offences including blasphemy, forming an illegal band and advertising against the system. At one point, they faced execution although Amnesty International have recently confirmed this is no longer the case. At the time of writing, they remain in prison and it's likely they will serve the maximum sentence.

"Of course it will change," Sina says, confident things won't always be this tough for Iranian metallers. *"What you see in the news about Iran is something that our government officially represent, but what's going on inside the country is completely different. This new generation has the internet, which we didn't have, and they are in touch with western people. They know what's going on in other countries and that's what they want. So of course it will change. Nothing will last forever. Things are changing slowly just because people want something and the government can't resist any longer. It's been almost 40 years since the revolution happened in Iran and they try to keep the country closed but nowadays it doesn't work like that. I'm hopeful. I don't know when, but I'm sure it will happen."*

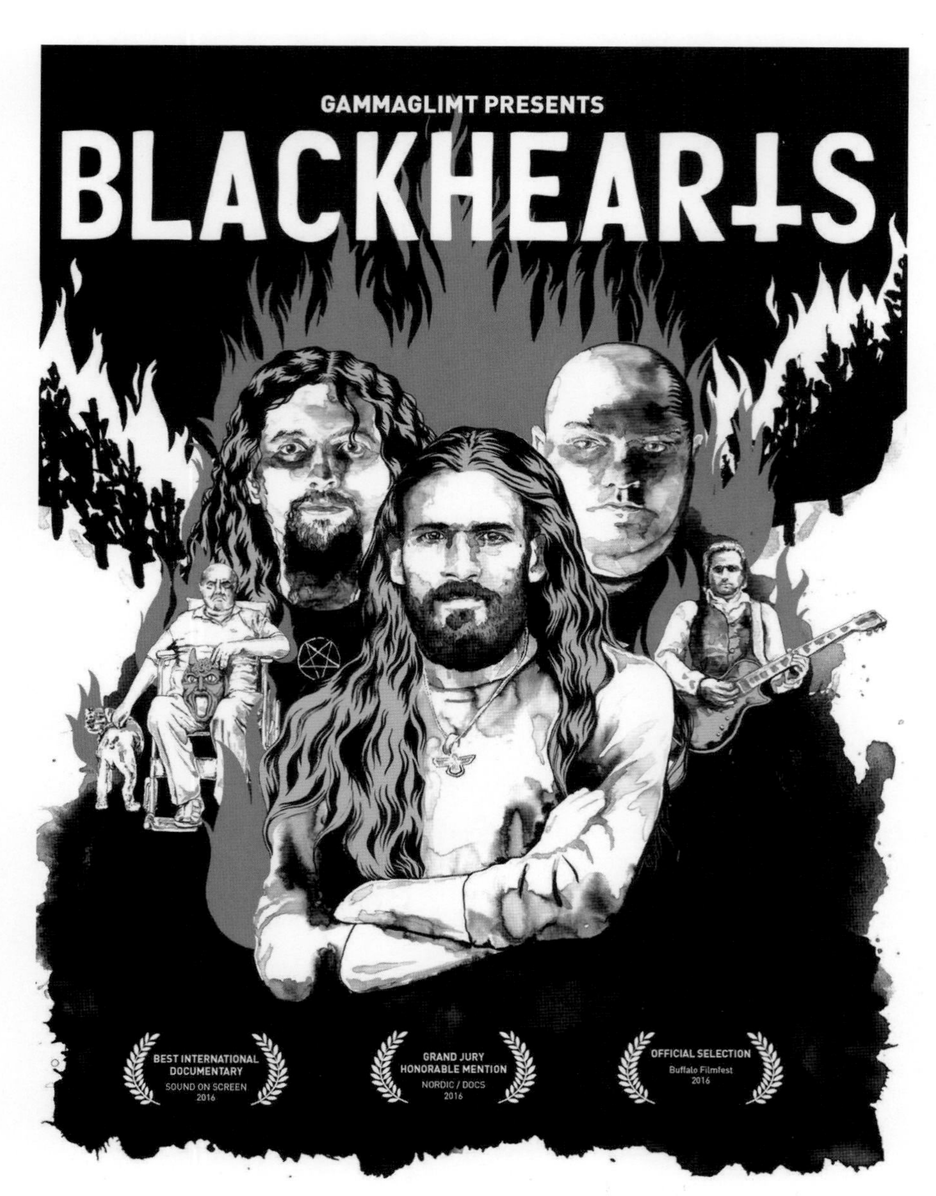

« A profound and wryly humorous film »
Decibel Magazine

For Sina, being a part of **Blackhearts** and assembling a band of Norwegian black metal musicians to play the first From The Vastland show at Inferno would prove to be life-changing. *"Meeting with all those legends like Arnt (Keep of Kalessin) and Nocturno Culto (Darkthrone), I was in dreams. I was not sure what kind of people they would be but I saw how they were nice and friendly and, after a couple of minutes, I didn't feel that I'm a stranger there."*

After returning to Iran from Norway, Sina found the pressure on him mounting. He was receiving death threats and, after an interview with him aired on BBC News (a channel that isn't blocked in Iran), he knew he had to leave or face punishment. With the help of Falch, he secured a special cultural visa and, in 2014, moved to Norway. *"I've released four more records since then and right now I'm working on the new album. Hopefully in a few months I'm going into the studio to start recording."*

"They accepted me," he says, of his new countrymen. *"Black metal is a small community, we all know each other and have become a family where we have everything. It doesn't matter where you are from or how long you've been making music. It's a brotherhood."*

Christian Falch concurs. *"Sina and I are almost next door neighbours in our little town up north in Norway. We hang out every day and he's become one of my closest friends. So you know, after all these years of making the film, I ended up with a documentary that I'm proud of but I also ended up with a new best friend. Sina is my source of inspiration really. His guts and his persistence. I have total respect for his passion. He's like a symbol of the positive effects of never giving up."*

And that's what makes **Blackhearts** such a great film, even for people who aren't into black metal. While the particular devotion the genre inspires may be unique, the film's message speaks to anyone who's ever been driven by a great dream. Its success at festival screenings proves that it's reached a wider audience than even Falch had expected. *"We wanted to include humour,"* he says. *"We wanted to bring down some myths perhaps, show a different side of the coin. We did a few things that are very unorthodox when it comes to documentaries about metal music but people understood and the negative response has been almost non-existent. That's actually the biggest surprise. We were preparing a page on our website to post all the hate mail but it never happened. We were looking really hard to find the universal achievement stories which involve all this black metal stuff and I think we succeeded, especially with Sina. His story has reached a lot of people."*

Blackhearts is now available worldwide on DVD and streams, including a free geoblocked minisite (link available directly from the filmmakers) for viewers who want to watch it in Iran where, of course, it's banned.

SATANIC MOJO MANIFESTO

JASON ATOMIC

Satanic Mojo is an art project that uses meta fiction to create artefacts that would fit into the history of Satanism and the dark arts in pop culture. So we're looking at things that have been accused of being Satanic, or are referring to actual events, cults or practices. We can get quite academic, but we do it in a really poppy way that looks like fun.

My passion and dream for most of my teenage years was to read and create comics. I drew and self published comics, up until moving to Japan in the early Nineties, where I wanted to get into the Manga trade.

However when I discovered what a soul destroying job working for a manga company would be I dropped the idea and I ran away from comics for about 20 years. I decided to focus on 'real life' & separated pictures from words sketching from life on a daily basis and keeping a series of journals in which to explore my adventures. I concentrated on finding interesting and exciting people to paint portraits of, sketched at live events, turned live sketching into a performance event.

That was all going fine until, the fateful day that I discovered an anagram of my name spells Satanic Mojo; as an artist I couldn't really take that information on board without it affecting my practice.

Photos:Beatrice Schleyer

I thought could go through my lifetime and create artefacts that respond to different key years within that period – I was born in 1967, which was the Summer of Love, when it seemed that the world was going to change, and then in 1969 we have what Hunter S. Thompson referred to as the 'Summer Of Bad Craziness' when 'the powers that be' jumped on the Charlie Manson thing using it to discredit hippies, and all that free love and sharing and being excellent to one another, as Bill and Ted would say. They tried to get rid of all of that and pushed us towards a more selfish, materialistic, capitalist, monotheist, patriarchal mindset. I feel that was done deliberately, so I'm trying to sow the seeds of undoing that in my own reality by examining that period. So I'm looking at 67 – 69 to start with, and then 69 – 72. There are these little blocks where it's gone from the hippy freakout, love-in, acid-fest to this stabby, murderous, big daddy world. From Woodstock to Hammer Horror. Later Hammer Horror – **Dracula AD 1972**, **The Satanic Rites of Dracula**. And you can see how that comes in after the Manson family. **Blood on Satan's Claw** and **I Drink You Blood** directly reference that social paranoia, with the kid-cult killers.

Next we lead into the misguided Satanic Panic of the Eighties and Nineties with an accusing finger pointed towards heavy metal and RPGs like Dungeons and Dragons. That's on my to-do list: a Satanic role-playing game. If they're going to accuse us of

SATANSPLOITATION PICTURES PRESENT AN L.S.D. 666 PRODUCTION
SECRETS OF THE HIPPIE WITCH-CULT
BLACK ACID
BLACK MASS
BLACKMAIL
SEX SLAVES OF SATAN
SATANIC MOJO 1972AD
WIDESCREEN · COLOR by DELUXE
Distributed by CINEMAGICK INDUSTRIES
SOUND by moog
Copyright (c) 1972 Satansploitation Pictures
X
NO ONE UNDER 18 ADMITTED
Printed in the U.S.A.

being that, why don't we do it? Why don't we make a game designed to ensare kids' souls?

But I'm getting ahead of myself, I took some time off and re-read all my old occult encyclopaedias and horror stories, and everything in between – Marvel horror comics, sixties undergrounds, **Malleus Maleficarum**, whatever. I re-immersed myself in all that stuff I loved as a kid, and realised that I really know and care about it, it has always been with me. They always say 'write what you know' so I made it my mission.

I found out that Jinx Dawson from sixties psychedelic occult rock group Coven is also a practising witch and will design sigils for people that she'll draw by hand, I figured that her involvement would give things a proper gravitas so my first act was to a have her craft a Satanic Mojo sigil.

I wanted to make a film, and so the next thing we did was to spread rumours of a lost witchsploitation movie ***Satanic Mojo AD 1972***, because I'm obsessed with Hammer Horror, and the work of Kenneth Anger… that Dennis Wheatley, Aleister Crowley black magic paranoia really impacted on the pop culture of the early seventies. **Satanic Mojo** should've been a film, so I invented this back story about this flame war between hippies and gangster Satanists, both trying to exploit the same market for different ends. Our photographer friend Beatrice Schleyer came to visit us and she has one of those large format cameras with the giant negatives. She wanted to shoot some old style analogue photographs of Manko & I. We built an altar in the kitchen of our Balfron Tower flat, blacked the place out, filled it with incense smoke and she shot us looking like Anton LaVey meets **Charlie's Angels**. The result was a set of amazing photographs, Before printing, for added authenticity she even threw the negatives on her floor and stamped on them for a bit so they'd have some random scratches… anyway, while the shoot was going on we also we shot a few seconds of black & white video footage, this was cut-up with shots of candles, our cat Howard, the moon etc. I leaked this footage online along with some of the pictures which were presented as backstage photos from this lost movie. It really took off. People genuinely believed it was real. Some even produced T-shirts bootlegging these images.

I'd still like to make the movie. I've got a lot of ideas about how the imagery & soundtrack should go. The real coup though was meeting Graham Humphreys, the legendary movie poster designer, he loved the idea and created real poster for our fake movie. It's legit. It says everything it needs to say.

I'd love to make a record. How about one where, when you play it backwards, it goes *"Jesus is Love"*. Because he was. This is one of the things we do in **Satanic Mojo**, Jesus is one of our icons within the comic. He wasn't a Christian. The Christian church was built by the people that murdered him in order to steal his power and discredit his methods and techniques. That guy was a magician who loved prostitutes and homosexuals, he wasn't this right-wing avatar that they've tried to make him into. We need to save Jesus from the church as much as we need to save the Swastika from the Nazis. These things do not belong to these people, they should not be allowed to have them.

Satanic Flea Market: Krent Able, Manko, Jason Atomic, Carla

I wanted to make clothes and this led to collaborations with the Tokyo based street fashion label Milkboy & Charles Of London. There were lots more things I wanted to do but I figured that as I already knew how to make comics, that was the place to start. And so began the saga of **Satanic Mojo comix**.

Using the contacts I'd made at Orbital Comics, where I'd already been curating group shows like (Jack Kirby tribute) Hail To The King, Magick Eye & Stripped, I started approaching comic artists that I thought might appreciate my vision of a cults and the occult themed underground comic.

As I knew I didn't have any money to pay anyone – I'm just treading water at this point creating the product and being able to represent it – I knew I had to have something that would make it special for the contributors. So I designed the Satanist cartoonist gang patch embroidered in sliver on black, a horned hand holding a Bic biro and a number two paintbrush on a field of flames, and everyone who contributes to the comic gets to fly these gang colours. They're quite coveted.

Satanist cartoonists is quite an expanding gang – we've got some famous artists, some lesser known underground creators and some surprising people from different areas. I think we've had over thirty contributors now – not all regulars.

Getting Savage Pencil on board was a major triumph for me because he's one of my favourite underground cartoonists when I did the first issue, he told me *"well, I'm not*

really doing comics any more" he was more into performance painting and abstract stuff, then he saw the first issue and was like *"I should've been in here"*, and he's been one of our main guys ever since. Krent Able has come to us in a similarly open minded and optimistic and enthusiastic way. Rufus Dayglo did a wonderful Charlie Manson/ Charlie Brown spoof for us. Rufus got James O'Barr of **The Crow** fame involved. Mike Diana, who is an absolute legend – it's so important just to be able to make a reference to his case. In the 1990s, he was sent to jail in America for printing comics, because people thought they were obscene, in a country with the constitutional right to freedom of speech! He was a teenager at the time, and fitted the profile of a serial killer the FBI were hunting. He had all his stuff impounded, was found to be completely innocent of that but the State of Florida decided that they had to do something about the comics – comics that he'd printed on the photocopier at the local cop shop while his mum was cleaning the floors. The only copier they had in his town, apparently.

He actually served time in jail and after being released was banned from drawing & could be raided at any time to make sure he had no paper of pens in the house. One of the crowdfunding stretch goals for the movie they recently made about him was to pay the still outstanding arrest warrant in his hometown.

Underground comics really blew my mind as a kid. I was into Marvel Comics first, and then in 1977 **2000AD** came along, actually that blew my mind first, but when I found full-on undergrounds, I was seeing stuff that was beautifully drawn it was exciting yet also upsetting and disturbing me, and I think comix should have that potential. I think that's right. People have lost the ability to debate and have conflicting opinions these days. Everyone's got to agree with me and my little bubble, or it's going to burst and I

just going to die, you know… I'd rather be offended by something than pandered to. I think the concept of censorship is more offensive than anything that cloud potentially offend me. Even if something freaks me out, I don't care, I'll go with it. The right to freak someone out should be stronger than the right to be protected from being freaked out.

But it's not just shock for the sake of shock, I don't want to publish anything that reinforces misogynistic, patriarchal stereotype bullshit. We have referenced the sacrificing of the virgin on the altar cliché, which is what you'd expect from a Satanic comic, and if you buy issue 1, there are a couple of references to that trope, but I'm not into that per se. I'm not interested in depicting innocents being victimised. One of my comics has a Catholic priest being given a blow job by an altar boy, another boy catches them at it but thinks it's the most beautiful thing he's ever seen. I'm more into that sort of subversive way of looking at things. A lot of culture will use these storylines as a gimmick – let's make a splash by using this victim, and I'm definitely not into that. That's going too far for me – victimising innocents. One strip that came in for issue 5 by the artist known as Weird Beard opened with a panel of a robed cultist raising a knife and saying *"I sacrifice this cat to the Lord Satan"*, and I thought oh shit, I can't print this. The next panel was the altar manifesting a pair of eyes and a voice saying *"forget the cat, I want the dog!"* That little bit of flipping I can deal with. I know people love dogs, but you wouldn't get a cat joining the police. Let's just say that. Dogs are pigs, man.

The comic turned out to be pretty gay, which I didn't see coming, but the heavy metal fans and comic geek punters that are buying it; despite being more used to adolescent heteronormative power fantasies they aren't put off by that. People are capable of looking at something different to how they feel in themselves.

As far as the name goes, I'm interested in things that have been described as being 'Satanic' – free thought, DIY, people taking control of their own lives and doing things in their own way. That's what it means to me. I like the idea of celebrating things that have been damned as Satanic. We have tarot readers at the Flea Market. I'd have a yoga class if we had the room.

There was an event I attended for the release of Alan Moore's **Jerusalem** novel, he was in conversation on stage with the comedian Stewart Lee. Lee was talking about the somewhat impenetrable prose that Moore uses in the first chapter and asked him about it Moore was saying how it was trying to evoke the feeling of dreaming, and how this dream sequence links up the various bits in the rest of the book. And Lee leaned over and said *"you told me backstage it was to keep out the cunts"*. And I think that's what we're doing. Putting the word 'Satanic' on something keeps out the cunts. The sub-heading on **Satanic Mojo Comix** is 'open-minded adults only'.

With the Satanic Flea Market we discovered if you charge three quid to get in somewhere and you put a scary name on it, the bullshit trolls and haters that just want to go and fuck your shit up won't come. They just won't enter. We had African priests in camo gear throwing holy water in the face of people entering Victor Wynd's Last Tuesday Society around the corner, the week before we did our Festival of Dark Arts. They didn't come anywhere near us. They probably thought that we'd turn them into frogs or something. They want to accuse someone innocent of being Satanic; they won't go near anyone who *says* they are Satanic. I like that. I guess it's a bit juvenile, it's like wearing a battle jacket – it's like, if I just wear this, douchebags are going to leave me alone.

So, I did the comic and when I launched it, I curated an exhibition that rapidly grew into a Festival Of Dark Arts because so many people wanted to take part. We did a Satanic Panic installation, which was a heavy metal bedroom with all the records and the RPGs and everything – basically, it was *my* bedroom from the Eighties, because I was that heavy metal fan into the video nasties & underground comics. My dad told me *"I don't want that shit back in my garage"* so we closed out the festival with a flea market, it was just an afterthought on the end of the exhibition. That became our breakaway hit, we had over 900 people queuing up that day and we've done it at least four times a year since then.

We also have the disco, ***Super Satanic Saturdays*** – we wanted something that reminded us of the manic enthusiasm that you'd have in the Seventies for those Saturday morning kids TV shows like **Swap Shop** and **Tiswas**. The basic design concept was The Manson Family meets **The Banana Splits**, in a blacklight poster environment, like the Disneyland orgy of Hollywood. That took off and we did a few of those, we did film nights with live music. Now we've got the Battle Jacket Sewing Club coming up. So we're picking up on all these different elements that people relate to and we're trying to cross-pollinate and team up with people.

At the moment, a lot of friends of mine are suggesting that the large Hadron Collider has pushed us into 'Earth 2' and we're now in the Evil Universe, like that classic **Star Trek** episode, which is why we're all wearing beards, which we never would've done ten years ago. It seems like so many crazy, bullshit things are being taken seriously in the mainstream, like Donald Trump or Brexit. Utter nonsense with people lying to your face, and not even pretending that they're *not* lying, and everyone going along with it. It's like reality is broken in some way. Anyway… I was looking at the classic Eliphas Levi Baphomet illustration, thinking about 'Solve' & 'Coagula' written on the arms – 'break apart and bring together' – and I feel like reality is really seriously broken. Any stupid shit can happen now. An orange hued buffoon from reality TV can be President, on the back of being a racist, misogynistic liar! But my point is, don't get hung up on the fact that reality's broken, *own* the fact that reality's broken and think now's the chance for us to put those pieces in a different order and say *"we want it to end up this way"*. I was told all my life that hippies were bullshit, thanks to Malcolm McLaren and punk rock, and they're not. Hippies had the fucking answer. There would not even be punk if it wasn't for hippies. That spirit of rebellion, you can trace it back through history and culture. This is basically Satanism. It's thinking for yourself, rejecting authority and trying to make a better world in *your* own image. That's the important thing that we have to do, and I think it's more possible to reshape our reality than I've ever seen it in my lifetime.

People say to me about Satanism, *"oh, it's killing cats, Lord's Prayer backwards"* that kind of bollocks. I reply *"You're thinking of Catholics"* - all that propaganda is from the **Malleus Maleficarum**, which was basically a wank mag for sickos in 1452. It's like that *Daily Mail* attitude. *"Oh, it's disgusting what they get up to… Tell me all about it in more detail so I can be properly disgusted"*. Their whole *raison d'etre* is supposed to be love and forgiveness, so where does all this hatred and torture come from? The point of Satan is to advocate personal responsibility and freedom. That's all we stand for. If you are going to worry about child abuse, then worry about established religion. Because religion *is* child abuse. Putting scary fairy tales into people's brains that they carry into adulthood, making them afraid of natural bodily functions, ruining their own lives and other peoples. You've got a legal age for sex, a legal age for alcohol – I'd put one on religion as well. If you choose religion as an adult, with an open mind and a proper education, fine. Maybe you'll get something good out of it. If you look at the words of Jesus Christ as an open minded adult, even if it's a fairy tale, there are still words of truth in there that can enrich our lives. But if Jesus Christ did the Process Church personality quiz, he'd come out as a Luciferian, he wouldn't be a Jehovan.

Disneyland After Dark

Too much of my life has been waiting for things to happen. Then I realised: actually, you *can* make it happen. I think of when I moved to Tokyo in 1996. Walking around, I'd see shops with fancy coats of arms above the door saying 'SINCE... 1992'. And I'd laugh at them, but a lot of those guys are still in business now, and it looks like something impressive. It is a thing. They'd put your foot down to make a stand, and it all builds up from there. If you start this afternoon, you can still change the world for the rest of your life. Before **Satanic Mojo**, I was doing most of the same things, but tagging along with other people's stuff – an artist adrift in the world. Now, I'm trying to do the best I can and move it up bit by bit. I'm still finding like-minded people and teaming up with them, and together we can spread out a bit further. Let's establish the foundation and spread out, using the ground that we've covered and not aim too high. The most depressing thing as a creative is to have a vision that you can't actualise. So I'll lay the groundwork for it, put the idea into the universe, and in the meantime I'll keep doing the comic and the flea market, Satanic-themed life drawing sessions, and this and that – whatever I can manage at the time. And hopefully build up. Aiming too high and failing is something we're encouraged to do – you've got to go for your dream, and then get shot down in front of everyone, and only one person is allowed to win. Everyone is going through the mincer, and it's not fair that the one that can suck dick and kiss arse and kowtow is the one that wins at the end. For me, the only success is for a society or a community to succeed. I want something solid and sustaining and creative.

That's what I'm pushing for. I'm not just trying to sell a comic. I want to change the world!

THE SATANIC REFORMATION

THE SATANIC TEMPLE, THE WESTBORO BAPTIST CHURCH AND THE ART OF PROTEST

LUCIEN GREAVES

We were already well outside of his jurisdiction by the time the Sheriff of Meridian, Mississippi announced that our arrests were *"imminent."*

Days previous, immediately following the so-called crime, my co-conspirators and I congregated - not far from the scene - at some lousy chain restaurant. (Meridian seems to lack any unique and quaint local flavour that can sometimes redeem American small-town squalor.) The bartender noted the novelty of receiving visitors to such an unattractive nowhere. *"Where are you all from?"* He asked amiably, *"what are you doing here?"*

There was a moment's pause as my eight companions tried to devise an acceptable answer. Nobody, of course, could have suspected what we'd done. Before any of them spoke I interjected with the unlikely truth. *"We came from New York,"* I explained, *"to visit the grave of the mother of the founder of the Westboro Baptist Church."*

Curious, he raised an eyebrow. Like most people, the bartender was likely aware of the Westboro Baptists and their controversial campaigns to protest the funerals of soldiers,

victims of terrorist attacks, and other high-profile deaths, in a general revolt against the 'sin' homosexuality. Under the motto of 'God Hates Fags', these bitter, bible-thumping simpletons furiously endorse a notion that the world's ills are God's righteous revenge against same-sex love. Achieving popular infamy in 1998 with a protest of the funeral of Matthew Shepard -- tortured and beaten to death for his homosexuality in Wyoming -- the Westboro Baptist Church [WBC] has ever since seemed to revel in the appalling role of sadistic religious zealots... a tribe of public villains -- consisting almost entirely of founder Fred Phelps's extended family -- thriving on enmity and the disgust of others.

Phelps, a disbarred lawyer, assiduously maintained the constitutional legality of his protests, ultimately finding his freedom to offend upheld by the Supreme Court of the United States in 2011. The trial was a result of a lawsuit brought against the WBC in 2006, following their funeral protest of fallen Marine Lance Corporal Matthew A. Snyder, whose family filed claims of (among other things) defamation and emotional distress. In an 8 - 1 decision the Supreme Court determined -- according to the majority opinion penned by Chief Justice John G. Roberts Jr. -- that while WBC's activities are *"certainly hurtful and [their] contribution to public discourse may be negligible,"* it is nonetheless important *"to protect even hurtful speech on public issues to ensure that we do not stifle public debate."*

The Westboro Baptist Church claimed to act upon positions born of sincerely-held beliefs, protected and inviolable. Chief Justice Roberts felt the issues highlighted by WBC's protests reflect legitimate discourse upon public controversies: *"While these messages may fall short of refined social or political commentary"* he wildly understated, *"the issues they highlight - the political and moral conduct of the United States and its citizens, the fate of our nation, homosexuality in the military, and scandals involving the Catholic clergy - are matters of public import."*

Surely, Fred viewed this vindication as a result of God flexing His benevolent might in Fred's own favour. More pickets, he vowed -- following the Supreme Court decision -- were forthcoming. Soldiers, Celebrities, high-profile victims of tragedy, whether they were homosexual or not; Phelps and the WBC would utilise their funerals to provoke uproar and spread the word of their divine tyrant's vengeful dissatisfaction regarding growing complacency toward - even outright acceptance of - 'sodomites'.

Having found his life's mission in battling the wicked scourge of homosexuality, Fred Phelps was at home with the angels, a humble reflection of his iron-fisted deity. Accordingly, Fred was known to beat his own children mercilessly - often while laughing in unrestrained glee - sometimes into a state of unconsciousness or shock.

According to the book **Addicted to Hate** by Jon Michael Bell, *"Sometimes Pastor Phelps preferred to grab one child by their little hands and haul them into the air. Then he would repeatedly smash his knee into their groin and stomach while walking across the room and laughing. The boys remember this happening to Nate [one of Fred Phelps's sons] when he was only seven, and to Margie and Kathy even after they were sexually developed teenagers."*

Summary punishment at the hands of the dour pastor involved being beaten with fists, kicked in the stomach, or having one's arm twisted up and behind one's back till it nearly dislocated.

Mark Phelps, an estranged son of Fred's, would recall *"coming back [home] once to find Pastor Phelps jogging around the dining room table, beating the sobbing [Nate] with a broom handle; while doing so, he was alternately spitting on the frightened child and chuckling the same sinecure laugh so disturbing to those who've seen him on television."*

In fact, Fred Phelps's biography is a litany of ignominious activity and mindless, dogma-driven vendettas. So why would we seek to visit the grave of such an odious personality's mother?, the bartender naturally wondered.

"We represent The Satanic Temple, and we have just finished performing a homoerotic Satanic ceremony at her gravesite," I informed him, most matter-of-factly.

Just as the rest of my table began to shift uncomfortably in their chairs, the bartender laughed, impressed by what he saw as my superior skills of impromptu storytelling. Clearly, he didn't believe a word. Soon after, however, we released a statement regarding our graveside activities, as well as photos of the event. Polarised scandal ensued. The national media ran images of me officiating the graveside ritual adorned in a horned headdress, gay couples groping and kissing over the stone, and - most offensively of all - an image of me with an odd, triumphantly bemused expression playing upon my face, looking off into the distance, during the climax of the ritual, with my bared scrotum resting upon Fred Phelps's mother's stone... Strange, profane rituals on sacred ground with lustful gays, open and menacing animalism… all intentionally made public in a provocation against the WBC. It was almost more than certain segments of red-blooded, fag-hating middle America could mentally digest.

Speculation ran rampant. While WBC may strike many as an entirely legitimate target of counter-protest and mockery, the spectre of Satanism still inspires panicked folk tales of anti-human bloodthirsty cults. What else were we capable of? What were our ultimate motives? Emails poured in, some of them from Mississippi and describing the local mob furore we had aroused. I wondered about the bartender and what he must have thought when the realisation struck him that I had told him the horrifying truth so nonchalantly, and point-blank.

The road to Meridian started with the Boston Marathon Bombing, really. Malcolm Jarry (co-founder of The Satanic Temple) and I were in Boston when the bombing occurred. Initially there were uncertain and undramatic reports that there was something that sounded, possibly, like an explosion near the finish line. There was also a small fire in the Public Library, and early speculations were that the two had been related. Soon, of course, the magnitude of the event was fully realised, and the city was swarmed with SWAT vehicles, circling helicopters, and a diaspora of runners and tourists marching in shocked silence back to wherever they were staying -- Public transportation had been shut down as the massive investigation began.

There was an odd phenomenon that manifested in the immediate wake of the tragedy: those with the simplest of minds were also the least confused by it all. While reasonable people were scrambling to understand the cause of this trauma, the Westboro Baptists claimed immediately to know who the culprit was and why. Happily co-opting the attack to promote their own tired, predictable message, they took to Twitter: *"The federal government is classifying the bombs as a terrorist attack"*, they stated, *"but they say it's unclear if it's of a domestic or foreign nature. Here's a hint - GOD SENT THE BOMBS!"* And, much to nobody's surprise, He, in His benevolent wisdom, sent the bombs because *"you"* (whoever you are) *"insist on nation-dooming filthy fag marriage."*

But, disappointingly, WBC was far from the only ludicrous group of smug shits to artlessly construct self-satisfying confirmation of their demented world views from the chaos of the day. The blood of the dead and wounded hadn't yet been cleaned from the pavement before syndicated radio host Alex Jones - a craven conspiracist clown who has spent his shameful career convincing a gullible mob of his bravery in the face of an imaginary enemy - declared the bombing to be a *"false flag"* operation. *"The Government"*, Jones suggested, had committed the bombing in an effort to frighten the American public into willingly surrendering their constitutional liberties for increased security. Social media put the degenerative

conspiracist spiral in full spin, and it wasn't long before a significant population of tender-headed bloviators asserted that the entire bombing was a hoax, the 'victims' all paid actors. The evil Government, according to this narrative, knows all, and It sees all. Nothing happens without Its knowledge, and nothing of sufficient magnitude occurs outside Its manufacture. It meticulously masterminds every significant event, bringing us a step closer, each passing event, to total dominion over each and every of our individual wills. One need only observe the events of the world with *cui bono?* in mind, and the undeniable truth will reveal itself. Fortunately, however, this nearly omnipotent force of absolute Evil is at least occasionally polite enough to see to it that real people aren't harmed in the making of their New World Order. Thus they create imaginary places like, say, Boylston Street in Boston, and act out horrendous terrorist strikes for the viewing satisfaction of the rural television-entranced, in an effort to convince them to yield to tyranny.

The evidence is clear. It's everywhere. You just need to learn to see everything for the evidence that it is.

From the comfort of self-aggrandising delusion, these simple fantasists see themselves as savvy realists and freedom fighters - the knowledgeable few willing to confront hard realities others refuse to face. They have an ironic word for those who don't uncritically swallow their asinine fantasies: *"Sheeple"*... and they uniformly bleet this word with unfailing diligence - like the neatly conformed flock they are - anywhere the 'official story' (or any story devoid of a New World Order conspiracy) might rear its ugly head... Assembling thoughtlessly in like-minded conspiracist cattle pens, shuffling about, bumping off one another, foraging in their own filth for ways to further simplify the world into one big, childish supervillain narrative in which they can cast themselves as the selfless heroes. They swarm like vultures, like the Westboro Baptist Church, toward tragedy with crass I-told-you-so pride.

Alex Jones was the first to crash a bombing-aftermath event in an open attempt to elevate himself upon a pulpit platform constructed of the victim's bodies, sending a reporter to harangue Massachusetts Governor Deval Patrick during the first post-bombing press conference. Jones's blustering, blank-eyed slob shouted senseless 'False Flag' theories, out of turn, as the morose assembly nonetheless attempted to maintain some dignity.

The Westboro Baptist Church, for their part, wasted no time in announcing their intentions to also join the 'fun'. Again, taking to Twitter - their prefered platform for public statements - they threatened to crash the funerals of the victims while (predictably) picketing against unGodly *"fags"*:

THANK GOD FOR THE BOSTON MARATHON BOMBS!!Westboro Baptist Church to picket funerals of those killed. #PraiseGod>> twitter.com/WBCFliers/stat…
— Westboro Baptist (@WBCSays) April 16, 2013

Naturally, none of this could be expected to sit very well with the citizens of Boston, nor did it gather support with the mainstream God-is-Love Christians who sputter in indignation at the very suggestion that their open demonstrations of anti-gay bigotry could possibly be motivated by anything less than the Lord's undying love for His misguided children. The Westboro Baptist Church, many mainstream Christians will maintain, aren't really Christians at all. However, according to their tortured rhetoric, the WBC is a negligible anomaly -- the true bigotry is in those who are attempting to curtail the freedom of practicing Christians… by insisting that Christians not be allowed to exercise their God-given right to deny equal rights to filthy fags. Philosophically, there's little difference between the Westboro Baptists and the American Evangelical mainstream - there's just this minor quibbling regarding tactics and Public Relations. The Christian Apologetics & Research Ministry (CARM) in Idaho explains on their website, *"While CARM agrees with Westboro Baptist Church's condemnation of homosexuality, abortion, unjustified war, and other sins, it does not agree with the methodology the church uses."* To wit, *"Westboro is overly abrasive, rude, insulting, and condemning."* There are more polite ways to assert the eternal universal wrath of their angry, other-worldly autocrat. In the case of the Westboro Baptists *"[t]here seems to be no grace and it shows very little love, if any."* [1]

It does rather seem that way.

"Love the sinner, hate the sin" is the platitudinous inanity that serves as the mantra of the pious anti-gay bigot. You see, God is willing to love his gay children, too, if only they accept the Lord and renounce their sinful proclivities. They'll love and accept the gays… so long as the gays stop being gay, and accept that homosexuality is a crime against 'God'.

Pat Robertson, of the famous conservative Christian 700 Club, is a perfect example of this bizarre dissonance. The puzzled old clown still feels the need to pretend that he doesn't actually hate gays, even while blaming the 'sin' of homosexuality for nothing short of the fall of civilisation, reminiscing fondly of the days in which gays were stoned to death. Robertson claims to actually believe that gays have *"become the oppressors of those who hold deeply-held religious points of view,"* [2] with their traditional-values-ruining *"agenda"*. That said, however, he points out that he's *"not anti-gay or anything"*... Heaven forbid. During a 2013 broadcast, he explained that homosexuals have regrettably *"forsaken"* God... but they can, thankfully, be repaired. *"It's not something that is natural and when people reunite with the Lord, the Lord will get their priorities the way it is supposed to be."* [3]

Until these queers get their priorities straight (so to speak), we have to recognise the Homosexual Agenda as the work of the Devil… And not just the Devil's work, but a forthright Satanic attack upon all that is decent on this Earth: *"The Devil is trying to say, 'I'm going to destroy your progeny any way I can,"* whether it be by abortion or non-reproductive gay sex. *"If you will kill your babies, that's fine, I'm with you; if you will deny the chance of having babies, that's fine too; but I want to destroy your opportunities to reproduce,'"* Robertson blathered on in March of 2014. *"It's a very serious thing and we're not talking about it, and we need to as a society, we have to realize where the attack is coming because it is definitely an attack."* [4]

Famously, in 2001, immediately following the September 11th attacks on the World Trade Center, Pat Robertson took to the air with popular televangelist and Moral Majority co-founder Jerry Falwell, who senselessly implicated homosexuals in the attack: *"[T]he pagans and the abortionists and the feminists and the gays and the lesbians who are actively trying to make that an alternative lifestyle, the ACLU, People for the American Way — all of them who have tried to secularise America,"* Falwell accused, *"I point the finger in their face and say 'you helped this happen.'"*

"Well, I totally concur," responded Robertson.

However, when the predictable angry public backlash returned, Falwell distanced himself from his comments by claiming that he was really saying something else - something completely unrelated to what he had actually said: *"I would never blame any human being except the terrorists, and if I left that impression with gays or lesbians or anyone else, I apologise."*

Falwell died, not a moment too soon, in 2007, just when everybody was beginning to think we'd never hear the last of his rancid apocalyptic paranoia. Robertson, unfortunately, carries on - a lightly animated corpse endlessly spewing stale outrage, sometimes followed by dissonant, nearly insensible apologies.

Robertson's comments surface regularly outside of his disturbingly large, insular medievalist viewership as the occasional civilized observer catches whiff of his constant idiocy and subjects certain bits of it to exposure, inevitably inspiring disgust and witticisms. However, it's important to note that, as co-founder of Christian Broadcasting Network, and long-standing host of its flagship broadcast program, **the 700 Club**, Robertson represents the views of a significant population of American Christians. The demon-haunted old fool even took a credible run at the presidency once in 1988, gathering millions in campaign funds, and ranking a solid second-place in the Iowa caucus. While few conservative Christians outside of Westboro's apoplectic flock will endorse WBC's pickets, it's clear that their disagreements are primarily semantic.

The big difference between the Westboro Baptist Church and these other passive terrorists - those who use death and destruction outside of their own making to nonetheless add the threatening weight of fear to their theocratic ultimatums - is that WBC is relatively honest in their approach. They know they revel in misery. They know they prefer cruelty to compassion. They don't feel the need to dissemble. The whole idea that 'God is love' or 'God loves everyone' is an acknowledged source of deep aggravation to the Westboro Baptists. They confront the issue unequivocally in writings on their website, making a strong case for God's bitter hatred, based directly upon Biblical text. In an online 94 page book titled **"God Loves Everyone": The Greatest Lie Ever Told**, WBC helpfully supplies readers with *"701 Passages Proving God's Hate & Wrath for Most of Mankind"*.

Looking back wistfully to simpler times, the book notes, *"Before the 20th Century 'God loves everyone' was largely a foreign theology to the United States even though they had the same Old Testament and New Testament that we have. The Puritans that stepped off the Mayflower at Plymouth in 1620, and their progeny that inhabited the United States for nearly 300 years, largely did not believe that 'God loves everyone.' Whether you call these early Americans, Puritans, Baptists, Lutherans, Presbyterians, Congregationalists, Episcopalians, or most other Protestant religions in the U.S., they read the Bible daily and believed in the wrath of God and they feared Him greatly. You never see 'God love's everyone' in their sermons or writings. Their books and sermons are full of the doctrine of God's wrath and judgment because the Bible is full of these notions."*

Say what you will, at least it's not inaccurate history. Somewhere along the line, the same appalling revelations about the Good Book that have led so many into convoluted apologetics or an outright renunciation of their faith stared Fred Phelps in the face, and he eagerly embraced them in all their deranged, savage glory.

"If God truly 'loved everyone' then everyone in the Bible would be loved and admired by God. If this was true you should be able to open the Bible anywhere from Genesis to Revelation and find everyone in the Bible going to heaven and receiving nothing but loving attention from God. Of course, nothing could be further from the truth."

The book then goes on to summarise some of the earliest examples of Biblical testament to God's cruelty before coming to the story of the Great Flood:

"God then destroys the whole earth (Woops!) and everyone on it, except for Noah and his small family, by a Flood, which means many of them died a slow agonizing death after days or even weeks of terror. Not only adults died; infants; elderly; men; women; children; newborns; because everyone perished! And so it goes. You can't even get out of the first book without the wrath and judgments of God consuming most of the book. So, it is throughout the Bible. Open it anywhere and you will see the wrath and judgment of God in every book and in nearly every chapter of the Bible. Below is a list of human beings in the Bible that God took exception to, judged or summarily executed." [5]

The whole rest of the book is one long, continuous citations list of Biblical passages, with brief summaries, establishing support for the Hateful God position. They make a convincing case. In any case, it's difficult to see how anybody can claim that the WBC aren't 'real' Christians.

Biblical justifications notwithstanding, Bostonians in general proved to be in no mood to host the Westboro Baptist celebration of the attack. Almost instantly following Westboro's announcement, numerous Facebook groups formed organising counter-protests - human walls, with the intention of blocking the WBC from approaching the funerals. The potential for violence was palpable. Shock and frustration easily transitioned, as they often do, into rage, for which the Westboro Baptist Church had witlessly offered themselves as the repositories. As of then, the perpetrators of the bombing were unknown. Confusion reigned. The WBC's proposed funeral protest gave an immediate sense of purpose to the otherwise helpless. The mention of it was sure to inspire vague clenched-fist vows of counter-action: Those motherfuckers will be sorry they came… Somehow.

Nobody I spoke to had a plan of action. Nobody said they were going to take a run at the WBC or pelt them with heavy objects. The plan, it seemed, was nothing more than to assemble into one large, angry mob, as a petty little team of ignorant picketers attempted to taunt the families of dead bombing victims. What could go wrong? Let's just go and see… let the events unfold as they may… see where the mood carries us.

When the day came, thousands were on the streets. Annoying, self-appointed 'organisers' walked through the crowds desperately circulating reminders that this was meant to be a peaceful, silent blockade in respect of the funeral taking place. Occasionally, they would approach specific people or groups - presumably those who looked potentially combative - to 'remind' them what 'we' were there for. I pushed through one such sanctimonious ass as he - for reasons unknown - attempted to block my path as I followed what turned out to be a false sighting of approaching WBC picketers. I had arrived at the scene independent of Malcolm and other Satanic Temple representatives who came to observe the potential riot, and we had underestimated the magnitude of the gathering. We never spotted one another in the crowd.

As it turned out, the Westboro Baptist Church never showed. As a funeral played out silently, and unseen, beyond the blockades, the crowd eventually dispersed, sullen and unsatisfied.

Offering no excuse for their apparent failure of nerve, WBC instead contented themselves by offering a tweet of a photoshopped image of a bitter old hag hovering ghost-like above the gathered Bostonians holding signs that read *"FAGS DOOM NATIONS"* and *"GOD SENT THE BOMBS"*. The tweet text declared: *"You showed up for us! And we're there in your hearts!"*

This inspired us to think on the idea of how we, too, could somehow counter-protest the Westboro Baptist Church remotely... in a way that would 'touch their hearts'... in a way befitting of them. For this specific purpose, the Pink Mass was born.

The publicly released images featured me, adorned in a horned headdress, presiding over the ritual, hands ceremoniously resting upon the heads of gay couples - one male couple, one female - as they knelt above the grave, kissing. Candles encircled the scene.

Arriving at the cemetery during daylight hours, we immediately began to scour the massive grounds for the grave. Internet research had indicated we were at the right place, but I had nearly lost hope by the time Malcolm located the actual stone, amongst the very last remaining in our sweep.

After the ritual was performed, the candles blown out, the robes removed… I felt a vague dissatisfaction with the event. As pointedly justified as a homoerotic ritual over the grave of Phelps's mother was, it wasn't nearly, I felt, a proportionate response to the ugly incendiary behaviour of the Westboro Baptists. We had travelled all this way, performed our ritual… but it was, I couldn't help but feel, altogether too tasteful.

As a final affront, and in a sudden surge of inspiration, I bared my scrotum and rested it upon the grave. Only then did I feel that the ritual was complete. Naturally, the impromptu tea-bagging would become the most controversial element of the Pink Mass as pictures of it, too, circulated internationally.

"It is an unusual crime that we haven't come across - to my knowledge - in a while," Meridian's Sheriff Dean Harper stated to the local news station, WTOK-TV, in a 'special report'. The implication that Meridian had ever before suffered the affront of Pink Mass-performing Satanists was puzzling.

"We brought you the story of The Satanic Temple's trip to a Meridian cemetery that's gaining national attention," an offscreen broadcaster solemnly intoned, *"[...] a group from New York's Satanic Temple made the trip to Meridian to protest the Westboro Baptist Church. You can see from pictures on their website that there they performed a ritual they call 'Pink Mass' on the grave of Catherine Johnston, mother of Westboro founder, Fred Phelps, Jr. The ceremony involved two same-sex couples kissing over her grave. They then declared Catherine Johnston a lesbian in the afterlife."*

Post-mortem sexual conversion was the ostentatious claim, but my descriptions to interviewers were more nuanced than most any of them cared to explain in their subsequent reports. The interviewers would typically open the topic with a question like, *"so, you believe that your ritual turned Phelps's mother into a lesbian in the afterlife?"*

"No. We believe that Fred Phelps and the Westboro Baptist Church now believe that Catherine Johnston is a lesbian in the afterlife."

"But you don't actually believe that?"

"The Satanic Temple doesn't endorse supernatural beliefs. However, we believe that the Westboro Baptist Church's own superstitions obligate them to believe that our ritual turned Fred Phelps's mother gay in the afterlife."

"So you don't believe that you turned her into a lesbian," the hapless reporter would stammer, trying to make sense of it all, *"but you believe that they believe she is a lesbian… because of your ritual?"*

Making clear that we fully respect the inviolability of belief, as put forward by the Westboro Baptists themselves, I would elaborate, *"we believe that they believe that she is a lesbian in the afterlife and, as nobody can challenge our right to our beliefs, we are free to believe that they believe she is a lesbian, regardless of anything the Westboro Baptist Church themselves may say to the contrary."*

One journalist helpfully likened the ritual to *"the Mormon practice of baptising the dead, only much gayer."*

Understandably, perhaps, almost none of the articles reporting the affair bothered to toil with this bit of pointed philosophical complication.

WTOK-TV seemed to suggest that there was something more sinister at play beyond a mere Satanic necrosexual graveyard ritual. Upon investigation the local broadcast journalism outfit revealed the vile motives concealed beneath the pageantry: *"They hope their actions will draw attention to the organisation's efforts to raise money to participate in New York City's Adopt-a-Highway program."*

Sheriff Harper sought charges of trespassing, malicious mischief, and indecent exposure - none of which the judge would sign off on. In the end, only the ill-defined charge of 'desecration' was accepted, though no material damage had been inflicted anywhere at the gravesite.

As I explained to **Vice** in an interview, *"The fact is, we were visiting an open cemetery, during the daytime, with no indication that visitors were unwelcomed. We caused no material damage to anything, and the cemetery was left exactly as it was when we entered it. I'm not sure which part of this is most problematic for the Sheriff - the displays of homosexuality, or the Satanism. I do know that the combination of the two is bound to cause absolute havoc among the superstitious homophobic."*

In the impossibly unlikely event that the police would extradite me to Mississippi, **Vice** asked if there were any Satanic magic spells I could work on the officers' sexuality, perhaps to increase their sympathy for our anti-Westboro action.

"I predict that if I were to be arrested and extradited to Mississippi," I replied, *"my very presence would raise unholy psychological Hell among the Sheriff and his colleagues. Just as medieval demon panics gave rise to episodes in which repressed people took the opportunity to act out in mindless abandon - exonerated from their own deeds by the idea of 'possession' - I believe it quite possible that I could find myself in a holding cell witnessing the Meridian Police devolve into a sweaty, grunting, savage orgy of uncaged homosexuality... all influenced by the idea that they were utterly powerless against my sexual conversion magic. Perhaps they are merely looking for such a scapegoat."*

Sheriff Dean Harper likely felt emboldened in his proclamations of immanent justice for a failure to recognise that a lewd Satanic graveyard ritual could possibly gain any public support, no matter what the context. If Satanists aren't the Bad Guys, by God, who is? One can only imagine his mystification at finding himself the butt of growing criticism for his reaction to the Pink Mass, and the vehement arguments against the notion that a crime had been committed at all. While Meridian locals, reportedly, were screaming for our blood, many commenters in the rest of the world were becoming increasingly vocally supportive.

"By now, everyone's just about had it with the Westboro Baptist Church, a group whose members use national tragedies as opportunities to forward anti-gay hate speech", began one piece by the Huffington Post before describing our retributive *"gay offensive"*.

"The Westboro Baptist Church may have met its match when it comes to public demonstrations," began an ABC News broadcast report, *"A group of Devil-worshippers giving them a run for their money. This, you have to see to believe…"*

Contempt for the Westboro Baptists emerged with varying degrees of subtlety even in standard objective reporting. WBC had become a symbol of the depraved, thoughtless, and cruel religious corruption of sense and decency. If my own 'indecency' was defined in opposition to that, I was looking rather justified. The inversion of roles seemed to make perfect intuitive sense in this context.

Indeed, in the years following the Pink Mass, the inversion of roles has become all too clear as theocratic lawmakers are ever more closely poised to entirely overturn secular constitutional democracy in the United States. Traditional mainstream religions bear the stench of medieval monarchism and backward superstition giving new life to the pre-Laveyan Milton-inspired Satan-as-rebel-against-tyranny archetype of the Romantic era. Satanism is more increasingly understood as a non-theistic religion that gives a mythical framework for Enlightenment values forever at odds with churches of superstition: science, progress, freedom of speech and inquiry, pluralism and individual autonomy are Satan's domain.

Narratively coherent as this perspective of Satanism may be, however, the comedic element of the Pink Mass naturally provoked skepticism regarding our authenticity. Common perceptions of religious attachment don't allow for it to co-exist with a sense of humour. Further complicating the discussion is the fact that The Satanic Temple wasn't begun by a self-aggrandising self-proclaimed 'Magus' who announced a series of etched-in-stone dictums, even while having no proven achievements upon which to justify a claim of leadership. No, The Satanic Temple, from the start, would earn its place, leading by example. Initially, we intended to do this by publicly releasing our activities in a documentary compilation of footage that would, hopefully, inspire trust in, and identification with, a new Satanic movement. That trust and identification came flooding in much earlier than we anticipated as The Satanic Temple swiftly moved into tackling more contentious, even dangerous, zero-sum battles against heavily-financed and well-organised theocrats, while battling to preserve pluralism, government viewpoint neutrality, and combat contemporary witch-hunts and pseudoscience.

The Satanic Temple has grown into a significant religious movement with a burgeoning membership and active chapters internationally. Looking back at our meteoric rise from the Pink Mass's ritualised antics to our high-profile legal campaigns, massive ritual events, establishment of a world headquarters, and my own televised engagements in current Culture War debates in mass media outlets, I'm sometimes asked about the perceived change from from a philosophy of pranksterism to one of religious conscientiousness. In fact, I was wholly motivated by a religious attachment to Satanism from the start, though with a deep respect for the value of humour, the tactical value of well-thought 'pranks', a sense of veneration for the Satanic Trickster archetype. My deeply-held belief in Satanism has obligated me to continue to dedicate my life to the causes I champion.

With a pre-existing expertise in the ongoing contemporary witch-hunt known as the Satanic Panic, I hardly took lightly the dissemination of the image of me at that grave in Meridian, Mississippi. My reputation, security, career possibilities, and possibly my life and freedom would evermore be at risk following that act. The Pink Mass was a declaration of lifelong war for Satanic values. My privacy and anonymity were instantly the stuff of nostalgic reminiscence, laid to rest the moment I rested my testicles on that fateful stone. My finances, obliterated in our legal bills and campaigns. None of that was a laughing matter at any given point, nor was it unforeseen.

It was an act of suicide.

It was, in a sense, from this act of suicide that the Satanic Reformation was born.

Notes:

1. http://carm.org/westboro-baptist-church. Retrieved 28 Oct, 2014
2. http://www.rightwingwatch.org/content/pat-robertson-recalls-days-when-gays-were-stoned-death-blames-satan-gay-rights#sthash.wgk3P3Gp.dpuf. Retrieved 28 Oct, 2014
3. http://www.mediaite.com/tv/pat-robertson-im-not-anti-gay-because-gays-are-just-straight-people-whove-forsaken-god/. Retrieved 28 Oct, 2014
4. http://www.rightwingwatch.org/content/pat-robertson-recalls-days-when-gays-were-stoned-death-blames-satan-gay-rights#sthash.wgk3P3Gp.dpuf. Retrieved 28 Oct, 2014
5. http://godhatesfags.com/reports/20060331_god-loves-everyone-lie.pdf. Retrieved 28 Oct, 2014

INTO THE OCCULT

SAMMM AGNEW

PHOTOGRAPHY BY ILYA FALCHEVSKY

The Occult describes the study of that which is hidden or secret. It refers to the knowledge of the unseen, the paranormal world. Historically it focuses on the study of a deeper spiritual reality beyond what we may ordinarily witness in day to day life.

Occultists believe that this world operates all around us either in conjunction to or alongside our familiar material realm that we inhabit daily as we go about our regular lives.There has been occurrences of practice in to the otherworldly in all cultures since the dawn of time serving the purpose of superstition, i.e. to prevent disease or to increase crop yield, and also of protection. These teachings were often kept hidden in secret societies, allowed to be accessed by the initiated individuals only, far from the public and their prying eyes. This enabled the respect and focus to be maintained into what is essentially a practice of the non-physical. Whether we are looking at voodoo, necromancy, communion with the dead, telepathy, the four clairs'- clairvoyance, claircognizance, clairaudience, and clairsentience - we are looking in to the depths of human potential the very frontiers of human experience.

Hallucinatory plants, herbs or substances may be used to invoke visions, and allow perceptions in to otherwise closed doors to the human psyche and to allow guidance, to strengthen ones perceptions and intuition into that which is held deep in our unconscious. By initiating contact we are able to tap in the information that we already know about ourselves, others and how best to act in our lives.

This photo series presents a few of the ways in which one might operate in occultist methods. One may use tools of divination to pursue an answer to a question, such as pendulums, reading tea leaves, using a divining rod or gazing in to a crystal ball. Here we have depicted the use of the tarot in which a deck of cards - each individually attributed to a character, usually painted beautifully on one side - will be picked one by one and placed in an arrangement on the table. The tarot reader should have an understanding of the various connotations that each card holds, depending on when it is pulled from the deck and therefore where it is placed on the table. They will then be able to read the cards and how they tell the story of the participant. This story may be of events that have happened or will occur in the future, and can offer advice as well as new perspectives on a vast array of problems the sitter may be concerned with.

One potential way of viewing the occult is that gazing at an object allows a focus and therefore a sense of power to be bestowed via that intent. It may then embody the received qualities, e.g. protection, sexual magnetism or confidence as if they were its own. It is believed that once an item is treated with high esteem it may rise to the challenge energetically and then house the emotion as a vessel. It is then enabled to be used as a totem or talisman to work in tandem with the occultist, for or against others.

The dynamic between the individuals in a practising coven may be the setting required to initiate a feedback loop of intent, increasing one's own level of power exponentially. With such mutual focus it is believed that there are many possibilities of what can occur to induce health or harm on another. An age old belief in black or dark magic, however, is that what one gives out will be returned by the force of three. Hence the user of these powers should not induce their spells lightly, and should treat their work with utmost respect. Deities, Gods and Goddesses may be invoked to multiply a coven or individual's power. These occurrences may not be tampered with and must be respected as with power comes responsibility. In order to hold more one must room for these stronger emanations than they are used to dealing with on an earthly level. Without such precautions of protection, offerings and thanks given the individual is simply meddling with things that they do not understand, and may be making themselves vulnerable in the process. Knowledge is power and to have power without knowledge may produce great misfortune in which the power one have seeked may be turned against the very user themselves.

Divination using the Tarot may be described as cultivating a conversation between aspects of the unconscious, archetypal energies or deities allowing them to speak to us mortals in a loud and clear here on earth. Some believe that as society and technology advance, we are losing touch with our natural selves. Some myths and legends talk about a time when gods and goddesses were within reach to the masses, but in time we have become more dense into the physical realm and they have become more subtle into the realm of imagination. Occult practices aim to bridge this gap and aid the materialisation of spirit and the spiritualisation of matter. This allows information to pass between the two more freely in a way found in the many stories contained within the perennial philosophy.

A fable that exemplifies the above passage is that of 'the Witch'.

The High Priestess depends upon her strong intuition and instinct. Whilst communicating and interpreting the will of the gods and spirits she is able to understand and translate signs and omens. She accepts what is and is her understanding of the divine order of the cosmos allows he to accept her place in the wider order of what is. She is humble, modest and is at peace; wanting for nothing, she is tuned in to what must occur through the path of least resistance. She embodies the positive ideals of a powerful and intuitive femininity.

However The Priestess is not safe from the energy of The Sorceress. The benevolent Priestess fell deeply into the hands of the malevolent energy of the Sorceress. This negative side of the powerful feminine gripped her tightly, allowing her power to be used for self gain and the attack upon others. Her ability to commune with the gods and spirits became a trapping that she could not escape from.

Left in her own narrowly defined world and using her power for evil and greed, she was unable to gain acceptance of what is in the light of love and peace. She wanted control at any expense and would use her power on mortals to get it. Operating in the realm of shadows, she can morph in to any creature of the night she chooses, using the power of the snake, the bat, the rat or the raven to pray upon the innocence of others. She appears in dreams and visions and symbolises the powerfully negative aspects of womanhood, inviting others in to her lair.

From birth, we primarily receive nourishment from what we digest. From the breast to the bowl, we take in what is applicable for us at that moment; drawn to that which we need most. When someone is no longer able to tolerate one element of nutrition, they must move to that which satiates them.

When the darkness of the Sorceress has snuffed out the light of its host and she has fallen victim to its wiles, the being must maintain its energy in the only way she can.

This low vibrational energy cannot make its own as she is no longer human, her demon side is almost complete in devouring her past identity.

Unable to operate in the realm of light, the Sorceress must gain her sustenance and take vampirically from the innocent. Ritualistic Cannibalism and Blood Letting; the way of the Vampire or Succubus.The dark arts become her lifeline and she feeds on light in order to survive, ripping it from the innocent souls of others too lost, weak and confused to fight back, they are taken into the depths of her lair between worlds for eternity.

Models and stylists: Sammm Agnew, Simret Cheema-Innis

SATAN SUPERSTAR - A PERSONAL VIEW

LYDIA LUNCH

If I was so intellectually impoverished as to have that much talked about "God Shaped Hole" in my heart which would result in a delirium so excruciating, as to lead me to believe in mythological creations, I would no doubt at this point be praying to the great Satan, to manifest herself into a Saturn sized bacterial infection that would rocket toward the earth and annihilate the infantile man babies whose psychotic temper tantrums could any day now result in a living hell for all the rest of us.

Photo: Sébastien Greppo

IF NEEDS MUST, THE DEVIL DRIVES

THE STORY OF THE SATANIC SLUTS AND BLACK MASS

NIGEL WINGROVE

Perhaps it was reading Dennis Wheatley, or listening to Black Sabbath, or watching Hammer films that set me off. But at sometime in my mid-teens I heard, or read, or, possibly, I made it up, that the way to reject God and to embrace Satan was to recite the **Lord's Prayer** backwards and spurn Christ by spitting onto the Bible at the end of the prayer.

Diligently I wrote the **Lord's Prayer** out backwards, word by word in my best handwriting, and then I recited it like a mantra each night and waited for the Devil to take me… Amazingly nothing happened, so I tried to get others to join me thinking that there would be strength in numbers; girlfriends and friends were equally encouraged to recite the **Lord's Prayer** with me. People either refused to do it, or made an excuse, or they would start to recite the prayer and then stop halfway, with some reason or other as to why they couldn't finish it. No one, it seemed, but me would read it out all the way through and I took pleasure in that. I was the bad one…

Years later I read the book **The Interior Castle**, written by the 16th Century Spanish Carmelite nun, Saint Teresa of Avila, a book in which Teresa describes her spiritual development through prayer, leading to a union with God. I thought that it was very beautiful and moving, so much so that I read all that I could find on Saint Teresa and went out to Rome to see Bernini's statue, *The Ecstasy of Saint Teresa*, which shows Teresa in the act of being pierced by 'a long spear of gold' which, in her writings, she says culminated in her body being filled with an intense pleasure.

I chose to make a film of that ecstasy, or her 'transverberation of the heart', in which her spiritual and physical presence unified with God. In my way I wanted to honour and praise her, to interpret her struggles and visions in my style. With that in mind, I made my short film, **Visions of Ecstasy**, with the aim not of demeaning Teresa but of genuinely trying to interpret her struggle and eventual union with her vision of Christ. That at least was my intention.

What I had done according the BBFC, some members of the Video Appeals Committee and later the European Court of Human Rights in Strasbourg who upheld their views, was to have *"outraged the Divinity of Christ"*. I had, in their eyes, committed a blasphemy.

So even when I tried to do good, I did bad.

Fourteen years later I did bad again.

"There are only two legal subjects left that you can explore that still, in this day and age when people have pretty much seen and heard everything, have the ability to

make people shiver with a kind of frisson or fear: Nazism and Satanism." So said the writer Gavin Baddeley to me, and that thought stayed with me long after the rest of our conversation had faded into time.

Then a series of events seemed to propel me towards, if not Satan himself, then certainly in his general direction. My film distribution company Redemption was, in the early Noughties, embroiled in a number of disputes, legal rows and debts. I had also lost most of my staff and things were generally, by 2003, in a bit of a mess, with both my UK and US businesses reduced to trickles and my main income now coming from sporadic R18 sales to licensed sex shops and direct sales of our horror titles through our main website.

It was the website that I decided to focus on. Having seen the then recently launched **Suicide Girls** site and noted the success of alternative models on sites like **Cam Whores** and **Gothic Sluts**, and the proliferation of really interesting alternative girls on sites like Live Journal, I wanted to do something similar with Redemption.

I chose the Satanic Sluts name as, at that time, it fitted in with all the other confrontational names girl groups were using and whether people took it ironically or not, once heard it wasn't easily forgotten. My motivation was to include the Satanic Sluts on the Redemption site as a way of bringing in extra traffic.

Having decided on the name and a logo, I contacted a few good looking and interesting goth girls that I knew to see if they would like a section of their own on our Redemption site where they could post pictures of themselves, write a brief biography along with some of their likes and dislikes and generally self-promote.

Nearly all of the girls that I approached said yes and the Satanic Sluts launched with about ten or so members. I then started approaching girls and models that I found on Live Journal and similar sites who I thought would be good to have in the Satanic Sluts and most, though not all, agreed straight away. In about a month we had some fifty or sixty Satanic Sluts from around the world and as the Satanic Sluts grew, so more girls started applying to join independently.

Then **Metal Hammer** magazine asked if I could send some of the London based Satanic Sluts along to their very first Golden Gods Awards event and in return **Metal Hammer** agreed to feature the Satanic Sluts in their magazine each month and on their website. The result

was a massive jump in traffic to our site and a equally massive jump in interest in the Satanic Sluts as a group. Hot alternative girls were, quite literally in some cases, beating a left-hand path to Redemption's door.

At this time several things happened, and it was the point that - with hindsight - I should have sought help to manage what was genuinely becoming something of a phenomenon. Several magazines from Europe, the US and South America asked to feature the Satanic Sluts; we were also getting requests for the girls to attend events, a calendar was produced and there was a real opportunity to monetise the group along similar lines to the Suicide Girls.

The girls - at least those that lived in and around London - now wanted not just to be in the Satanic Sluts but to be *seen* to be in the Satanic Sluts and they wanted a place to meet up. I had somehow managed to turn Redemption around: at this point (2004) it was starting to make money again and so I was able to subsidise the Satanic Sluts and look seriously into the idea of giving the girls access to some sort of venue and equally importantly giving them a 'look'.

Three things then happened. Out of the blue, a friend who ran a lot of Soho's bars and clubs asked if I would like a Sunday night once a month at the Green Rooms, a members club for Actors, that was relocating from Covent Garden and reopening in a large renovated house in Romilly Street in the centre of Soho. The second was an opportunity to redesign and publish an official UK based Church of Satan magazine, **Rule Satannia**; and the third was that after talking directly to Peter Gilmore, the administrator of the Church of Satan in the US, I was given permission to use the Church of Satan's endorsement in the promotion and marketing of my new club, now to be called Black Mass.

Black Mass came together like magic, at least initially. The logo, which incorporated the Redemption face, an inverted crucifix and the Baphomet symbol looked amazing. I was able to redesign **Rule Satannia** and link it visually with Redemption, Black Mass and the Satanic Sluts whilst hopefully not damaging the magazine's Satanic integrity; and the girls, at least some of them, were really keen to be involved and suggested putting on shows.

It is about now that the first signs of Gavin Baddeley's predicted 'shiver' began to appear. Firstly, it turned out that my friend at the Green Rooms didn't have quite as much power at he had intimated, and when the actual owner of the club - a rather pompous and affected man - heard that an event was to be held there called Black Mass, he had hysterics! Not least because 'Dickie', as in Attenborough, would apparently have a fit he heard about it. I explained that we had already had expensive flyers printed promoting the event, but these only upset him further and that was that. Black Mass was banned from the Green Rooms.

That night I was moaning about losing my venue to friends in a bar and was approached by someone who had heard my wailing. He said he ran the Astral Bar in Soho's Brewer Street, a former adult cinema which had been converted into a classy lap-dancing club and which was now a gay night club with a small stage. Our benefactor said that he was fine having a Satanic themed club there once a month and that, importantly, he was also fine with the Satanic Sluts performing and that furthermore, he had no problems if some of the Satanic Sluts shows involved nudity. Given what had happened with the Green Rooms I wanted to be absolutely sure this

REDEMPTION FILMS IN CONJUNCTION WITH RULE SATANNIA MAGAZINE AND THE OFFICIAL CHURCH OF SATAN PRESENT:

black mass

Satan finds Redemption... Presenting **Black Mass**, an exclusive monthly event in one of the darkest corners of central London where damned souls can gather to indulge their blackest fantasies and view some of the most twisted live acts this side of Hades. Featuring **Redemption** film visuals, debauched performances by some of our elite **Satanic Sluts** including at **Black Mass V** a Countess Bathory Blood Bath, a tormented and sick performance from one of our new **SS** recruits, a lesbo Frankenstein gorgasm show and an atrocity xzibit of unbelievable cruelty and perversity involving some of our most twisted **Satanic Sluts**, an iron maiden and a St Andrews Cross.

On top of this family fare there will be numerous **SS** pole dancers, an initiation to Satan by drinking blood from the wounds of the elite **SSDD** (Satanic Sluts Depravity Division) and, we hope, some Black Mass goody bags for our devotees to clutch in their claws as they crawl away into the darkness at the end of the night...

DRESS AS IF YOUR SOUL DEPENDED ON IT.

A unique environment combining the aesthetics of horror, perversion and Satanism where true believers can reclaim the night.

Tickets: Members £5.00 Guests £6.66

OUR UBER GOTH SATANIC SLUTS RESERVE THE RIGHT TO REFUSE ADMISSION TO ANYONE!

"Scenes from Hell" Black Mass I, II, III & IV

An important announcement - Due to the nature of Black Mass and the performances staged there, we have been advised to make it a members only event and this will be the case from Black Mass V oawards. Membership costs £10.00 and is valid for 12 months from the membership date. This admits members for £5.00 and members can sign in up to two guests on any night. Guest admission is £6.66.

Details are listed below and you are advised to apply quickly as membership is limited and members will get priority at all times.

You can apply to become a member of BLACK MASS by paying either by credit card or by sending a cheque for £10.00 made payable to REDEMPTION FILMS LIMITED. Send to Redemption Films, BCM BOX 9235, LONDON WC1N 3XX.

Membership is £10.00 and is valid for 12 months from the date you join.

Visa/M.Card
Name: Expiry Date:
Address:
Email: Contact phone number:
Date of Birth:

time that all was OK before printing new flyers and promoting the new venue. Finally, after umpteen confirmations and assurances, I took the plunge and had new flyers printed, booked DJs, told the girls and so on. All systems were go - Sunday 26th September 2004 was to be the first Black Mass.

On the Friday before, the 24th, I was directing a shoot for **Rule Satannia** at a studio in Camden and at about four o'clock took a call from our benefactor. *"Would the girls at Black Mass be showing their breasts?"* he asked. *"I hope so"* I replied flippantly. That was it. He cancelled. Apparently he couldn't, despite everything he had said, allow any kind of nudity, which was probably nonsense as the Astral had previously been a lap-dancing club. But he was adamant, there was to be no Black Mass at the Astral Club on his watch.

I remember calling our offices in Soho straight after in a complete panic. I should say now that Redemption's office and where I lived at the time were about 100 yards from the Astral Club. A girl who worked at Redemption said *"leave it to me"* and ran around to Madame Jo-Jo's club, which was literally across the road from the Astral Club - and somehow, she persuaded them to let us hold Black Mass there. Hallelujah!

On the night of that first Black Mass we had to put up directional posters on the Green Rooms' ans Astral Club's doors saying *"It's Behind You"*. I guess in the end maybe a hundred or so people turned up to that first Black Mass. Those that did saw a somewhat shambolic collection of Satanic Slut shows that would set the tone for the future of the club. In one, a nun was tied to a crucifix, stripped, covered in (fake) blood and implied rape with a crucifix. The other shows all had similar exploitation film themes: nudity, blood, blasphemy, rape nuns, more nuns, violence, vampirism, Nazism, lesbianism and more nudity and even more blood - the Satanic Sluts had arrived.

Madame Jo-Jo's had insisted that, because of the nudity, Black Mass was a members club so we had made people pay, I think, £5 or £10 for that first Black Mass membership. By Black Mass II, to be held on October 31st, Halloween, we had posh Black Mass membership cards, a semi Satanic Sluts uniform which, with its armband and transmuter books, made them look like a cross between satanic SS officers and gothic stormtroopers. We also had a great friendly venue with a good-sized stage. Word had also spread and Black Mass II was packed.

Black Mass II was also the official launch of **Rule Satannia** magazine, so a lot of genuine Satanists were attending. In recognition of this we had arranged for a real Black Mass to be held; a truncated version, but real nevertheless. Also present were The Nuns, a completely over-the-top all girl goth band from New York that I had taken on, and maybe thirty or more members of the Satanic Sluts, including many that I was seeing and meeting in real life for the first time. I was also filming everything.

It was initially great: the shows, shambolic and shocking, were better and bigger than Black Mass I and the audience, I think, were just enjoying the madness of everything. And then came or happened what has ever since been referred to as the 'incident'. I should point out at this juncture that I rarely got involved in the actual content of the shows other than booking props or costumes or paying the girls. So when this particular performance was outlined to me, it sounded as if it would be a standard Satanic Slut show featuring some sort of simulated rape, or stripping of a girl with some vampirism and lesbianism thrown in for good measure.

I filmed from amongst the audience, as the side of the stage didn't give much of a view. The show looked OK, though a bit chaotic with maybe too many girls on stage, not all looking like they knew what they were doing. But otherwise it was fine. The show finished, the DJ started up again, people started dancing and I went to the bar to get a drink. Then, a long term colleague with a theatrical background who made many of the props and decorations for Black Mass and our shoots came running up to me saying that they had had to call an ambulance and that there was blood everywhere back stage, as one of the girls had cut herself.

At this point I just assumed that a girl had accidentally cut herself coming off stage - but ridiculously, two of the girls had arranged for one of them to cut the other with a scalpel as part of the performance, as they thought that the blood would look more real! The cut girl, had the blade gone in fractionally deeper, would have died. Luckily, she was OK - just - and taken straight to hospital while the police gave the other girl a sound talking to.

All this drama happened backstage and in a police station, while on stage The Nuns, more Satanic Slut shows and a Black Mass were performed making Black Mass II, despite the carnage, one the best ever. Nevertheless, Madame JoJo's very nearly lost their license as a result of the incident and Black Mass was banned again.

Black Mass III was scheduled for December and with Christmas in mind, the girls decided to reenact the Nativity; also planned were Nazi Go Go dancers and other outrages. The problem was not having a venue. At this stage in Black Mass's history it was proving helpful not to mention the club's name or the Satanic Sluts to potential venues, so instead Black Mass was described as just a 'gothy' night. On this basis we were finally able to book the Stork Club, a small traditional night club off Regent Street that was infamous in the Fifties and early Sixties as the venue where politicians like John Profumo and Harold MacMillan could rub shoulders with film stars like Elizabeth Taylor, Peter Sellers and Frank Sinatra - as well as less reputable women like Christine Keeler. Now it was about the get the Satanic Sluts.

By Christmas 2004 the Stork Club was definitely showing signs of age and was a bit frayed around the edges. It was also very small, with a tiny stage overlooking a square dance floor. Yet for Black Mass it was perfect, and even a crowd of perhaps a hundred people made it seem crowded and buzzy. It was then that Black Mass's 'gothy' crowd seemed to worry the club's Middle Eastern management,who started making arrivals remove 'dangerous' jewellery and anything else they considered offensive. But despite this, after about an hour the management settled down and watched the unbelievably warped antics of the Nazi Go Go dancers - which they seemed to enjoy.

By the time of the climatic Nativity show things had calmed down nicely, with all parties seemingly happy with the general state of affairs. Indeed even the drunken debauchery of several top Satanic Sluts was greeted with benign smiles, so I was hopeful that Black Mass had found a new home - but alas the evening's main theatrical event soon put paid to that.

The Nativity initially started off very much like a school performance, with Jesus and Mary seeking shelter before settling down in a stable - all accompanied by suitably reverential music. The Nativity reenactment was also - by Satanic Slut standards - actually quite a show and had attracted the attention of the club's management who had all gathered to watch. This was perhaps unfortunate, as their arrival coincided with the baby Jesus being booted out into the audience and replaced with a horned goat, accompanied by blaring Black Metal, while Mary was stripped and ravished in the usual way by a horde of satanic disciples. The booted baby Jesus - by some miracle - landed in the lap of the manager. Black Mass was banned again.

Yet despite all the bans and chaos, Black Mass and the Satanic Sluts were growing, with more and more girls asking to join and more magazines wanting to feature them. There had also been a major escalation in the level of press being generated as the launch issue of **Rule Satannia** had featured an article on a Satanist sailor in the Royal Navy, who had been allowed to worship in his way while at sea in his ship, the aircraft carrier The Ark Royal. With agreement from all concerned parties we arranged an exclusive with the **Sunday Telegraph**, who in turn got an excited Ann Widdecombe, at that time still a Conservative MP, to condemn everything. By Sunday evening Rule Satannia was on Channel Four news and the story went worldwide. At this point, the press focused on the Navy and Satan. For the Satanic Sluts, their moment was to come…

Black Mass finally found a venue that would tolerate their behaviour, the new Marquee Club in Leicester Square where, from January onwards, the club would be held once a month throughout 2005. The Satanic Sluts at this time were on a roll, in the sense that opportunities were coming in almost every week. It was as much as I could deal with and still run Redemption, which had now expanded its range to include the Japanese film label Sacrament, increasing my workload even more.

Around this time Redemption was offered the night slot on a shopping channel, from ten in the evening until six in the morning during which time the channel would be named Redemption. Naively I thought it was free and that all I had to do was supply our films. I was wrong of course - the shopping channel wanted a fee for the airtime and was effectively just trying to rent Redemption the time slot. However, I had the TV bug now and went out to get the money, which I did very quickly, but not without incident and not without the Satanic Sluts almost getting the channel closed before it actually started.

The media company I had approached, and one of its key staff who was considering funding what would become Redemption TV, had bizarrely walked passed a big queue outside Black Mass a few weeks prior to my approaching them and remembered being very impressed by the number of people lining up to get in - so much so that he pushed very hard for my project.

The net result was that they agreed to fund an alternative film, music and lifestyle channel to be broadcast on SKY which would be called Redemption TV. I was to be in charge of its creative image and, after auditions, suitably photogenic and eloquent members of the Satanic Sluts would be its presenters. To cement this agreement, all the bigwigs of this media company decided that they wanted to attend the next Black Mass club...

I was given a friendly warning that it would be best if there wasn't anything too risque going on when the financiers arrived, and tried hard to avoid any obvious performance ghastliness. However, two of that night's Satanic Sluts were the same two who had been involved in the attempted limb removal at Madame JoJo's at Black Mass II. Rather foolishly, I hadn't considered that letting them perform on this of all nights might be a bit rash.

So as the financial muscle walked in, a girl dressed as a Jewess with a Star of David stencilled on each arm and - for good measure - a larger star stencilled between her breasts was pushed out on stage. Then another girl in a full and proper SS uniform from the waist up and black stockings and boots from the waist down goosestepped around her before she attempted to gas the Jewish girl.

At this point, the financiers had quite literally stopped in their tracks and were watching opened-mouthed as the SS girl was attacked by another Jewish girl, who was in turn joined by the semi-gassed girl who staged a remarkable recovery and proceeded to mimic sodomising the SS officer. I did quiz my delinquent thespians later as to the meaning of this show and it was apparently supposed to represent various aspects of the Holocaust, though exactly which ones I am not sure.

Somehow this faux pas was allowed to pass and Redemption TV went ahead, at least as a concept. Very soon, it became clear that the meaning of 'creative control' actually meant very little as everyone, like cooks, had a suggestion when it came to the channel's artistic direction ideas - and first to go was Satan. Investors do not, I was told, like Satan, nor do they like oblique references to him - so out went a lot of the initial animations and graphics that used genuinely Satanic symbols.Then out went the 'Satanic Sluts' - not the girls, as they were good, but their overall name least it offend. Then came the deal breaker - instead of really alternative music and underground material, they wanted 'rock' and just 'rock', no more films or anything in fact other than 'rock' and 'rock' related material. For me, that was a step too far and I decided to part company. The channel became 'Rock World' and I and 'Redemption TV' were gone.

However, it lost me nearly two years and broke both the momentum of both the Satanic Sluts as they were and Black Mass, which I ended on the twelve (actually eleventh) show. One of the Satanic Sluts was going to come out on stage in a burka and blow-up, but the theatrical man that we used could not get the explosive element to work; so perhaps fittingly, the last performance at the last mass was a fan dance by Dischordia, one of our first and best Satanic Sluts.

By now it was 2007, and FAB Press had agreed to publish **Blood and Dishonour**, a photographic book on the Satanic Sluts - while in turn Redemption released two DVDs cobbled together from footage shot over the previous three years. Satan's cheerleaders then were still there but not as focused. Some of the girls were by now smitten with wanting to be presenters while others were just getting on with life away from Black Mass. I too was beginning to see DVD sales

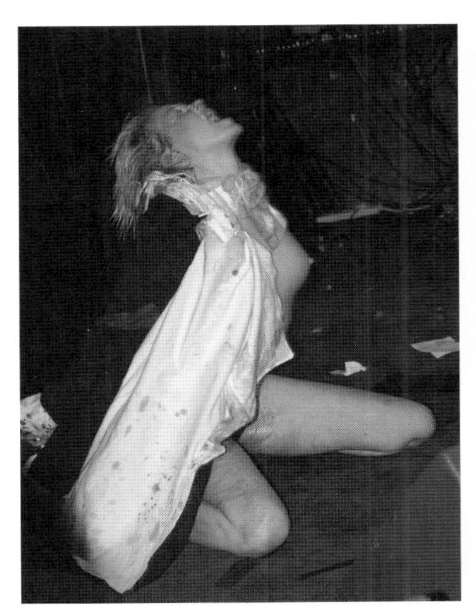

declining and suffering as one of our distributors after another started going bust. But Satan had at least one more throw of the dice to make.

Amongst the London core of Satanic Sluts was a girl called Voluptua, a sexy, curvy girl who had appeared on the scene at Black Mass some time in 2005. This was Georgina, Andrew Sachs' granddaughter, and soon to be Russell Brand's lover, Jonathan Ross slayer and national news story.

At sometime in 2008, Georgina asked if I would support a Satanic Slut performance group of some five or six girls who could represent the Satanic Sluts at clubs and events. I said yes, and they got on with it. As with all Satanic Slut ventures it was a bit chaotic, but generally they were finding their feet and, as the 'Satanic Sluts Extreme', they were getting bookings. Separately to this I had given the main Satanic Sluts their own website and was building up a new membership with a new generation of girls; but without Black Mass, and with the pressures of running Redemption increasing, it should have been obvious that something was going to give. In the end it was events, and a major event, that did for it.

The Satanic Sluts Extreme were booked to perform at a nightclub in Vienna in October and I remember Georgina coming into the office complaining that Russell Brand had been saying rude things about her grandfather on his radio show with Jonathan Ross, and she was really pissed off about it. She also mentioned that the **Daily Mail** had been calling her. I told her that she ought to call them back but she wanted to wait until she got back from Austria, so we left it at that. That was on a Thursday. On the Friday, the girls flew to Vienna.

IS THAT A FACT? Inflation has increased 'penny for the Guy' to £6

BABIES? YOU'RE KIDDING SAYS JEN

GEORGINA'S GUTS!

Babe eats fake intestines in stage shocker

Sacked for a year of double pay

Cokeheads get free nose jobs

Actor's granddaughter hits back at Brand show 'prank'

I'M ANGRY, UPSET AND BETRAYED

Joke is on Woss

That Sunday, the 26th October - which is also my birthday - I went to get the Sunday papers and saw that the front page of the **Daily Mail** was all about Jonathan Ross, Russell Brand, Andrew Sachs and Georgina. I knew instinctively that this was going to be massive, though not perhaps how massive.

I called - unfortunately, given later revelations - Max Clifford, as I felt if anyone could handle this it was him. And for this story, I think I made the right call. However, on that Sunday I just had to leave a message on his company's answer machine and for me, despite the **Mail**'s front page story, the day was quiet. I couldn't get hold of Georgina and no one called me.

Monday, however, was like the end of the world. I stepped out of my flat and walked around the corner into Charlotte Street where Redemption's offices were and people I didn't know ran up to me asking if I was me, saying that reporters were everywhere. There were reporters on the pavement outside our building, there were reporters inside our building. The phones, and we had six lines then, were ringing off the hook - every news channel you can think of, every newspaper, radio show, and more called.

They all essentially wanted or said the same thing - if Georgina wasn't around could I speak for her? Her grandfather, Andrew Sachs was apparently under siege. And then, of course, there was the Satanic Sluts! What were they? Who were they? What did they do? Were they Satanists? Were they into perversion? Who many were there? What was Georgina's role and so on. I even got interviewed by Terry Wogan for the **Times**. It made the brouhaha around my blasphemy ban seem like nothing.

This was a full-on media storm and people got scared - and then Max Clifford called and we were to meet on the Tuesday with Georgina, who was flying back from Vienna and

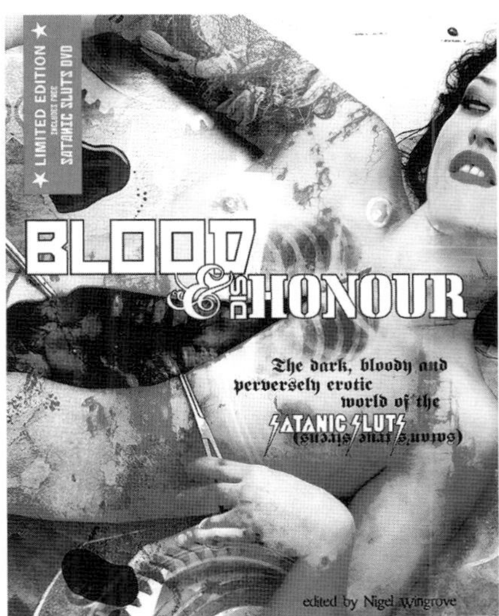

staying with one of the other girls who also worked for me in the office. Once Clifford was appointed, things quietened down for us very quickly, with all calls rooted through his offices. **The Sun** and the **Mail** got exclusives, and Ross and Brand got the boot from the Beeb! I got some money but lost the Satanic Sluts - or rather, many of the original girls panicked at the press spotlight and - being good girls under their Satanic veneer - moved back into the light. The rest just got on with their life, or perfected their shows and moved into burlesque or whatever, but essentially I had to either save my company or run the Satanic Sluts as a business. I had to choose the company, so Satan and I had to part.

I got to make another Satanic Slut film with Georgina, **Scandalised**, and then really had to focus on Redemption as circumstances forced me into administration in 2009. I was able to buy back the assets and Redemption lived again, launching on Blu-ray in the US via distributors Kino Lorber while I reinvented the Redemption brand yet again in the UK - but none of these involved Satan or his black-clad, nun-raping little helpers...

I still get emails from girls wanting to join the Satanic Sluts and asked if I'll ever stage another Black Mass club. It could happen, but in a way Black Mass and the Satanic Sluts happened organically at the right time, the result, I suppose, of a series of (un)fortunate events. Now in 2018, with people taking offence at almost anything, I think that it would be even more difficult than it was to allow the Satanic Sluts the freedom to essentially go crazy and do what they wanted to do - and if they were restricted creatively then it would be against the whole concept of the Satanic Sluts, Black Mass and the eternal motto of 'Do What Thou Wilt' ... and that really would be blasphemous.

Black Mass photographers: Dave Murphy, Paul Xerode - xerode.net, Brian Southam - ag-1.co.uk, Andy Dendy, Andy Meyers and Belladonna, GMK, Adrien Judd - adrienjudd.com

THE GOLDEN AGE OF GROTESQUE

THE OCCULT PHOTOGRAPHY OF WILLIAM MORTENSEN

DAVID FLINT

William Mortensen is a photographic artist who has, to a large degree, been written out of history. In a world where the phrase 'the camera never lies' is taken as some sort of mission statement for realist photographers, Mortensen's staged works of pictorialist grotesquery have been widely ignored or dismissed by all but the most ardent connoisseur of the bizarre.

It wasn't always so. At one time, Mortensen was a big deal, as both a portrait photographer and a creator of fantastical, monstrous works that often combined the occult and the erotic. He was a pioneer of seeing photography as an art form equal to painting, and one that could be manipulated and warped. His printing method often allowed his photographs to transcend the medium and become more like illustration, and his technique involved staged scenes, costumes and fantastical scenarios. They were the very antithesis of photojournalism, and so it it no surprise that he was considered to be *"the antichrist"* by Ansel Adams and his fellow Group f.64 purists, who would come to define 'serious' photography a decade after Mortensen's glory days.

During the 1930s, Mortensen was a big star – one of the first big names of photography, in fact. He wrote books about 'the Mortensen Method', and The Mortensen School of Photography was where every aspiring photo artist wanted to go – here, you could get first-hand instruction on his techniques from the master himself. It was the peak of a career that began in the late 1910s as an artist and etcher, before a move to Hollywood – in the company of a fourteen-year-old Fay Wray, the sister of Mortensen's fiancée Willow – brought him into the film industry. Here, in 1920, he had his first encounter with manipulated photography, albeit in the motion picture medium. Predicting the current trend for green screen filming and computer-generated sets by almost a century, director Ferdinand Pinney Earle hired Mortensen to paint backdrops for the film **The Rubáiyát of Omar Khayyám**, a film that had the actors shot against a blank black background and then matted in over Mortensen's art. The film, now lost, immediately hit legal problems, as backers battled for control of the film and Allan Dwan sued over what he considered a breach of his copyrighted matte process. The film didn't emerge until 1925, when it released in an edited and inferior form as **A Lover's Oath**. Unsurprisingly, it had little impact on how films were made at the time.

Mortensen's connection to Fay Wray ended when the mother of the now fifteen-year-old arrived in Hollywood, convinced (wrongly, as it turns out) that Mortensen had been sleeping with the underage girl who was in his care. She destroyed photographs (including implied nude shots) that he had taken of her, and the two would only meet again for professional portrait engagements. Wray would, of course, achieve immortality a decade later as the leading lady of **King Kong** (and to her credit, always defended her photographer friend who was unfairly maligned by her mother, and lazy writers, for

Untitled, 1927

Preparation for the Sabbot - photogravure 1927

years); interestingly, in 1935 Mortensen created his own 'woman and ape' image with his provocative photo **L'Amour**, in which a drooling, giant gorilla leers over an unconscious topless woman. One wonders if he was thinking about his former charge at the time.

In the mid-1920s, Mortensen met photographer Arthur Kales, who taught him the photographic and bromoil printmaking techniques that would see him move away from painted art and into the newer medium. Mortensen, apparently a quick learner and a man with social connections in Hollywood, would soon be an in-demand portrait photographer for movie stars, and his work appeared in all the leading magazines of the day. His success saw him open his own studio on Hollywood Boulevard, where he began to experiment with his style and subject matter – by his own account, the studio was frequently populated by the same sort of sideshow human oddities that would later be seen in Tod Browning's **Freaks**. Browning and Mortensen seem to have been similar characters, though there is no record of them working together. But the photographer did form a working relationship with Cecil B. DeMille, with whom he worked as stills photographer for **King of Kings**. DeMille was impressed enough with Mortensen's work to publish it as a limited edition book; Mortensen, similarly, was influenced by DeMille to think that he could direct a photograph just as a filmmaker directs a movie; he also took on board many of DeMile's fascinations – religion, sadism and eroticism.

Mortensen began to explore the bizarre and the grotesque for what would ultimately be a frustratingly unfinished book – **A Pictorial History of Witchcraft and Demonology**, which he began work on in 1926. In this, he worked with occult expert and writer Manly P. Hall, who gave the photographer access to his library of black magic volumes as he investigated the subject. Hall had previously posed for Mortensen, who provided the frontispiece image for the author's 1930 book **The Space Born**. The **Witchcraft and Demonology** book was also influenced by legendary horror star Lon Chaney, who Mortensen had photographed on several occasions. Chaney's innovative use of make-up to change his face and create new monstrosities particularly inspired the photographer, who was already fascinated by the bizarre – studying Chaney's techniques showed Mortensen how to create his own monstrous creations for his work.

The final influence on this occult project was Mortensen's soon-be-be second wife and muse Myrdith Monaghan, who would be the model in many of his most iconic

The Mark of the Devil, 1927

photographs from 1926 onwards. A comfortable nude model, Monaghan seemed to immediately click with Mortensen, and she became his main model for the **Witchcraft and Demonology** project.

Much of what Mortensen shot for this book has vanished, but what remains is a remarkable collection of images – from joyfully sexy witchcraft to grim mediaeval tortures, all dramatically posed and quite brilliant in execution. In his book **The Command to Look**, Mortensen states that:

"fear, secrecy and converse with the evil powers were characteristic elements of this mysterious cult that is as old as man. These elements are the very substance of the grotesque. The early wood engravers did much with themes derived from witchcraft. Brueghel has worked with this material; also has Goya; but little has been done with it by photographers."

Indeed, he was right. What's notable about Mortensen's pioneering exploration of this subject is not only how much his work looks like a photographic representation of the earlier art that he references, but also how much if it eventually filtered into the popular consciousness, and cinema in particular – occult films from **I Walked with a Zombie** to **I Married a Witch** have a (toned-down) flavour of the work that he was creating over a

Untitled, 1926

decade earlier, and subsequent movies have – almost certainly unknowingly, through second-hand inspiration – continued to use the visual style that he helped create. It's a great pity that the book was never completed – possibly lost in the complications of his private life, that included a divorce from his first wife and another ugly incident with Fay Wray's controlling and manipulative mother in 1928, which saw him having to publicly state that photos of him and Wray together were faked (they weren't), while having both the fame-hungry stage mother and the executives from Paramount threatening all manner of punishment even though the photos and the relationship were both entirely above board. This was a humiliating moment that probably influenced his decision to leave Hollywood behind.

Above:Untitled, 1926
Below: L'Amour, 1935

At the start of the 1930s, Mortensen relocated from Hollywood to Laguna Beach, where he opened his photography school and his career continued to flourish. He continued to develop his techniques of manipulation – something now familiar to anyone with even the most basic photo editing software, but revolutionary stuff at the time - and his set ups became ever more elaborate. For him, the photograph itself was just the starting point, to be manipulated and transformed into a piece of art.

Throughout the 1930s, Mortensen's style was something to aspire to. As well as his bestselling instructional books, he was able to lend his name to lights, developer and other photographic products. Mortensen was a brand. Not all his work was fantastical, of course – he was justifiably famed for his excellent nudes, and was still taking portraits of stars (or wannabe stars). But his time was almost up.

Mortensen's work was the antithesis of photo-reality, and a new generation of ultra-realists – for whom any sort of manipulation was anathema – went on the attack. With surprising speed, Mortensen fell out of favour with publishers and galleries, for whom

Untitled, 1926

the purity of unretouched, photo-vertité became the new standard for the medium. It would be a lie to say that Mortensen's career was over – he still had his admirers, and his nude work – now the bulk of his output – remained popular, if not especially respected. But as the neo-realists strengthened their grip on what photography was supposed to be – reportage and authentic – so Mortensen's work and style began to be marginalised and, increasingly, ridiculed as classic examples of Bad Photography, in much the same way that 'serious' film critics have long sneered at the phantasmagorical and the high camp, in favour of turgid realism. By the time of his death in 1965, he was a niche figure, though the short documentary film **Monsters and Madonnas** (named after his most famous book) did attempt to revive interest in him. It was narrated, rather appropriately, by Vincent Price, another intelligent artist associated with the grotesque and the baroque.

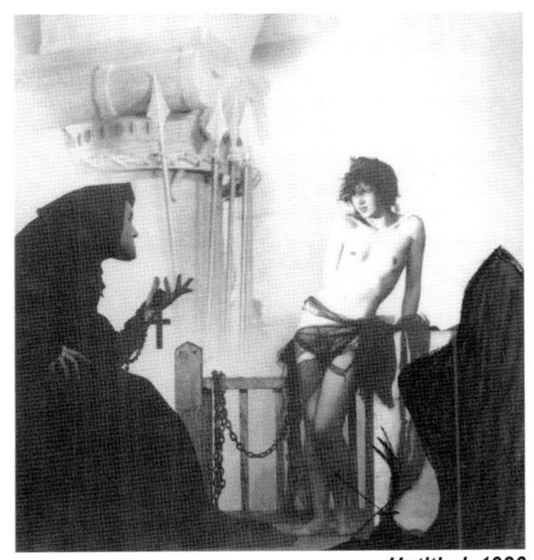

Untitled, 1926

Yet we might think now that Mortensen's time has come. The fantastical is in favour, and the Calvinist stranglehold of Adams and others has long been broken. Artists like David LaChapelle routinely create the sort of manipulated, carefully directed photographic works that Mortensen pioneered, and the idea as the photograph as art has been accepted for long enough now that we can allow all schools – the realist and the pictorialist, the reportage and the grotesque – to co-exist and be appreciated on their own merits. Yet Mortensen is still, to a large degree, a marginal figure for most people – if they have heard of him at all, it is likely to still be in disparaging tones. Thankfully, there are those who are championing his work – the Feral House book **American Grotesque**, by Larry Lyttle and Michael Moynihan, is an essential introduction to his surviving work.

William Mortensen's imagery is as startling now as it ever was – and seems surprisingly modern, more so than much of the work of his detractors. He may never quite be respectable – thank God – but he deserves to reclaim his place in the history of photographic art, and to be seen as one of the great creatives of the 20th century.

HOLY ORGASMS

DIVINE INTERVENTIONS AND THEIR RELIGIOUS SEX TOYS

GIPSIE CASTIGLIONE

Divine Interventions is a company that produces sex toys. But not just any sex toys. Oh no. The Divine Interventions line is a gloriously blasphemous selection of erotic novelties, like the Baby Jesus Butt Plug, the Jackhammer Jesus, dildos based around God, the Devil, Buddha and the Virgin Mary, plus – for the gentleman – the Bible Thumper, a masturbation sleeve. They also produce Holy Water Lube to help ease these sacrilegious silicone delights into your orifice of choice.

Naturally, we were intrigued to find out what the idea behind these unique toys was. And so we got in touch with Divine Interventions main man Nigel to submit him to the question…

What's your background? Had you worked in the sex toy industry before, and what brought you to the industry?

My background is in law. Prior to Divine, I had never worked in the sex toy industry. Dare I say that the Good Lord spoke to me and said *"ye shall have a career, albeit, not a great one, in the sex toy industry"*. What's a good lapsed believer to do? I mean, sheeite, one cannot ignore the Word.

Where did the idea for Divine Interventions come from?

There I was, I believe it was a nice summer day, sitting on the can (I find I receive her Word best when I'm evacuating my bowels) and there on the bathroom cabinet was what I thought was a Jesus dildo. After a quick, and probably not complete wipe, I jumped up and rushed into my roommates room to find out where he got this amazing Jesus dildo.

He first asked me to pull my pants up and then told me that it was not a Jesus dildo, but merely a Jesus night light. I was both disappointed and elated; and thus the Jackhammer and the Baby Jesus Butt Plug were born (though it did take me longer than seven days to birth them;

turns out that while the Good Lord and I commune, I don't share his Godly powers).

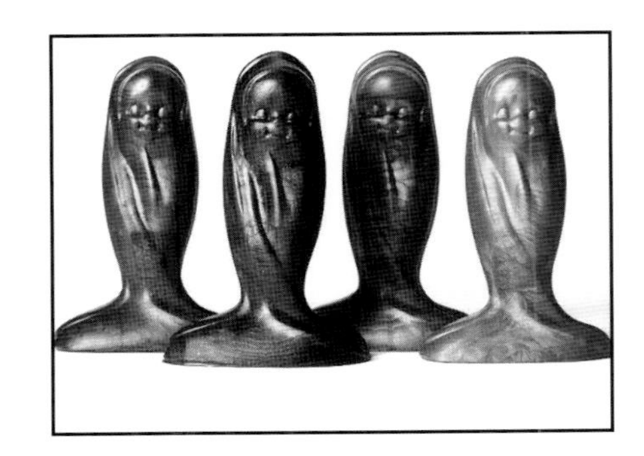

Do you have a religious background?

I was raised Church of England. I'm a believer now, just not in religion. I believe that a glow-in-the-dark Baby Jesus Butt Plug can be a guiding light in one's life. I've learned that the religious have no sense of humour. I'm concerned that the religious are weak mentally as their faith is shaken so easily

What was the first piece you created?

The Baby Jesus Butt Plug was first, and that remains the most popular, alongside the Jackhammer Jesus.

What sort of customers do you have (assuming you know)? Are they believers, blasphemers or atheists?

I'm going to guess all of the above. At street fairs I've had loads of lapsed Catholics come up and thank me making the toys.

There is an obvious humour to the collection, but are you also making a more serious statement about sex and religion?

Glad that you get the humour, some folks don't. I wasn't intending to make a more serious statement about sex and religion, but I can't stand how fucked up we are over sex, especially here in the U.S. Sex/intimacy is a wonderful thing and we're so afraid of it. These right wing fuckers truly scare me.

Religion is notoriously full of sexual repression that all too often results in abuse. Do you think that your toys - and sex toys in general - could help loosen up believers and allow them to have a healthier relationship with sex?

Do believers have an open mind? I don't know that they do; if they did, they probably wouldn't be religious. I don't know that the toys/toys in general can help loosed up believers. Believers seem to have too much shame around their bodies and sex.

I assume you must get some 'interesting' mail. How have people reacted - both good and bad - to what you do?

Interesting is a nice way of putting it. We mainly get fan mail, but definitely get our share of haters. Some are pretty extreme, describing the bullet type they're going to use, others just call us cowards for not having any Muslim toys (quick lesson: if the carpenter ever existed, he was a Jew -who never converted- and was also an Islamic prophet).

There's a long history of religious erotica, both serious and scurrilous - from nunsploitation to tales of lustful vicars and hypocritical priests. Where do you see your work within this tradition?

Not on the serious end of the spectrum, we're more on the 'just get over yourself and your silly ideas' end of the spectrum. I mean, if you truly believe that the Bible is the Word of God, you should seek psychiatric help. There's also a long history of sexual abuse by the religious - and folks get mad at us? Our toys have never raped anyone.

Are there religions, figures or ideas that you wouldn't touch? And if so, why? What remains taboo for you?

Muslim toys are something we won't touch. Their religious nutters really can't take a joke and it's simply not worth it (not to mention, what does the fucker look like?)

Presumably, there are people who would be deeply upset by your collection. How would you defend yourself to them?

I don't, what's the point? I don't care if your religion is personal to you, but do keep it to yourself. This world would be in such a better place if people just shut the fuck up about their religion.

Do you think that you are part of a Luciferian tradition of questioning and challenging religious dogma and control?

I wasn't intending to be, but I fully support it. I love what the Church of Satan has done in the US to point out religious hypocrisy. We need more Satanists.

If you had a dream stockist for the collection, where would it be? The Vatican gift shop, perhaps?

Ha, we'd sell so well at the Vatican gift shop! Years ago we got an email, allegedly from someone in the Vatican, stating that we would be taken to court for copyright violation because the Church owns Jesus. Sadly, we were not sued. I would love to get the Pope's seal of approval ...

What next - are you planning on expanding the collection further or is it complete?

It's pretty complete, but we've wanted to do a nativity scene and anal rosary beads. Have a Ganesha prototype, but he's a big boy, so not sure there's much of a market. Going to be working with some adult film producers in the near future ...

SATAN SUPERSTAR - A PERSONAL VIEW

GROOVIE MANN (THRILL KILL KULT)

And this is what the devil does…

Satan for me is the power of opposites, negativity inspired power from Satan & through taboos.

Taking a chance on facing & challenging the opposite/ negative power into a positive work/creative energy.

Without the Satan/Hell system of sin/punishment the church fall silent without the rebel of ignition.

It's like when your environment causes you upset and you can't escape it and you are going in circles — that's Satan.

Figuring reversal of feeling or using its power good or bad will empower it because of your force being motivated by a positive or negative, energy placement ,of your response.

Satan is a reaction to a game [that] always automatically stems from [the] eXsistance of Good & Evil.

Satan is the Rebel… Satan means No.

Photo by Larrabee Reed.

FUN IS THE LAW

THE MAGICAL WORLD OF THE PARTRIDGE FAMILY TEMPLE

BILLY CHAINSAW

Extreme fun flashback to 1991… I was travelling across North America with Siouxsie and The Banshees on the first Lollapalooza tour when my eyes beheld the light of The Partridge Family Temple for the first time. If my memory serves me well, it was at the Fiddlers Green Amphitheatre in Greenwood Village, Colorado, and I was drifting around the showground in search of freeky fun when I was handed a Partridge Family Temple sticker. Intrigued, and, being a fan of the TV show, I pocketed it with glee and a grin.

The Partridge Family Temple is also known as The All is Flowing Family of God – flash by Pika Partridge

Fast-forward almost three decades to the full tilt realisation of why I was handed and accepted that Pft! sticker. It was preordination in motion. It was my ticket to ride the Pft! bus to where all roads lead, to Albuquerque… and my allocated driver for the journalistic *trip* is none other than the Pft!'s exultant HIGHness Shaun Partridge– accept no substitute.

Part One: Shaun Partridge on the Pft!

In light of the tragic death of the Pft!'s beloved David Cassidy on 21 November 2017, my leading question has to be… where were you and what were you doing when you heard he had died?

Like all people who do very important things, I was on Facebook and someone posted something. I wasn't sure at first if it was an update on his present condition, or that he had in fact passed on and was in Albuquerque. Apparently it was both.

How did David's death effect you personally?

When I realised that David Cassidy had split the skin poncho scene, I was surprised how hard it hit me. You realise how much this person has had an influence over your life. How powerful that voice is. One thing that surprised me and made me happy was that all the news articles I read about David Cassidy weren't saying he was just some flash in the pan, or a curiosity note about how he used to be famous. Over and over again the articles explained how important and hugely famous David Cassidy was and how he affected so many people. The outpouring of love was phenomenal.

How will David's death impact on the Pft!?

The Partridge Family eats its TV dinner in front of the Eternal Reality TV show, so we understand that Keith is Dead, Long Live Cassidy. But his death impacts the Temple in the sense that we should always live 24 hours a day and to keep his songs singing in our hearts for many years to come.

The Partridge in the Pear Tree & Boyd Rice communing with the Great Mother backstage at her concert in 1993 – photo by K is for Kaleidoscope Partridge

Thank you for sharing Shaun. Now… please flashback through the psychedelic mists of time and recall your earliest memory?

Albany, New York. Pushing myself on a rabbit push toy into the living room and looking at my Uncle Corky and his wife.

Everything was dim and dark which may have done something with the lighting or memories., but I remember thinking that my Uncle Corky and his wife were Gomez and Morticia Addams. This was because my uncle was wearing a suit and had a mustache. The thing about memories is I don't think I'd know why it was the **Addams Family** because I was only one or two at the time.

Would you care to share a bit about your life pre-Pft!: how you were raised, your loves, your hates, and any run-ins with the authorities.

I was a very pleasant child who loved running through the meadow by our house. I was very fond of apples and would bring flowers to my mother everyday. My first loves were Underdog, **King Kong**, Spoon Candy and Ice Cream Bubblegum that came in strawberry, vanilla and chocolate flavors. The commercial was of a psychedelic cartoon clown laughing, as a volcano flowed with chocolate, vanilla and strawberry lava.

When I was a wee lad, one of the first things I hated was when they brought the cartoon **Popeye** back and there was a interview with some of the people responsible, who reassured everyone that Popeye was new and was no longer going to be violent, which didn't seem like a good idea to me and I thought, *"No one asked me about this."*

I later told my father and he exploded in a rage screaming, *"Popeye was a fucking sailor man! He got his eye popped out in a bar fight!"* This was one of the things that started me on my path of disliking meddling kids, do-gooders and tattle-tells.

All my run-ins with authorities were joyous occasions because where I grew up all the police officers were Irish. and everyone in the neighborhood would wave at the Irish

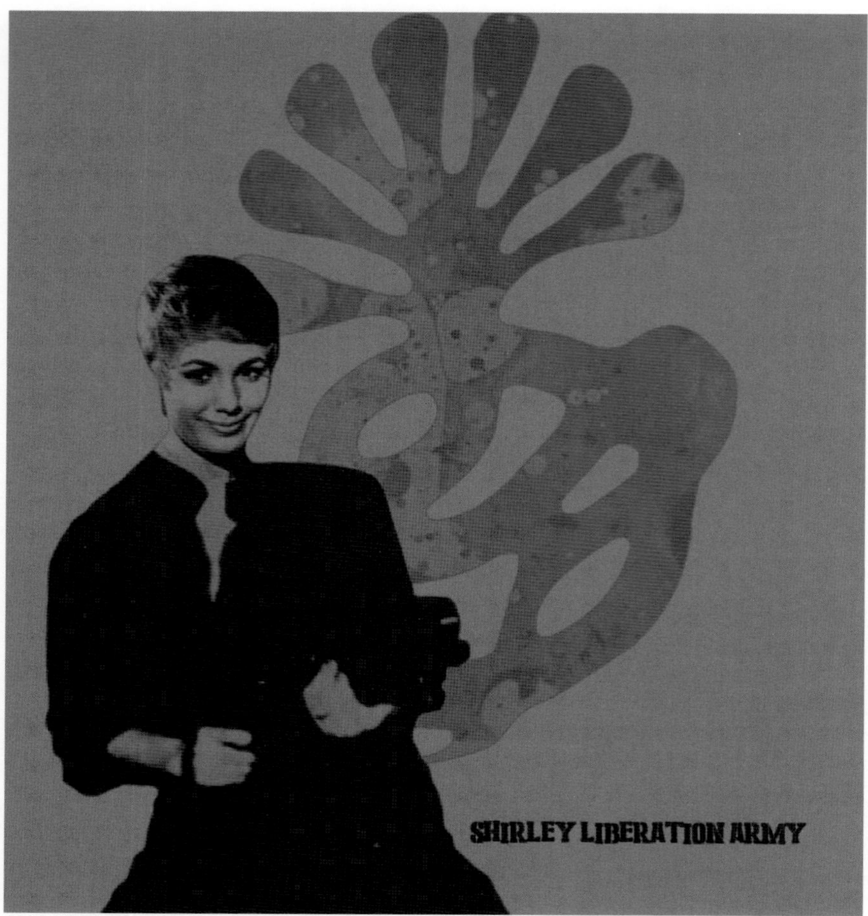

Shirley Liberation Army - artwork by Whale Song Partridge

police officers and they would wave back, whistling and so happy they were doing their job for the entire community. But I would say, my biggest run-in with the authority was when I accepted Keith Partridge as my Lord and Saviour - but I'll tell you about that later.

Were you a fan of the Partridge Family's music and TV show when they first came into existence?

When I was a child, I was very disturbed by people with red hair and freckles, so Danny Bonaduce [Danny Partridge] horrified me. I remember the first time I saw **The Partridge Family** I was three or four and living in La Crosse, Wisconsin ('71 or '72). For some strange reason, the opening credits actually frightened me: the images floating out of the screen, red and vivid on a black background. And the music for some reason at that age, reminded me of a horror movie which I later realised was a beautiful thing. I think this was God showing me my future and saying, *"You can turn away from the television now, but your path has been written in honey."*

Here's a two-parter question…What made you change your mind about ***The Partridge Family*** *and who was responsible for the formation of the Pft! ?*

When I was seventeen years old I became a Jesus Freak. I lived with friends in what was basically a Jesus Freak commune. My fellow commune roommates were musicians and they all went on to to be in different bands like Sixteen Horsepower, Slim Cessna's Auto Club, Wovenhand, The Denver Gentlemen (but when I lived with them they were called Blood Flower). We used to eat a lot of acid and smoke a lot of grass and read the Bible, listening to **Satanic Majesties Request** and Donovan all the time. Eventually we stopped doing drugs and the Holy Spirit took over. It was a beautiful experience for almost three years.

Slim Cessna's childhood friend, Adam Sleek moved in with us, and while sitting in the living room one night, I noticed in his box of records were some Partridge Family LPs. I asked Adam if he actually liked The Partridge Family. It seemed so disturbing to me at the time that somebody actually listened to this band.

Adam looked at me and asked, *"Have you heard them lately?"* Which is something he'd ask people every time they insulted The Partridge Family. I remember Slim looking at me and shaking his head saying, *"Adam listens to some horrible music."*

A few years later, Adam Sleek moved to Denver and I soon followed. There was a coffee house called Cafe 13 where we used to hang out. One day Adam Sleek noticed they had The Partridge Family '45 on the jukebox with the songs **Twenty-Four Hours a Day** and **I Woke Up in Love This Morning**. He became very excited and kept putting quarters in the jukebox. This went on for days. At one point I remember this strange sense of submitting. All of a sudden the music made perfect sense to me. I guess Adam Sleek was using classic, breaking-down tactics and I snapped and got it.

At the time, a friend of ours who later embraced The Temple, had not gotten the music yet and finally became so angry he unplugged the jukebox. Then it got to the point that one day we went in there and somebody actually removed the '45. I guess they didn't realise that persecution and religious movements go hand in hand.

So then Adam, at his apartment, started playing **Shopping Bag** and **Notebook** over and over again, teaching me, making me understand. I ended up drawing a huge image of the **Shopping Bag** LP on his wall. One day, my friend The Risen Keith came over and I said, *"You have to listen to this band. It'll blow your mind."*

Adam put it on and Dan instantly saw the light. One night we were driving down the street listening to it on The Risen Keith's cassette player and I said, *"People always say The Clash and Eric Clapton are God but The Partridge Family are actually gods!"*

However, if it wasn't for The Risen Keith Partridge, I'm sure The Temple wouldn't exist. For a couple of years I went around spreading The Byrd, but when I came back from New Orleans, City of Gold, The Risen Keith had made Partridge Family stickers and flyers. He had switched up his black hot rod for a mini van so we could spread The Gospel a little easier and with more Partridge Freaks.

Is Pft! a registered religion?

No, but we have been looking into that because in this new day and age of religious persecution maybe it's an Uncola idea.

Does the Pft! have a specific recruiting method or is it something that has changed with time?

In the beginning, classic Hare Krishna harassment and good old fashioned screaming. Later we advanced to flyers and stickers and a more professional street preaching session.

How did you come into contact with Boyd Rice, and what is his role in the Pft!?

When we moved back to Denver, we went to The Lion's Lair one night, where Boyd would DJ, and The Risen Keith put a Pft! sticker on Boyd's turntable. We later heard that he was excited because he loved The Partridge Family and thought it made perfect sense that there'd be a religion based on them.

We later met and ended up doing a Partridge Family interview in front of the **Mork and Mindy** house. Mork came to Earth in a giant egg, which he cracked open when he landed. This was to symbolize Mithras, who was hatched from a stone egg. Also, the egg is the white stone that fell from the sky that Jung talks about on his inscribed cube at Bollingen Tower.

One of the most important things that Boyd ever did was turn us onto Bobby Sherman. We were hanging out in his basement pad and he asked if we'd ever heard Bobby Sherman. We said no, and he said, *"Oh, my God. Bobby Sherman is like the flip-side to The Partridge Family.They're like one coin."* He instantly got up and played **Unborn Lullaby** and Bobby Sherman took his natural place at the table of God.

Have you ever run into any trouble/opposition when publicly spreading the Pft! gospel?

We've had all kind of hassles but nothing too crazy. We've been kicked out of malls and public places, but when you're a new-and-improved religion that's to be expected; basically people screaming and yelling who were born with a I Hate TV sticker on their souls.

What was the breakthrough moment when the Pft! stepped into the media spotlight?

Besides the show running from 1970-1974, I would say when The Risen Keith and I were persecuted for our beliefs at Toad's Place in New Haven, Connecticut. David Cassidy was performing and Danny Bonaduce was opening up doing comedy. The Risen Keith was passing out stickers and the bouncer said he couldn't do that and was kicked out. He came over to where I was sitting and told me to be really careful. So I walked in very peacefully and couldn't believe Danny Bonaduce, the Devil himself was about to take the stage.

I was just coming onto some very strong ecstasy when the bouncers asked me to talk to them. They found some of the stickers in my pocket and said, "*You're not supposed to put them up.*"

I said, *"I know, they were just in my pocket."* But it didn't matter. I was so frustrated. Then the fuzz told me to split. I wouldn't. The next thing I knew I was on the ground being persecuted by The Pig for my love of Keith Partridge and Danny Partridge.

Danny in an interview with Boyd later told him he heard the stickers were dipped in LSD, which he said was, *"Really cool, man."* But David Cassidy decided in his wisdom to kick us out, so I would be arrested and it would make the Connecticut news. Also, apparently it was in one of those calendars that have a new word for every day of the year. This one had weird things in the news for every day of the year and one of them was something along the lines of *"Man Arrested at David Cassidy for Worshipping The Partridge Family TV Show".*

Do you consider yourself to be a provocateur?

No. I don't consider myself a provocateur, but I do consider myself a part-time employee of God looking to pick up fulltime hours. I think people are Audio-Animatronics and we are designed to react and do certain things. It's always an added bonus when they happen to be fun.

There will always be haters, especially with regard to belief systems, so… what are some of the most heinous accusations that have been leveled at you personally regarding the Pft! ?

I'm not going to go into stating the obnoxious things the Brown Goblins bring up but I went to Mordor, hung out and made the scene. You can't get to the Land of Enchantment unless you do that. Of course you run the risk of coming back the Fisher Price King but on the path to Albuquerque there are many bus stops.

Why was it degreed that "Fun is the law"?

The Risen Keith and I really enjoyed having fun and over time we had met a bunch of [Aleister] Crowley Heads and they didn't seem to be having much fun. Then one day, Danny Partridge whispered in our ears, *"Fun is the law!"*

Aaron Partridge knew from a young age that the early byrd gets the Ouroboros. When his sons Loki Partridge and Guru Partridge came into the world, he built a Shirley Tachyon Chamber Ritual Room." – photo and artwork by Aaron Partridge. Shirley Jones painting by Jim Blanchard

As the Pft! appears to driven by symbolism resented to you via TV shows, can you give a breakdown of some of the key elements.

We believe that all symbols are one; it's God's way of guiding us back home. A simple quick breakdown: The CBS Eye is the all-seeing eye of God. The McDonald's Arches symbolize many different things. One of them is the Death card from the tarot, the 'M' being the 13th letter and because to most people, McDonald's represents un-ending death, which it is. But after death comes the Golden Arches, the Resurrection, un-ending golden triumph. The NBC snake logo from 1959-1976 represents the Serpent Power. Besides being a wonderful logo, the NBC Peacock has many groovy meanings. Some members tend to enjoy the Luciferian session, others enjoy the peacock's association with the Goddess Lakshmi, a.k.a. Laurie Partridge.

As television plays a big part in the Pft!, please explain how and to what lengths.

First, let me say I speak from a personal journey. Television has been a part of my life since I was a little kid. When I was five, I went to my friend's house and his mother said he was not allowed to watch TV. When I asked about Saturday Morning Cartoons she shook her head and said, *"No"*. At that moment I looked at her and her white blouse and brown hair and thought she was a witch.

The Risen Keith and I bonded over our television viewing and after watching Mary Tyler Moore we'd call each other and compare notes. So yes, television is very important. Not to mention TV means transvestite and for Pft! Freaks, the goal is to be androgynous.

The Pft! talk about reaching a state of Albuquerque. What is it… how can one achieve it… and does it have any link to extraterrestrials?

Albuquerque is just another say of saying Holy Grail or Samadhi. And of course in merry old England it's called Narnia which can only be achieved by stumbling upon a magic wardrobe. Also, the Pft! practice a form of meditation called MIND CONTROL. We find that it's very helpful when dealing with everything the Late, Great Planet Vietnam throws your way. I did see a UFO at Villa Italia Mall while eating Dairy Queen in the car with my mother on Saint Patrick's Day. I was eating a medium butterscotch sundae and she was eating a medium hot fudge sundae.

There's an undeniable psychedelic aspect to the Pft! Have/do mind bending drugs play a part, or is it a purely visual aspect of the Pft!'s ethos?

As a child of the late Sixties/early Seventiess, TV was full of psychedelic commercials and cartoons so it was like being on acid at a very young age. A lot of the Pft! Heads dig the psychedelic scene and view The Partridge Family Temple as a psychedelic religion.

On the subject of visuals, the Pft! artwork is exceptional and really elevates your 'brand' appeal. Why are the visuals so important to you and who is responsible for the artwork?

Well, visuals are important because God is an ad man and the advert scene knows what we need to see. Whale Song Partridge is responsible for the way-out God Ads. He has been completely mind-blowing, completely switched-on to the pulse of the Pft! Generation. He has brought so much kosmic interest to the Children of the Fun.

Do your dreams inform what you do?

I was hatched very lucky and I've always had amazing fun-filled dreams. When I was 29 I had a very specific dream that led me to a whole new All-You-Can-God buffet. I started having dreams about alchemy and the Serpent Power Yoga Scene; things I had no interest in at the time. In fact, things I thought I'd never have any interest in. But I didn't disobey because we all know it's not nice to fool Mother Nature.

I see how the Pft! can be perceived as being a magical means of transformation, a form of alchemy, if you like. So… are there alchemical aspects at play here?

Yes, The Partridge Family Temple practices alchemy. We wake up and everyday we're offered the raw material of lead. This could be politics, movies, mass killings, clouds, food co-ops; and the goal is to transform that lead into gold. And that can be very difficult but the Pft! believe there's always a silver lining.

To quote Robert Hunter, *"Once in awhile you get shown the light in the strangest places if you look at it right."*

There's no more perfect display of alchemical transformation then when the original brown-haired Christopher was transformed into the blonde-haired Christopher. This was The Partridge Family explaining to the masses the Great Work.

Anne Frank features prominently in your life… why?

When I was young, I read all the Judy Blume books, and for some reason the **Diary of Anne Frank** seemed to fit into that book scene. When I moved to Portland, Oregon a movie came out that actually had the only found footage of Anne Frank at a wedding waving from a window. For some strange reason I had a compulsion to see this flick. They made an entire movie around one quick clip of Anne Frank waving.

And oddly enough, I still have the movie ticket. I never save movie tickets, but for some reason I saved this one. I truly believe that people are vessels. None of these ideas are ours. God moves across still waters, searching for the correct vessel.

And slowly but Shirley Partridge I started become really interested in Anne Frank and then starting painting psychedelic paintings of her. I realised she represented the Occult; The Hidden.

Is there an occult aspect to the Pft! and if so, is it connected to The Partridge Family?

The Partridge Family Temple has always been an occult happening. It's seeing God hidden in a Seventies TV Show and it's seeing that that same God is in everything. If you can see the Divine in a so-called hokey Seventies sitcom, then you can see the Divine in everything. No matter what occult trip you're into, it all leads back to The Partridge Family, and The Partridge Family is making its way to all those occult bus stops.

It really just comes down to what your preference is. Some people really love Kali and some people really love Laurie Partridge. But the Temple says, *"All is fun."* We believe in a well-balanced, All-You-Can-Eat Occult buffet. You have to eat all of this to see that The Partridge Family is truly a gift from God.

When you watch it or listen to the music, it's like actually watching every holy book and writing come to life in the here and now. People always say, "*Wouldn't it be great to see what ancient Egypt was like?"* But you can turn on The Partridge Family and see Isis and her goofball son Osiris arguing with Set about who ate the brownies as their manager Thoth sets up a concert in Las Vegas on the telephone. All Roads Lead to Albuquerque.

The thing is, for years people have thought the Pft! was a joke religion or a weird art prank, and it's not. It came from a sincere place and it keeps growing and becoming more realized. I flashed in '98, a religion or spiritual practice should help people. I hope that The Partridge Family Temple brings people to a bus stop that's on a convenient route for them and they are nourished by the honey that flows from the Honeycomb Hideout of Shirley.

The Order of the Goldie Hawn - artwork by Whale Song Partridge

Artists always choose their own colour palette… is there a reason why you ride the ultra vivid colour route?
I'd say because it's what I would like to see. The world is much more fun in Day-Glo.
What Medium do you work in, is it digital?

Yes, all of my artwork is done digitally.

I'm particularly intrigued by your Order Of The Goldie Hawn artwork, the juxtaposition of **Laugh-In***'s Ms Hawn and Aleister Crowley's sigil is inspired. How did the idea come to you?*

The idea for The Order of The Goldie Hawn was Shaun's. Not the artwork, but the name. When he pitched it to me I had never seen **Butterflies Are Free** (the Milton Katselas movie starring Goldie Hawn), but after watching it I loved the idea! From there I just went with what I thought would work best. I believe that image was what I came up with on my first try. I was already familiar with the Golden Dawn imagery and that picture of Goldie from **Butterflies Are Free** was just perfect.

Whale Song Partridge – photo by Austin Kimbrough

Do your dreams ever inform your work?

No, I rarely have dreams, or at least ones that I can remember.

What do you do creatively outside of the Pft!?

I've contributed to a few issues of **Estrellita Mia Zine**, which is run by Leo Casas, another Temple member. I've also been involved with Frank Greens and his music project :TROTH:, he had me contribute spoken word to an album recently and we discuss artwork often.

Tell me about your recent work with Boyd Rice… did you know Boyd before your involvement with the Pft!?

I knew about Boyd before joining the Pft!, I was already a fan. But I did not know him personally. I've been honoured to help him re-release his book **NO**, which is my absolute favourite book, and to work on other projects with him. We just re-released some material as **The Spoken Word Album**, these are recordings that were only released with 100 copies of his book **Standing in Two Circles** - and it's great stuff, people needed to hear it! I've also helped set up his online store with NON merchandise, and my artwork is scheduled to be on his next full length LP.

Boyd is another person that I just work really well with, I can bring up new ideas with him and see where we can take them, or he can pitch something to me and our ideas usually sync.

It appears that you have something of an obsession with Paris Hilton… why is that?

I definitely do! Paris is such a fascinating character to me, and a real inspiration. Did you

know she had the same vocal coach as Michael Jackson? How amazing is that! To me she just does everything right. She was one of the first reality TV stars, and she created that character herself. She understood what would sell and what wouldn't, and marketed herself accordingly. I remember reading that she would pretend to be drunk without really drinking, just to make the headlines. She created an empire by branding herself, which was something rarely done at that point - now it's everywhere. To me it seems she's always ahead of the curve, and having a blast no matter what she's doing.
If you weren't Whale Song Partridge, who, out of anyone that's ever existed, male or female, would you love to be – and why?

That is a really though question and I thought about it for quite a while. There are tons of people throughout history that I'd love to meet, but swapping places might not be my cup of tea. I'm quite happy in the here and now. Maybe one of the two guys that invented Helvetica, it would be neat to see something you helped create everywhere; people come into contact with that font so often without even thinking about it.

What was it that attracted you to the Pft!?

Everything about the Pft! is right on the mark. It combines all of these different elements that I'm interested in into one delicious recipe. That's what drew me to it and what has kept me so involved to this day. The further you dig into any of this the more it all connects.

Part Three: Boyd Rice and the Pft!

Have you always been a fan of the Partridge Family's music and TV show?

It's strange. I can't remember a time when I wasn't very skeptical about the world of man, yet I always had an affinity for pop culture. I was still watching **the Partridge Family** at the same time I was going up to Hollywood to see the New York Dolls and the Stooges during the glam rock era. I was still watching children's shows like **The Banana Splits**, because I genuinely like them and thought the music was great. I remember when **Sugar Sugar** by The Archies pushed The Rolling Stones out of the number one spot on top 40 radio. So I already had all these sort of points of reference before meeting the Pft!.

When did you first become aware of the Pft! and how did you get involved with them?

A short while after I arrived in Denver, I was waiting for a light to change and saw a car drive by completely covered in bubblegum. I commented that the people in the car were obviously fun-niks, and that I wished I knew their story. The girl with me said they were members of a weird cult, and that they worshipped The Partridge Family. I was immediately intrigued. I loved cults and I had always loved The Partridge Family.

Shortly thereafter, I began to see day-glo stickers for the Temple all over town. And graffiti. I decided I needed to know these people. At the time I was a writer on the staff of a free music newspaper available all over town, and I suggested to the paper's editors that I interview this strange sect. They thought it sounded like fun and okayed the thing. A week or so later, I drove to Boulder, Colorado to interview two of the Temple's main founders, Shaun Partridge and Dan Partridge. We met for breakfast and then proceeded to the **Mork & Mindy** house in Boulder where the actual interview took place.

When the interview was printed they made the cover of the paper. I think the only press coverage of them up to that point was when they were kicked out of a David Cassidy concert on the East Coast for passing out Pft! stickers that the security people suspected were dipped in LSD. They showed the stickers to David Cassidy and he freaked out.

But Danny Bonaduce was opening for David and thought it was totally cool that young people might be distributing day-glo photos of the Partridge Family dipped in acid. Danny and Shirley loved the Pft!, but I think David Cassidy was afraid they were going to kill him or something.

When David Cassidy came to Denver in some stage play, some mega-fan bought front row centre seats for every single performance. And on the first night he brought several dozen roses and walked to the stage to lay them at David's feet. He did the exact same thing the second night and Cassidy assumed he must be a member of the Temple. And he had the guy banned from the theatre!

Whale Song Partridge and Boyd Rice after discussing that Walt Disney is in the details

The same week that show opened, **Entertainment Weekly** in Denver (Westword) did another cover story on the Temple, and it was obviously the first thing David Cassidy was shown upon his arrival here. And he was evidently paranoid about it all.
What was it about the Pft! that made you want to get involved with them?

Someone once observed that once you understood Warhol's concept of pop, you realized it was all around you – it was everywhere. And you could never see the world the same way again. I think the Temple operates on that wavelength in the same way.

I've heard it said that culture trumps politics, and that's something I wholeheartedly concur with. And pop culture is great anyway, but when you realize that it constitutes a kind of modern mythology, you move into another realm altogether.

Cite something that you personally bought to the Pft! table.

I turned Shaun onto Bobby Sherman. Bobby was on an episode of **the Partridge Family**; and had a spin-off series where he drove a psychedelic hearse. So Bobby became part of the Temple pantheon. Then we were listening to a lot of the Banana Splits and Shaun realized they were part of the same reality; after that it expanded to include Marcia Brady, The Bugaloos, McDonalds, Ty Cobb, and god knows what else.

You mention Marcia Brady, a member of another famous American TV family, ***The Brady Bunch****... Shaun was already a fan of hers, wasn't he?*

In the Nineties I had worked on and off as a bodyguard for celebrities appearing at a retro festival in Denver. I'd meet them at the airport, drive them around town, emcee Q&A sessions with them and sit next to them at autograph sessions. It was mostly people I loved anyway, like Julie Newmar. One year, it was Marcia Brady and I was sitting next to her when Shaun got her signature then showed her a tattoo of her face on his upper arm. She was gobsmacked! *"Is that me?"* she asked. When Shaun said yes, she couldn't take her eyes off it. And every interview with her I've seen since on TV, she mentions Shaun and his tattoo. It was one of the high points of her life!

Do you regard the Pft! as a religious organisation?

I once read the factoid that it takes twenty-five years for cults to become mainstream religions. The Partridge Family Temple has been around nearly thirty years, so by accepted standards it's transitioned into legitimate religious thought. But it's still got the allure of a cult.

Is there a message that you want to send the world about the Pft!?

Jean Cocteau said something to the effect that history is a truth that eventually becomes a lie, but that myth is a lie that eventually constitutes the truth.

ADVENTURES IN DEMONOLOGY

THE STRANGE WORLD OF THE OCCULTIST INSTRUCTIONAL LP

DARIUS DREWE AND DAVID FLINT

From the late 1960s and throughout the next decade, the boom in Satanism, black magic, witchcraft and the occult not only entertained the masses – it also educated them. There were countless books on the shelves offering advice and instruction to the potential witch and Devil worshipper – often, it must be said, aimed at those who saw witchcraft as a way of propping up a sagging – or possibly non-existent – sex life with books like **How to Become a Sensuous Witch**. On the more serious level, Paul Huson's **Mastering Witchcraft** was a gateway volume for many practioners, while countless large format hardcovers and paperbacks alike set out to tell - with extensive illustrations, of course - the history of assorted occult practices. Older, academic volumes were retooled for the mass market, while just about anyone with even a passing knowledge of the dark arts seemed to be having book contracts dangled before them.

But not everyone likes to read, and this was also the era of the instructional LP. In the days before home video, a spoken word record was the most immediate way of getting direct instruction from the masters of the art, without actually meeting them. This wasn't just true of witchcraft and black magic – pretty much any hobby or interest was captured on LP, even seemingly unlikely examples like train spotting. But the occult had the added bonus of being a sensational enough subject to appeal outside the confines of the enthusiast – and the the twin promises of sex and the supernatural that many recordings hinted at made these records predictably popular with sensation seekers.

While Aleister Crowley had made wax cylinder recordings in the early 1900s (now available on a variety of CD editions for those who can put up with the scratchy, whispy sound), the boom for occult spoken word recordings really began, as perhaps was only right given his role in the wider occult revival, with Anton LaVey's 1968 release of **The Satanic Mass**. Recorded when the Church of Satan was a new and exciting arrival on the Hollywood scene, **The Satanic Mass** was guaranteed to be snapped up by sensation-seekers who had read about LaVey in the press, and wanted to be part of the whole 'Satanic ritual with naked girls and Hollywood celebrities' scene without actually having to travel to San Francisco.

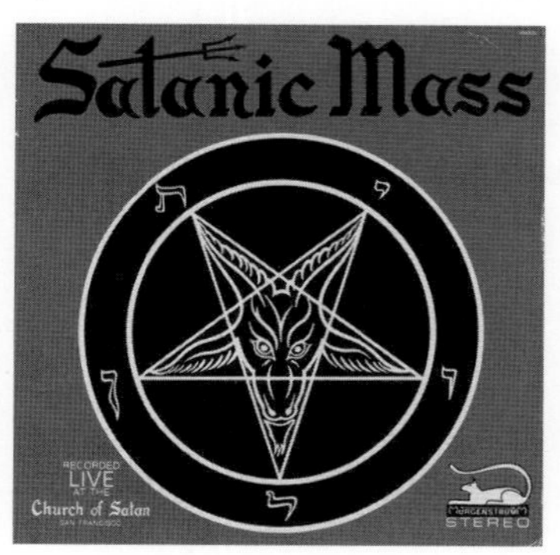

Satanic image aside, LaVey was a relatively clean-living individual who drank and smoked relatively little, eschewed all drugs and hated the sound of any rock music, even of a diabolist nature. This in turn may be why this album, the first of four recorded during his lifetime, features no concessions to such sounds: however, the spoken passages (divided into **the Mass**, **the**

Prologue, the four-part **Book Of Satan** and the **Hymn Of The Satanic Empire**) are interspersed with electronic twiddly-diddly, neo-classical allusion and sci-fi FX that wouldn't have sounded out of place on a BBC library record (or its nearest American equivalent). For those reasons alone, it's worth hearing.

Admittedly, **The Satanic Mass** does eventually lose its way somewhat, a problem that besets many of these spoken word albums: though far more declamatory and grandiose (some may say downright camp) than the Alex Sanders album that we'll discuss shortly and closer to the imagined sound of a Satanic ritual than possibly anything else ever recorded, it still overwhelms the uninitiated listener with far too much hocus-pocus, the ultimate effect being that, rather than gaining any true insight, their attention simply ends up wandering by the start of side 2.

Of course, LaVey's version of Satanism was more philosophical than supernatural. For those in search of a thorough history of - and DIY guide to - actual Devil worship, none other than Vincent Price was here to help, on his 1969 double LP **Witchcraft and Magic – An Adventure in Demonology**. While Price had done many a spoken word LP in his time, and later would crop up as narrator on albums by Alice Cooper and Michael Jackson, this is his magnum opus – a book length study of witchcraft, produced by Roger Karshner and released by Capitol Records. Terry d'Oberoff is credited as both composer and director, while the impressive stereo sound effects were supplied by Douglas Leedy, a pioneer of late Sixties electronic experimentalism. There is no credit for the text, though it seems likely that this too is d'Oberoff.

The LP consists of Price telling tales of witchcraft and devil worship – not fictional horror stories, but factual accounts of historical events and aspects of the occult, helpfully split into various chapters on the sleeve – **Hitler and Witchcraft**, **Women as Witches**, **The World of Spirits and Demons** and so on. Price seems to have fun with the more lurid descriptions, his voice and (most likely) tongue in cheek attitude giving a gleefully macabre and somewhat leering tone to lines like *"fornication with the Devil, child sacrifice, feasts of rotting human flesh"* and *"the tearing of her flesh with pincers, her body broken on the wheel, her fingernails ripped off, her feet thrust into a fire, whatever horrors the twisted mind of the hangman could devise"* in the two-part section entitled **Witch Tortures**.

A surprising amount of the album actually seems to be a 'how to' guide to witchcraft, with handy chapters on *"How to invoke spirits, demons, unseen forces"*, *"how to make a pact with the Devil"* and *"Curses, Spells, Charms"*. *"Of course you should never resort to this… except in the case of the most dire necessity"* says Price of selling your soul to Satan, giving a little chuckle as he does so, before going on to give full and frank instructions nevertheless. What would constitute a 'necessity' to sell your soul to the Devil is, perhaps wisely, left to our imagination. With atmospheric music and sound effects, this is one of the most entertaining 'Satanic' LPs out there.

Less lurid, though still knowingly sensationalist, was another 1969 LP. **Seduction Through Witchcraft** was 'performed' by Louise Huebner, who revelled in the dubious

title of *"the Only Official Witch In The World"* - the use of the word 'official' here stretching all credibility. But the stunningly beautiful and publicity-aware Californian adept Louise Huebner (1930-2014) was certainly several cuts above, appearing on both the Johnny Carson and Joey Bishop shows, promoting outdoor concerts and even helping the LAPD with 'psychic crime detection'. She was eventually granted the title 'Chief Witch Of Los Angeles County' in 1968. Given her marketable popularity, it came as little surprise when Huebner was eventually signed by Warner Bros: her initial remit was to deliver a 'spoken word' record concerning the manifold elements of her craft, but what they ultimately got was something quite different. Rather than anything so functional, what we have here is a deeply erotic album, outlining numerous methods by which female Wiccans might seduce, charm and keep their menfolk.

After appearing alongside the likes of Alan Watts, Anton LaVey and Black Widow on the cheesy United Artists cash-in album **Occult Explosion**, the divine Miss H published a series of books before retiring and opening, like all the best apothecaries in American TV horror films, an antique shop. Yet her legend endures- and though **Seduction Through Witchcraft** sounds impossibly dated and twee by modern-day neopagan standards, we still recommend you hear it (if only for the reverb and phasing rather than the actual content) at least once.

Regardless of her 'official' status, Huebner wasn't the first witch to hit the recording studios. 1968 saw the release of **Barbara, the Gray Witch**, with the titular performer (Barbara Roehr) offering up a mix of magical tips, female empowerment and a capella folk songs. As a double album, it somewhat outstays its welcome, even with a guest appearance from 'JC, The Warlock', but the album remains an intriguing curiosity, produced by Ed Hansen, who may or may not be the same Ed Hansen who later directed films like **Eroticise** and **Takin' It Off** starring Russ Meyer favourite Kitten Natividad. Roehr is still practising - in 2010, she was in her local South Bend, Indiana newpaper blaming the economic crash on *"Saturn coming too close to Earth."*

While both Huebner and Roehr's recording were sold to a gasping public as much for the looks of their artists as their Craft, the same probably can't be said of **The Hour of the Witch**, recorded by Detroit wiccan Gundella in 1971. It would be fair to say that the more mature and motherly Gundella was less glamorous – and so a harder sell to the more fickle record buying public - than her more media friendly rivals, though she still managed to carve out a successful career in the 1970s as both a practitioner and a writer. On this self-released LP, she mainly deals with love spells, though there is also information on discouraging unwanted attentions. It's probably one of the more sincere witchcraft LPs, genuinely trying to spread the Craft without any sensationalism.

Maxine Sanders

Considering that at one time or other, he was considered to be *"the most powerful witch in Britain"* (a title oft-disputed by his closest rival Gerald Gardner) one might possibly expect Alex Sanders' sole recorded album **A Witch is Born** to sound a lot more terrifying than it does. Then again, Sanders was not a Satanist, but a Wiccan - and thus, his perspective, much like that of his wife Maxine (at time of writing, still alive, teaching and practicing the Craft) was always going to lean further towards education and information than pure sensationalism.

That said, neither were strangers to the publicity or notoriety their activities engendered: if anything, they encouraged such reactions, appearing in tabloids, on television chat shows, and even in their own feature-length documentary **Secret Rites** (1971) And, of course, they made this LP, documenting the initiation of the now similarly-exalted Janet Farrar. Granted, the sleeve states that the aim is to provide a *"signpost to the ways of Wisdom"* for those who *"seek to know more of this faith that is older than history"*.

Where the album triumphs is in its indispensably accurate description of said initiations, the histories of the mysteries, and, ultimately, the Great Rite. Where it loses house points, however, is in its musical backing, which simply consists of the same piece of classical music looped ad infinitum and betrays either a basic lack of imagination or a hint of unwelcome record company interference. After all, we know that Sanders' coven included at this point a group of more than proficient musicians known as the Spindle (who provided the excellent soundtrack to the aforementioned 1971 movie) - so why he didn't use them for this remains even more of a mystery than the Great Mystery itself.

As tastes and technology changed, interest in these occult spoken word LPs fizzled out by the middle of the decade, and the records were deleted and forgotten for years. Inevitably though, these original recordings are now highly sought after by collectors – and some have been reissued by specialist labels on CD and vinyl. And let's not pretend that the audience for spoken world occult instruction doesn't exist – there are now countless YouTube videos and podcasts offering a variety of voices giving advice, information and opinion on all matters witchy and Satanic. The message has been democratised as the medium has changed. Of course, few podcasts can quite match the florid tones of Vincent Price or the Satanic majesty of LaVey, but we can't have everything.

SATAN SUPERSTAR - A PERSONAL VIEW

CARL ABRAHAMSSON

The symbol is no longer merely symbolic

It's not so much about aligning myself with all the great defiant and creative men and women of history – the devil's representatives. It's not so much about cherishing a resonance with an antithetical attitude (and aesthetic) that always allows for new revelations and syntheses. Neither is it about taking pride in being unique, creative and intelligent. And it is certainly not about believing in some compensatory monster originally designed to bully people into submission.

Today, I pledge intuitive allegiance to the ultimate scapegoat simply because it's relevant. And important. Satan simply makes too much sense to be discarded. Satan is a force to be reckoned with, mainly because it is a pro-human force. Residing deep within the human psyche, Satan represents the liberation from restraint. Not the petty, externally imposed restraints but the deep-rooted ones holding us back as individuals. Who do I want to be? What holds me back? The consciousness that allows us formulation in this process of liberation is spelled S-A-T-A-N.

It is sometimes useful to provoke by fear. Many simple-minded people still fear the bully's projection: the terrifying monster stemming from deranged biblical minds. The bullies themselves fear their own shadow more than anything or anyone else. This denial turns them into monsters. Their own dark perversions are unfortunately still claiming real, tangible victims. Satan as a symbol of resistance to this kind of criminally abusive behaviour is perfect and to the point. What these people fear will come back to haunt and destroy them. Satan is the avenging mirror of ultimate justice they fear to look at – for good reason.

Why the need for cathartic symbols at all, the contemporary savants wonder. Many Satanists probably agree. Perhaps better to work in silence and darkness, if that's how one gets one's kicks and satisfactions? But at the same time the overall tide has turned and the pendulum swung. Satan represents human initiative and achievement more than ever before. A pythagorean, luciferian spirit still resounds and is growing stronger by the day, connecting us with the pioneers, artists and scientists of history; the real movers and shakers. In times like ours, permeated by potential dangers and destruction, it's important for those who should be in charge to take charge and shove the greedy fear mongers down to the Hell and misery of their own self-reflection. In the sulphurous pit of stripped smokescreen splendour, these cowardly do-gooder cheapskates will finally suffer to the full extent of their actual desire.

If the evangelical masochists of every religious persuasion eagerly await the apocalypse, and in doing that actually ruin for the rest of us, let's speed up the process of their suffering and demise. The symbol is no longer merely symbolic, and we welcome this stark and powerful transformation of reality. Responsibility will now and henceforth be handled by the responsible. This is a beautiful planet but one that has sadly been abused for too long by shortsighted moral messiahs with fingers firmly inside other people's honey pots. Our planet deserves better. Much better. Vade Ultra!

Photo by Vanessa Sinclair

THE LIFE AND DEATH OF PETER SOLHEIM

BRUCE BARNARD

'It is my belief Watson, founded upon experience, that the lowest and vilest alleys in London do not present a more dreadful record of sin than does the smiling and beautiful countryside'
The Adventures of Sherlock Holmes (1892)

Prologue:
In the murky world of Satanic Ritual Abuse and its believers – and, indeed, its naysayers – the question of memory is everything. Opponents of the dubious phenomenon would point out that memory is a trickster, especially when 'recovered' or otherwise nudged by news headlines and imagination; supporters counter that the whole idea of 'false memory syndrome' is an invention of abusers to deflect from reality. In a court of law, where much depends on who has the best solicitor, whether or not the defendant is a bit shifty looking and the emotional pull of the accusations against them, such niceties are often forgotten. Sometimes, as we know from numerous cases, the innocent are falsely accused and convicted; other times, the guilty go free. And sometimes, what might otherwise be a genuine case is conflated with fantasy and exaggeration, needlessly making a grubby crime into something more disturbing than it already is, effectively libelling an entire community and providing solace to conspiracy theorists in the process. Whether that is the case with Peter Solheim, German Pete and the claims of ritual abuse is something that remains a matter of debate. But the story is awash with superstition, supposition and the linking of unconnected lifestyle choices.

I

Dawn Jewell, the owner of Erik, a two year old stallion she had loving raised from a six week old foal, found her beloved pet butchered in 2012 when she went to feed him at his paddock in Sithians, a picturesque rural village near the south coast of Cornwall. Initially she thought he was sleeping, but as she walked closer she became aware that the ground around the body was covered in pools of blood - the result of a frenzied overnight attack that consisted of numerous knife wounds to the animals head and body. Following an equine post-mortem at the site, the vet reported that Erik's genitalia had also been badly mutilated. One eye had been removed from the socket, along with the horse's teeth, all of which had been taken from the crime scene by the perpetrator. *"He was like a baby to me"*, a distraught Dawn said. *"I knew when I found him he was the one for me. I absolutely adored him"*.

Inspector Chris Strickland, the senior investigating officer on the case was quoted as saying that *"he couldn't rule out any link with a Satanic ritual"*, but was keen to clarify that *"it was not the only line"* his officers would be pursuing. Some people in this isolated community, a place where rumours tend to spread quickly and set as fast as poured concrete, started to undertake their own detective work online as soon they heard about the incident. Perhaps motivated by the £10,000 reward offered by Graham Rickard, a local horse lover who said he felt compelled to act due to the appalling nature of the crime. The crime even made the national news, the broadcaster and horse racing pundit Claire Balding tweeting her sympathies to Dawn and suggesting that people maintain a close watch over their animals in the area.

Within a few days, Dawn's mother, speaking reluctantly to a local journalist, said that she had *"been told about the speculation that there might be a Satanic link"*, but seemed to quickly dismiss the idea, most likely unaware that the reason people were so fervent in believing that dark forces might be at play had much to do with the date on which the attack took place, a few days after January 7th. Celebrated by some as St Winebald Day, an event named after an obscure Catholic saint that some people claimed had historically been devoted to offers of sacrifice in the satanic calendar. Although this was an idea challenged by experts on the occult as a nothing more than a dangerous myth, local conspiracy theorists were encouraged when Commander Peter Spindler of the Child Abuse Unit of the Metropolitan Police suggested on the Radio 4 Today programme that it was a day *"where there will be animal or human sacrifice and dismemberment"*. Spindler was not an expert on the ocult, but he *was* one of a number of officers from a variety of different forces who had recently attended a national conference on identifying Satanic abuse, one of many such courses organised by a US based fundamentalist Christian group. Like many a police officer and therapist, he was fed unproven – in fact, often disproven – ideas about Satanic abuse by believers who are not only unqualified, but often evangelical Christians. Spindler would later be promoted to lead the investigation into the crimes of Jimmy Savile.

Regardless of the motivation of Erik's killer, the wide ranging national newspaper coverage of the case meant others soon came forward with similar, often equally horrific stories of attacks on livestock in the area. Jo Barr, an RSPCA spokeswoman added to the wild speculation when she said, *"there have been a couple of recent attacks on sheep and there was a suggestion that the bodies were left in a formation. I believe it was a pentangle. It has been said that these are linked to Satanic practices or witchcraft"*. This belief has not been verified independently, and Barr did not explain who it was who had linked the attacks to Satanism.

A few months later, just as rumours about the motivation for the crime was finally dying down, the area was hit by a new spate of animal attacks, increasing in brutality to the point where some of the local press were initially reluctant to publish full details, leading some to conclude that there was a news black-out in place. In May of the same year, a decapitated horse, the head removed with near surgical precision, was found on the beach at Pentewan by lifeguards. A cross made with driftwood forced into the sand next to its body and a dead seagull with its wings removed placed on its chest. One shocked local who had stumbled across the macabre scene whilst walking his dog was quoted as saying, *"it was such a grotesque and disturbing sight, I don't think I will ever forget it. Whoever did this to a defenceless animal must be pure evil"*. Much was made in the media at the time that the attack had taken place on the night of a full 'super moon', with even well respected national broadsheets like the **Daily Telegraph** choosing to lead on the Satanic angle.

Just a few days later, fifteen or so miles away in the tiny hamlet of St Tudy, a farmer woke to find that three of his cattle had been killed by someone brandishing a blunt instrument. One of the animals was missing its tongue, hacked free from its base and once again taken from the scene. Reports of further horse and pony mutilations flooded in, representing something of a pandemic of animal cruelty cases across an area usually renowned for its natural beauty and the warm welcome it reserved for the thousands of tourists who visited every summer.

Despite the number of unsolved cases now piling up, with no sign of any suspect being caught, the police seemed to be adopting a different approach, playing down any idea of a ritual element to the crimes. Instead they continued their investigation without reference to any occult motive behind the attacks, releasing a statement that blandly stated, *"detectives are following all lines of inquiry to find the offender and would ask livestock owners to be particularly vigilant and report anything suspicious to police"*. This change of tone came even as a notorious court case took place in the area that seemed - on the surface – to have all the trappings of an occult crime. The murder of Peter Solheim and the resulting claims that came to the surface during a later trial seemingly confirmed the cliché that truth is indeed stranger than fiction.

II

"I always though he seemed normal. Until the time he told me his mother's house had flooded because the river spirits were angry" - Peter Solheim's neighbour

The first sign of the gathering storm came when a boat was found floating adrift in June 2004. The keys were still in the ignition when it was boarded by the coastguard just outside Falmouth, a popular tourist spot and vibrant university town on the South Cornwall coast. The small vessel, called the 'Izzy Wizz', was traced to parish councillor, retired printer and antique gun salesman Peter Solheim, 56, who lived in a nearby village. Bearded and stocky, Solheim suffered from strabismus, meaning in layman's terms he was cross eyed and because of this, he tended to project an image of looking constantly confused and disorientated. Despite this, he managed to be quite the hit with the ladies; in fact he had a reputation as something of a lothario, a man not to be trusted around your wife or girlfriend, a fact not lost on his long term girlfriend Margaret James.

Solheim was viewed by some as something of a fantasist, often holding court in the local pub and telling anyone who would listen about his money-making schemes providing illegal weapons to shadowy criminal gangs or bootlegging dirty videos that he would buy mail order and sell on for a profit. When the police entered his house, recently renamed Valhalla by its owner in reference to his Nordic heritage, they were surprised to find an attic room containing a large library of books dealing with the occult, along with a selection of ingredients used to produce potions and a collection of ceremonial swords and daggers. Although he never purposely kept it as any kind of secret, people in the village were surprised to learn that Solheim had for many years been a practising pagan, referring to himself as Thor's Hammer at the various covens he attended all across the county, although his welcome had been worn out at a number of locations due to his frequent clumsy attempts to seduce female members. One coven member remembers being terrified of him, especially after he arrived at a ceremony wearing a helmet and metal breastplate rather than the more traditional white gown, before theatrically telling the group, *"I make a very good friend, but a very bad enemy"* - something she saw as a veiled threat to intimidate them. *"He seemed to be heading in a direction that was very dark"*, she said on the subject of his occult interests.

Peter Solheim

Solhiem's mutilated body was eventually found floating five miles out to sea by the crew of The Clairvoyant, a local trawler. When they hauled it onto the deck they saw that his knees had been smashed by either a blunt axe or a machete, and one of his toes was hanging by just a thin thread of skin. A forensic examination of the body indicated that there were eighteen separate hacking wounds across his body. His ribs were also broken and he had sustained head injuries, although these weren't thought serious enough to kill him before he was thrown in the water. The pathologist reported that he was most likely held captive somewhere for at least two days before being thrown in the sea to drown. Initial toxicology reports showing that he had been heavily drugged with Lorazepam, a commonly prescribed drug used to treat anxiety and depression. If the trawler hadn't been passing at the time it was unlikely that the body would have been recovered, probably being dragged by the strong currents out further into the English Channel.

"SATAN-CRAZED PARISH COUNCILLOR MURDERED", read **The Sun**'s lurid headline on July 2nd, 2004. The article going on to say that the police were probing links with *"Devil-worship rituals"* as a result of what they claimed *"was an obsession with black magic"* - paganism and Satanism being one in the same for newspaper journalists, it seems. This tabloid embellishment was immediately contradicted by the police when they issued a statement which said that the murder victim's paganism wasn't even being considered as part of their investigation. Detective Inspector Neil Best briefing the media said, *"the occult is a subject we are trying to focus away from"*. In reality the police's attention was already drawn to a much more mundane line of enquiry, one that developed when the son-in-law of Solheim's partner Margaret James walked into a local police station. A long term heroin addict and petty thief, long rumoured to be a police informer, he was keen to tell them of a conversation he had a year or so before, where his mother–in-law had asked how you would go about finding someone willing to commit murder for money.

Solheim and Margaret James had first met after he had placed an advert in the lonely hearts column of a local newspaper. They seemed a perfect match, both were best diplomatically described as 'colourful local characters'. James, a petite vegan divorcee, could often be seen swimming naked in the sea close to her coastal home and Solheim's cottage industry selling bootlegged pornographic DVD's was common knowledge in the area. *"We were at it like rabbits"*, James had giggled in a police interview, although later she would claim in court that he often forced himself upon her in the later stages of their relationship.

Jealousy had started to become an issue quite quickly. James had been known to search Solheim's house from top to bottom looking for evidence of affairs, once finding video recording equipment hidden among the books in his attic, along with a wax doll dotted with pins that she thought had been made in her image. Then there was the money, thousands of pounds hidden away in antique tea pots and vases, cash he made from his trading in vintage guns and sex films. When she was finally arrested, a police search found bundles of cash James had stolen from her lover hidden around her house, all because she had finally realised that he was intending to leave her and marry a secret girlfriend he had been seeing for the last few years behind her back.

Pleading innocence, despite being caught in possession of her dead lover's phone - which she used to send texts to herself, in order to give the illusion that he was still alive and had taken off on a fishing trip - James claimed that Solheim often took off on unscheduled trips, saying that once he had spent three whole days at a stone circle reciting the **Lord's Prayer** backwards over and over again in an attempt to raise demons.

What was clear however, a theme discussed frequently both in police interviews and court, was the fact that there was no way Margaret James could have practically committed the crime by herself. Physically she wouldn't have been capable of dragging Solheim any distance, but despite intense questioning she refused to give any information on who had helped her commit the crime. Sentenced to a twenty years for conspiracy to murder the police say the case is still open and they are actively searching for one or more accomplices, even offering a reward that currently stands at £10,000 for any information leading to a conviction.

III

"He used to invite you in and offer to offer to read your tarot cards. He did mine once, but to be honest I thought it was a load of bollocks" - Pete Petrauske's neighbour

Pete Helmut Petrauske, or German Pete has he liked to call himself, was not someone who believed in hiding his beliefs. On the contrary, he was known to walk around the estate he lived wearing an elaborate purple gown with gold edging, complete with an embroidered pentangle on his chest. The self-proclaimed 'High Priest' would have cut quite a striking figure even without his ceremonial robes, given he had bleached blonde hair and maintained a year round mahogany tan the colour of well brewed tea. He was

Pete Petrauske

happy to be photographed as something of a novelty item by the local press in his small council flat, a framed painting of a horned satanic figure taking pride of place on the wall behind him. This visibility may have come back to haunt him as time went on.

German Pete, or Lord Murak, as he was known in local pagan circles, was so outraged by the recent negative coverage of his faith in the press following the Solheim case he took it upon himself to set the record straight by making himself available for interviews with anyone who asked. *"Any suggestion that Peter was murdered as a sacrifice is a load of crap and so is all this crap about Satanism and black magic"*, he told a reporter from the Falmouth Packet. He said that he'd met Solheim a number of years before, but had distanced himself from him because he tended to cause havoc at meetings where he would arrogantly claim to have superior arcane knowledge to everyone else and always insisted on carrying around his selection of large swords. *"His murder had nothing to do with black magic"*, he said. *"Knowing what he was like he was probably killed because he made someone angry"*.

Fast forward eight years, and the knock - as always in cases like this - came early for German Pete, the police executing a warrant as dawn broke over the Beacon estate in Falmouth, with a mixture of uniformed and plain clothed officers searching his flat and removing items of evidence in plastic bags. People were shocked when they heard he was facing charges relating to historical child sex abuse charges that were claimed to have taken place over at least three decades. Especially as he had a blemish free criminal record and was always described as a 'true gentleman' by the females in his coven, all of whom were very keen to state on the record that at no stage did they ever perform ceremonies naked. Within half an hour of the police leaving his flat windows were smashed by stone throwing local youths and the word 'NONCE' had been spray painted in red across his front door. This did not bode well for him facing trial by a jury of his peers.

Sometimes people tend to judge you by the company that you keep, something German Pete, 72, was made acutely aware of when he found himself charged along with his friend, Jack Kemp, 69, an ex-tin miner who had a previous conviction for a sexual offence against a young girl. Kemp had been given the nickname Popeye locally due to his resemblance to the spinach eating cartoon character. He and Petrauske had known each other for a number of years, close to the point where German Pete would occasionally sleep with Pamela James, Kemp's wife, whilst he sat downstairs watching soap operas in the living room.

The arrests of both German Pete and Kemp came about after a boozy birthday party on the Old Hill estate in Falmouth. Economically deprived, the local shop windows covered in rusting metal shutters, it was only the towering palm trees planted by the council that gave the place an air of faded seaside glamour. Late into the night, after yet another run to the off licence for supplies, an argument broke out and fists flew. More significant than the punches thrown during the fracas was the allegation of rape aimed at Jack Kemp, who quickly left the party and returned home. It was only when he woke up later the next day that he realised word had spread and other alleged victims had come forward to the police. Some of these named German Pete as a historical sexual abuser who had prayed on generations of local children since the 1970s.

This accusations differed from the usual sordid narrative of paedophile sex rings, if only because the esoteric and disturbing elements of their crimes seemed to hint at something darker that mere sexual exploitation.

IV

"While those that don't follow the crowd are criticised, it is not yet illegal to be a weirdo" - German Pete's defence barrister

Most people, you would think, would start to worry about their chances in a criminal trial, if their own defence barrister started his summing up of the case by calling you a weirdo. As blunt as this was, it was followed by a statement meant to draw a strong historical precedent. *"Just remember the people over the years who have been subjected to medieval justice when the finger of accusation has been pointed"*.

As Kemp and German Pete stood in the dock, they listened to witness evidence which was given from behind a protective screen or presented via video link. The judge decided that it would just be too traumatic for the adult witnesses to stand directly opposite the accused; such protection does, of course, also have the effect of immediately demonising the accused. The judge also decided that given the disturbing nature of the evidence the trial should be subject to a media blackout and a reporting restriction was placed on the case. A decision that was challenged and eventually overturned following the intervention of a local BBC journalist.

The jury and the packed public gallery heard from the first witness that the abuse had taken place in many different locations over a number of decades. Manor houses, stone circles, woods, open fields and abandoned quarries. *"The chanting stuck in my head for weeks"*, the witness said. *"I didn't understand what was happening. I just thought they were weird"*. She said she was taken to a garden at first, where there was an area with big stones and a fire in the middle. There were people dressed in *"gown things"*. She thought they looked like Ku Klux Klan hoods with necklaces. *"I was with eight or nine other kids. We didn't understand what was going on and we were scared. I was warned that if I was naughty they would hurt me. That they had special powers"*.

She gave evidence that there were 'high priestesses' present when the abuse took place, although no female suspects were ever questioned or charged during the investigation. It was said that they had bound their hands, drawn knives and poured hot wax over the victims' bodies. The court heard how the men were said to have told one young victim that if she was a good girl, *"she would see their snakes spit"*. She also said that during one attack, which took place in a quarry, she had sat next to a boy, no older than three who had tears streaming down his face. *"That was when I first learnt about witches"* she said before breaking down. The judge taking a break so she could compose herself before giving further evidence.

The second prosecution witness, known as Witness A, had previously given evidence in the trail of paedophile Stanley Pirie a few years earlier, although at no point had she ever mentioned to the police any ritual element to her abuse in the many hours of interviews she had given. When asked by the defence why she had never mentioned it she simply stated, *"no one asked"*, though one might wonder why such a significant aspect of the case would not seem worth voluntarily bringing up once the initial accusation was made and the police were, presumably, collecting all the necessary evidence. There is no record of whether she had undergone any 'recovered memory' therapy or not.

Her evidence spoke of her being about three when she was first abused, and five when she went to a ritual attended by a number of men and women, together with up to twelve children, where Kemp and Petrauske had acted as high priests. Rumours of a 'third man' being a constant figure in her abuse had been evident throughout the trail and a week or so into the case during a long cross examination, Witness A made it clear just who this was.

"I was taken into a big house", she said. *"There was a weird incensey smell and I passed rooms where there were chains coming off the bed, and whips. I was in a room where there was a big double bed with ropes coming out of it and a black whip with star things on the ends. I was scared. He pushed me onto the bed and I knew I was in trouble. I did what he told me, he tied ropes around my feet, they were really tight, hurting. I was telling him 'please don't hurt me' and he slapped me across the face. His eyes were looking evil"*.

Victim A said she suffered pain for weeks after the attack which happened when she was nine. She spoke of being scared of being thrown into a fire. Seen as being naughty. Raped by a man that years later she had only recognised after he was murdered and his picture was shown on television. When she saw the picture she was *"hysterical"* and couldn't tell anyone. *"It made me hate men"*, she said.

The Solheim connection seemed to join all the dots, at least in the eyes of the press who rushed to cover the trial in forensic detail now the press reporting restrictions had been lifted. **The Sun**, as always, lead the field in terms of headlines, leading with *"SEX CULT OF PAGAN PAEDOS"* as a header and trawling through their library to cut and paste the worst excesses of their reporting of Solheim's murder years before.

Sometimes the court records read more like a passage from a Dennis Wheatley novel than a criminal trial. Every 'witchcraft as evil' trope seemingly used by the prosecution to signal that this was no ordinary child abuse trail, this was much worse, because here dark forces beyond our usual understanding of the corruption of innocence were at play. As if the abuse itself wasn't lurid and disturbing enough, the prosecution case focussed mostly on the ritual aspects, despite the jury hearing from an expert who stated clearly that he didn't recognise any pagan practices outlined in the evidence of sexual exploitation given by the witnesses. Such evidence would probably have been buried amongst the sensationalism. Yet there are uncomfortable questions that arise from the evidence. Is it possible that blurred, buried childhood memories of genuine abuse was conflated with the well-publicised pagan beliefs of Petrauske and Solheim, both subjected to sensationalist news reports that emphasised their 'Satanic' interests? The emphasis on the ritual elements – which, even in the evidence given, sound more like costume drama inspired to create shock and awe in victims than the stories of Satanic Ritual Abuse that abounded in the 1980s - seems odd, given the unquestionably horrific nature of the crimes in question. Take away the ceremonial robes and many critics thought the case was little more than repugnant historical sex abuse.

But what became clear during the trial was that some of the victims were said to have been as young as three as four and according to court transcripts would have represented dozens of local children who had passed through the hands of Kemp, Petrauske and Solheim over the years. Apart from the 'ritual' elements there was evidence given about photographs and videos being taken, although none had ever been found when the homes of the accused had been raided. Alcohol and sweets were given to buy silence, threats made.

Kemp's defence team were keen to point out that the ritual element was little more than a 'red herring' and that their client thought paganism was 'silly' and had never shown any commitment to the faith beyond attending a few meetings with Petrauske. *"It just wasn't my cup of tea"*, Kemp was quoted as saying. This dismissal of the 'occult' elements of the case might have been more admirable if it wasn't being done to try and show the innocence of their client – the inference being that he was not guilty because he was not a pagan.

In the witness box Petrauske told the court that he had been a pagan for 55 years and had an altar in his bedroom, he had always been proud of his faith and was well known locally for his frequent appearances in the press. He also accepted he had a dagger and whip, but insisted they were for ceremonial purposes. He was very keen to clarify that he had no doubt the victims who gave evidence had been abused by men in robes but said he was never involved. His defence, essentially, hung on the fact that he was the victim of mistaken identity, singed out because he resembled other abusers. This claim did not, unfortunately for him, wash. The jury found Kemp and Petrauske guilty as charged.

Insisting that his combined sentence of thirty-two years for rape and indecent assault would see both men die in jail, Judge Graham Cottle said: *"The offences range from the extremely serious to the truly horrifying. You are two of the surviving members of a paedophile ring that operated in Falmouth in the 1970s and 1980s. I'm satisfied that you have both had a life-long sexual interest the ritualistic, sickening abuse of young, young children."* Kemp, who already had a prior conviction for child abuse, received a lighter sentence than Petrauske – fourteen years rather than the eighteen handed to the pagan 'High Priest'. Some people on the local estates around Falmouth could be heard openly expressing the view that it was Solheim who had received the most appropriate justice out of the three and that the £10,000 reward money to find the other protagonists in his brutal murder was now never likely to be paid.

The pagan community was appalled by many aspects of the case, especially the reporting. They focussed on what they saw as a vicious and unfair attack on their faith, terming it a 'blood libel', the same pernicious lies that had seen them persecuted for thousands of years. In this case it was purely due the actions of men engaged in what they saw as simple, if repulsive child abuse, cloaked in faux ritual which bore no relationship to their own belief system. Many made the point that abusive Church of England vicars, Imams and Catholic priests didn't tend to send the media into such a frenzy. Interestingly, just one day after Petrauske and Kemp were sentenced, an Anglican priest, John Haley Dosser, was convicted of abusing three boys under his care in the 1990s, and was sentenced to less than two years in prison. Perhaps because cases against mainstream religious figures were now so commonplace, with hundreds of prosecutions over the years, they were somehow seen as less sensational, and less to do with religious belief than individual culpability. In contrast this case seemed to be the first recorded instance of a practicing pagan being charged for child sexual exploitation, and everyone involved seemed to be a little too keen to link the religious belief to the crime.

Epilogue:

As the trial came to its conclusion and as quickly as they stared, the animal mutilations in the area seemed to stop. Some more cynically minded observers believe that there are still regular cases but the local press have been warned off reporting them for fear the coverage would inspire copycat attacks.

Following the Kemp and Petrauske verdicts, no one else has been charged, or indeed questioned, about their involvement in the ritual abuse of children in the area, despite witness testimony that claims many other people, both male and female, were present at events where children were sexually exploited. There appears to be no current, open investigation into the case by Devon and Cornwall police.

Petrauske attempted to appeal his eighteen year sentence in 2014, claiming that the evidence given by a witness who claimed he had bragged about having sex with girls as young as nine when in the navy should never have admissible in the trial. It was nothing more than drunken pub bragging and had turned the jury against him. His appeal was denied.

Margaret James has kept her silence throughout her prison sentence, despite repeated police requests to name the rest of Solheim's killers. A recent appeal against her conviction for conspiracy to murder was also denied.

WALPURGIS
THE SATANIC SABBAT IN ART
KERI O'SHEA

If 'the Devil has all the best tunes', then, historically, he's made quite the mark on art, too. Sure, the story of Jesus has dominated the art world for a millennium or so, but there are only so many biblical scenes you can take on board: walk through the halls of any of the most esteemed galleries in Europe, and you eventually begin to turn a blind eye to the rows of dead Christs, looking instead for the grotesques, the monsters and the fallen souls. Artists, too, many of whom would have received lucrative patronage in order to create mile upon mile of annunciations, crucifixions and resurrections, must have longed for the day when they could turn their hands to goings-on in Hell, giving free rein to their imaginations and painting gleeful demons, damned hypocrites, and all manner of salacious goings-on. Even when beloved saints are getting set about by laughing demons, there seems to be a kind of *joie de vivre* involved which is lacking from all the sober renditions of a political prisoner being tortured to death by the government of the day. Some of the only figures to smile in medieval art come with forked tongues and cloven feet: possibly there weren't many other people who had much to smile about, back then.

But, as diverting as these demons are, they're still just the henchmen. When the boss himself turns up in art, he's often accompanied by his very human followers: depictions of witches' sabbats have long been particularly delightful to artists because, as well as affording the option to paint different kinds of subject matter, particularly 'fallen' and often disrobed women (like the **Daily Mail** today, it's not lascivious if it comes with a moral judgement), it was also a place to explore other issues. Sabbats provided an opportunity to play with the anxieties of the day. They were often gatherings of women who did not content themselves with rigid moral mores, those who were believed to have strayed from the flock, or otherwise to have rubbished the roles they were meant to play. As such, the sabbat was an expression of anxieties about outsiders, people who played outdoors at night and those were actively involved in plotting against their pious neighbours. At different times, more specific anxieties cropped up in art, too, as we will see.

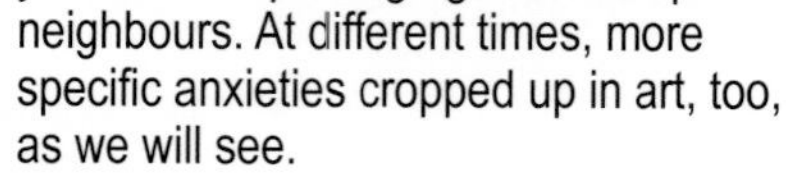

Whilst this feature isn't intended to be the definitive guide to these Satanic get-togethers, it nonetheless features some of the most appealing and interesting. We start with the early 17th Century.

Woodcut taken from Francesco Maria Guazzo's Compendium Maleficarum: Witches Kissing Satan (1608)

Medieval Europe knew a thing or two about the rich cultural significance of arse jokes: just ask Geoffrey Chaucer, whose **Miller's Tale** contains one of the finest examples of such. By the dawning of the 1600s, however, despite the burgeoning Renaissance, with all of its improvements, more sinister developments meant that a belief in witchcraft had remained steadfast. The renowned **Hammer of the Witches** text - **the Malleus Maleficarum** – was over a century old, but its influence was still incredibly pernicious. It acted as a manual for the increasingly brutal persecution of witches during the century to come; the increasing numbers of printing presses also aided its reach, as well as affording new opportunities for illustration.

Medieval and Renaissance society understood that low literacy levels amongst the people necessitated some form of illustration in order to communicate effectively, and the arrival of the woodcut had been a new, relatively easy means of doing this. Many of these woodcuts are unattributed, but they are still striking examples of folkish beliefs (as well as, to an extent no doubt, fuelling the imagination and spreading knowledge of alleged occult practices). The arrival of cheaper media, like pamphlets, also helped to place fantastical images at last into the hands of the people.

The 'obscene kiss', whereby gathered witches were supposed to greet Satan by kissing him on the backside, is illustrated in this particular example of a woodcut, where a group of women (and a man) have gathered at night to offer the 'osculum infame'. Believed by the god-fearing to show the complete degradation of the devil-worshipper – you know, the god-fearing ones who regularly ate the flesh and drank the blood of their Saviour – it seems to show a kind of liberation as well, playing to the long relationship between humour and obscenity. Old Scratch himself certainly seems to see the funny side, and appears here in his most infamous guise – a cloven-hooved, winged being. It's a look he would stick with over the ensuing centuries.

The Great He Goat - Francisco de Goya (circa 1822)

Goya started his career as a courtly painter, but through the course of his life he increasingly turned to darker imagery, bemoaning what he saw as the death of rational thought amongst his countrymen which had culminated in the Penninsular Wars. This is why he revisited the theme of the sabbat several times: for him, these moonlight gatherings neatly encapsulated irrational thought and behaviour. Rather than illustrating literal Devil-worship, as some of his forebears had done, Goya used the sabbat in a symbolic sense, showing how, even in modern times, people would quickly flock back to sinister and arcane forces.

However, his earliest depictions of same are all light and colour: by the time he painted **The Great He Goat** during his 'Black Paintings' period – a time of great personal anguish and introspection for Goya, by now losing his sight and painting directly onto the walls of his villa - we see only oppressive sepia tones and darkness. The sabbat in this painting is crowded, frantic; a seated, goat-like figure presides over what seems to be an initiation, as the only young, beautiful face in this mob sits apart from the others, presumably awaiting whatever comes next. There's a touch of bureaucracy here, albeit made monstrous, but most of all this is an ugly and unreasonable gathering, about to subsume the youth in front of them into their midst. The Devil at the heart of this ceremony is bathed in shadow, but unquestionably controls the clandestine meeting. This is above all a startling, stark painting of degeneration: the belief in the Devil here may not be literal, but it's nonetheless rife with paranoia and unease.

La Danse du Sabbat - Émile-Antoine Bayard (1870)

Parisian draughtsman Bayard was a cartoonist and book illustrator, perhaps most famously turning his hand to illustrations of characters from Victor Hugo's **Les Misérables** – but book illustrators inevitably go where the work is, so when Paul Christian's volume entitled **Histoire de la Magie** surfaced in 1870, Bayard was enlisted to design the accompanying artwork. At this time, there was a burgeoning renaissance for all things magical, and reprints of this work developed a reputation for their particularly attractive, engraved artwork, with plates featuring themes such as Mélusine, mid-transformation from woman to serpent, and the mythical death of Faust.

Alongside these, Bayard's **Danse du Sabbat** revisits a now-familiar theme, but renders it in meticulous detail, with numerous captivating details emerging from the gloom of the night-time scene. Satan now performs his role as the Master of Ceremonies on a raised plinth, possibly an ancient stone structure, with a gibbet – corpse still swinging – barely visible behind (Satanic rituals were often rumoured to take place near such ill-fated sites). Clad in monastic robes, similar to the **Great He-Goat** of Goya's imagination, Satan here also seems to have a go-between between himself and his admirers, though this time just a solitary, stooped woman, cradling a skull and brandishing a wand. The revellers themselves are a diverse bunch, comprising barely-clad women and all manner of demonic beings, arm-in-arm and circling the raised earthworks where the Devil stands. Bayard's work has been occasionally attributed to that master-engraver Gustav Dore, and it's not hard to see why: the murk, the shadow and the unpalatable aspects of irrational thought looming up out of the great Industrial Age all call to Dore's own preoccupations.

Luis Ricardo Falero – Witches on the Sabbath (1878)

Falero's oil paintings are renowned for their nudity; most of the work he ever displayed featured ample naked flesh, so when he began to experiment with occult themes, he clearly saw no real reason to rock the boat. Falero's work might be notable enough for that, but what's particularly interesting in his own depiction of a witches' sabbat is that he has by and large left Old Nick out of the equation altogether. Like a twenty-first century media narrative, Falero is chiefly interested not in the destination, but in the journey, and it's the journey he has chosen to illustrate.

The resultant work is quite unlike anything else featured here: rather than grotesque beings or dark shadows being prominent (although they are there), you could be forgiven for thinking that these flying witches aren't really defying Christianity at all. The moonlight is so bright, it's close to daylight; beautiful and healthy girls make up most of the group, although in the interests of fair representation, we can see one man and one old woman; the whole scene is rich with floating drapery and picturesque clouds, more reminiscent of a scene from Classical lore than the sabbats we've come to know and love.

Yes, it's doubtlessly a salacious piece, but it's also complex and stylish enough to set it completely apart from other depictions of the theme. Falero was pleased enough with his handiwork that he used a very similar melee of intertwining female bodies for a later work, **Faust's Dream** (1880). Good work if you can get it, I suppose.

Otto Greiner, Satan Presenting Woman to the People (1898)

And so we come to the end of the 19th Century, and our final illicit gathering – though admittedly, one which has transformed the image of the sabbat into something altogether new. Here, the raised plinth has turned into something which far more resembles a stage, and as such calls to mind the popular modern pursuits of the day – the music halls, the bars, the salons. Certainly, for many outraged observers, Satan held sway over all of these new places, so it's eminently fitting that he should appear, by now far more man than animal, to join forces with the woman at his side. Long associated with the femininity, the devil and the woman here look like a pair of sidekicks, as she perches on his knee.

And make no mistake: she's a modern girl. The illustration and its title may deal in absolutes, and may call to that long association of women with carnality and evil, but here the woman is wearing stockings and fashionable footwear. Her hair is curled. The scene is even rather well lit, enough for us to see the smiles of the performers and the adulation of the gathered male group at the feet of the Devil and the woman. Through the course of the illustrations considered here, women have moved from being supplicants, to adherents to, finally, taking their place alongside the Devil, not beneath him. It's a career progression of sorts, and one worthy of the 'New Woman' which so alarmed reactionary society during this era.

Perhaps most of all, though, it's via this piece of artwork that we see Satan toasting in a new century, surviving all the way into modernity, still a preoccupation and a source of fascination for artists and commentators alike. The 'People' alluded to in the illustration's title hadn't forgotten, and nor would they over the coming years. Satan was 'alive', and belief in his arcane worshippers would persist – for good or ill – into the years of our own living memories.

SATAN SUPERSTAR - A PERSONAL VIEW

BOYD RICE

I am very much aware that within the Judeo Christian mindset, there are people who view Satan as a romantic or heroic figure. But I'm a monist. As such, I've long seen Satan as one half of the divided mind, one half of a false dichotomy.

Good vs. evil is a concept you tell children about to frighten them, but has no reality beyond that. Man's so called dark side is part and parcel of human nature, and always has been. History proves as much.
Human nature hasn't changed in millennia, and for all that time humanity has always said one thing and done another. Don't pay attention to what people say, observe how they actually behave (and always have). You'll find that those who proclaim what nice people they are, are the biggest liars. And it's never the devil that made them do so.

When you have even the most minimal understanding of human nature, you realize there is no need for a devil.

Boyd Rice and Anton LaVey. Photo: Carl Abrahamsson.

THE NIKOLAS SCHRECK FILES

DAVID FLINT

Nikolas Schreck is a writer, musician, filmmaker and artist, now based in Berlin. He formed the band and occult movement Radio Werewolf (and The Werewolf Order), has authored books including **The Manson File**, **The Satanic Screen** and **Flowers from Hell: A Satanic Reader**. His musical collaborators have ranged from Death in June to Christopher Lee. He has a monthly show on Berlin's Radio On, and is now – after rejecting all forms of occultism – a Tantric Buddhist teacher.

David Flint met with him during his visit to London in January 2018, and talked to him about his occult past, his involvement with Anton LaVey and the Church of Satan, and his personal interpretation of devil worship.

Let's start at the beginning. When did the Devil first enter your life?

Even as a very young child, before I could articulate what I was thinking, and based on no outer influence, I was instinctively drawn to everything to do with the realm of supernatural beings, whether they be gods or demons, and with the practice of magic, sorcery, the invocation of spirits. At first, I became obsessed with the minutiae of first Greek and then Nordic myth, especially the darker side of those traditions, such as Hecate and Circe, Loki, the Fenris Wolf. I'm certain this was just a matter of me returning to a field of study and practice I knew in a recent past life before this current incarnation. My parents were bohemian free thinkers, swingers, and psychedelic enthusiasts who instilled in me an early detestation of organised conventional religion and societal institutions. So they were open to and encouraging of my pint sized early experiments in paganism. I've noticed a lot of people attracted to Satanism come from very repressive religious backgrounds. That was the exact opposite of my experience. Which is probably one reason why even when I was a part of that subculture, I never felt much affinity with many other so-called Satanists, who always struck me as reactionaries rebelling against their upbringing rather than genuinely committed devotees of the Devil.

I was originally mesmerised as a child by the Northern pantheon of gods, something which later resurfaced in the Werewolf Order. Luckily Sixties pop culture fed my obsession. One anecdote will illustrate how much my parents encouraged me in this pursuit. In 1966, I was enthralled by the Marvel TV cartoon of **The Mighty Thor**, particularly the trickster Loki. I watched this cartoon about Asgard with truly religious fanaticism. One day, the **Mighty Thor** show was preempted by a special broadcast about Pope Paul VI. I was outraged. My father called the TV station and complained, in his usual confrontational irreverent way, *''My son wants to watch The Mighty Thor and you're showing some guy in a white dress and funny hat instead!"* The operator at the station said, *"But sir, that's the Holy Father!"* So that sort of attitude shaped my own spiritual penchant for the old gods in opposition to the newer Abrahamic religions from an early age.

Nikolas Schreck, 2017.Portrait by Zeena Schreck.

At what point did this fascination start to take on more occult leanings?

My emphasis was always on the underworld, the casting of spells, calling forth the gods, everything to do with ascending from what I saw as the ignorant mortal human state to a higher level of being. This was not only an interest but a fascination, in the literal Latin sense of the word, an enchantment. When I was working musically with Christopher Lee in the Nineties, he once asked me much the same question you did about how I got into all this, and I told him *"It's partially your fault!"*. He was somewhat appalled when I explained that when as a child I saw his performance as a sinister black magician in the

Nikolas Schreck as a child, in Devil costume

hallucinatory Mario Bava film **Hercules in the Haunted World** at a kiddie matinee in 1965, I aspired to become a black magician too. Another landmark at this early stage was my intense and far from innocent childhood crush on the beautiful Evil Queen in the Disney film **Snow White**, which began a lifelong magical entanglement with the figure of the femme fatale as sorceress. That earliest phase as a magical apprentice was largely informed by European paganism.

In 1966, however, due to the infernal intervention of my first initiatrix, a teenage babysitter who fashioned herself a witch, I fell under the Devil's spell. She was not only a self-styled witch but an ardent admirer of supernaturally themed horror films. She would let me stay up until well after midnight to watch the classic Universal monster movies of the Thirties and Forties on the late night TV broadcasts which, in the mid-Sixties, was the only way you could see them at that time. While we watched these films, she would very seriously explain the diabolical folklore of the werewolf and the vampire to me. Or the basics of Egyptian magic when we watched **The Mummy**.

I can trace the very moment that I became a Devil Worshipper to an experience I shared with her. One late night, we were watching Tod Browning's **Dracula**. I'm sure you remember the scene where Dwight Frye as Renfield quotes his master Dracula as telling him, *"All these will I give you! If you will obey me!"* Well, for some reason this phrase captivated me. She explained that Bram Stoker took this line from the scene in the Bible about the Temptation of Christ where the Devil promises Jesus Christ in the desert, *"All these things I will give you if you fall down and do an act of worship to me."* Jesus, of course, responded to this offer by saying, *"Get thee behind me, Satan."* Upon learning of this deal, my immediate reaction was, *"Okay, where do I sign up?"*

From the beginning of that phase of my spiritual journey, I was focused on literal worship of the person of the Devil, in exchange for forbidden wisdom. Which is why I underscore that I preferred to be called a religious Devil worshiper rather than a Satanist, which is a word that can be misused to describe an atheistic secular worldly philosophy or the member of an organisation rather than mystical engagement with a real spiritual being, which was my only interest in the phenomenon.

From that point on, for many years to come, I sought out every possible source of information about the Devil I could get my hands on. As this coincided with the general occult revival of the mid-Sixties, a wide selection of previously obscure traditional grimoires and magical treatises on the Black Arts were suddenly easily available and I devoured them all, trying as best as I could to put them into practice.

At the same time, that era's popular culture exploded with positive portrayals of the Devil in cinema and literature, from the open practice of black magical rituals on the afternoon TV show **Dark Shadows**, to the scantily clad diabolism drenching the Hammer films of that time. So my devil worship was very much a product of its time. The time of **Sympathy for the Devil** on the radio, **Rosemary's Baby** in the movie theaters, and a thousand gothic paperbacks of enticing damsels escaping from Satanic covens on the bookshelves. I must point out that in those years, the Devil was portrayed as an elegant, erotically charged aristocratic being, not the crude and brutal creature he was soon reduced to later after being taken up and dumbed down by thuggish heavy metal culture.

Nikolas Schreck as Christ performing with Radio Werewolf at Roxy Theater, Los Angeles, 1985, Photo by David Hermon

How did you interpret the Devil at that time? Was it entirely pop-culture based or did you develop your own ideas about who Satan was?

My working hypothesis at that time, very much shaped by the revolutionary aspirations of the counterculture I grew up in, was essentially Gnostic. In that I believed that the jealous bloodthirsty tyrant Jehovah was an impostor god, a demiurge, and that the Devil and his minions were liberatory dissidents helping mankind to escape from the killjoy God's puritan prison. I know now that was a wrong interpretation, as I will explain, but that was my stance then.

This wasn't just theoretical, as I experimented with magical rites and spells to see if ceremonial magic invoking demons could really effect change in the material universe. One crucial experience in the early Seventies was when I visited Haiti during the time of the Duvalier regime. My father, knowing of my magical studies, arranged for us to attend a genuine Voodoo rite, in which the loas were called down to possess the celebrants. Actually witnessing the entrance of spiritual beings into human beings during that ceremony demonstrated to me that the occult playacting going on in the civilised west at that time was just a charade compared to the real thing rooted in ancient tradition. Seeing how Haiti was a society completely ruled by magic transformed my understanding completely, and set me even more firmly on a theistic approach to magic.

Around the same time, I had a friend who was a Southern Baptist – he didn't necessarily believe in it, but his family did. My family and I went to his baptism, where he was dumped in water. Just to give you an idea of how people saw me, afterwards he came up to me and said *"I'm very sorry that I had to renounce the Devil and all his works, and I hope you weren't offended by that"*. Because I was so grimly serious about my devotion to the Devil. An odd thing is, I found many Christians – and I always have seen this – if you are seriously a devil worshipper and say *"yes, I believe in the Devil and serve him"*, they have a kind of respect for you. They think, well, that fits into our framework, I can understand you. They don't understand or make any sense of it when you say *"I don't believe in God or the Devil"*.

What were the wider social attitudes like toward Devil worshippers at that time?

The first time I was aware of the social significance of Satanism was during the Manson trial in 1970, and the weird coincidence of my being in New England where the original witch trials happened and seeing that this was just more American puritanism. These people are having sex, taking drugs etc., and therefore they are witches. Now of course, I wanted to think that they were – if the myth was true, it would've been more interesting. But I found out it's really not very interesting – it's a bunch of squalid drug dealers with Mafia connections doing what criminals do. There wasn't anything occult about it. I feel like a parent telling kids that Santa Claus doesn't exist when I have to puncture the balloon of the devil cult and Helter Skelter. It's crimes that are happening down the street right now – drug dealers get into arguments. It was done in a particularly vicious way, but – and this ties in to understand the context of the times – at the time it just seemed completely normal that there would be a murderous Devil cult. Now it wouldn't. Who would believe that? If you found a bunch of people murdered, and two of them were drug dealers, you'd know what it was about in ten minutes. The interesting thing about the Devil mystique in Western pop culture is that it actually broke into reality, where people thought *"well, I saw **Rosemary's Baby** last year, and according to this film, your next door neighbour could be a Satanist"*.

And of course, Polanski connects the two.

Of course. I talked to Gene Gutowski, Polanski's best friend for years who was deeply involved in the whole production of **Rosemary's Baby**, and both of them were secular atheists. To them, it was just a story. He said that Anton LaVey had nothing to do with this film, they didn't have any occult adviser. He thought that was laughable. But **Rosemary's Baby**, when it came out in 1968, everyone believed it was a documentary – that on every suburban street, there must be a coven. So that's how the prosecution could say *"this was a cult of Devil worshippers"*. Now, people think it must have been true, because who would believe it if it wasn't? But that was in the air.

The idea of Anton LaVey as advisor became reality too in the 1970s. His presence was a seal of approval for films like **Race with the Devil**, **The Devil's Rain** *and so on, even though the Devil worship that they portrayed was entirely removed from the beliefs of the Church of Satan.*

In all of these subjects, there's the myth and then the reality. The myth is that he was the technical advisor for **Rosemary's Baby**, the most influential Devil worship film ever. In fact, he wasn't involved with the film at all save after the fact for a local promotional appearance at the San Francisco premiere, but right at the end of that wave of Satanic films, he was involved in one of the most unsuccessful films in that cycle that showed in drive-ins for a few weeks then disappeared. But people don't care about the reality, and I've found it doesn't matter that I have spoken to each and every one of the people involved, on every level, and can tell you that it's all bullshit. I know, from bitter experience, they'll tell me *"that's what YOU believe – I know better."* They have a vested interest, emotionally, to believe the myth. 'Print the legend' is the famous journalism thing. I've given up on my earlier naïve idea that the truth matters – it doesn't. I can say the truth all day, but people prefer the colourful legend.

But the main point is watching the Manson trial and seeing it as being similar to the Salem witch trials. That was the first time that I knew being what I am is going to be dangerous for me now. Before, it's fun and colourful and part of the counter culture. Suddenly, this could lead to problems. To me, that was the beginning of the Satanic Panic, though it didn't actually occur until decades after. I saw then the Christian Right in America, which to English and European people is hard to even conceive of their fanaticism, and I already saw the backlash.

I guess the Satanic Panic had to evolve slowly. It didn't just emerge from nowhere.

It began during the Manson trial and the first reports of sensational nonsense about the Devil and witches. In a way, Dennis Wheatley was more positive – he's saying Devil worshippers are wealthy aristocrat elitists who run the world, but they are very cultivated people – they've got art collections and fine wine in the cellar. But suddenly now, they are filthy hippies living out in the desert somewhere coming to kill you. It changed the whole mystique of it and it made it a criminal phenomenon rather than a spiritual one. That helped plant the seed for the Satanic Panic.

Nikolas Schreck and Charles Manson

Radio Werewolf Youth Propaganda, 1985

Of course, in the early 1980s, much as now, the Sixties was blamed for society's ills, opening the door to sexual freedoms and promiscuity that apparently invariably leads to abuse.

Right. The Trump era is still fighting the Sixties. They think all the counter culture liberties of that time need to be wiped out. That's what Nixon began. The Nixon administration was literally voted into power to get rid of the counter culture, which it did. So for me, I couldn't even think consciously of it. It was just everywhere and I was attracted to it. But it was just a part of the counter culture, just like many other things. It could have been Eastern mysticism, it could have been any number of these things that people were looking into.

So in the 1970s, you knew that your beliefs were potentially dangerous, but you then chose to publicly embrace them rather than hide in the shadows.

Even by the early Seventies, I was doing all-out ceremonial magic according to the book – according to the exact instructions. And I did encounter forces. Nothing dramatic, but I did learn that if you do this ritual, it will make this happen. I did it in an almost scientific experimental way – I don't really care if it does happen, but let's see if I do this ritual, will such and such happen. And I found it did work. In 1981, I had a specific experience where I thought OK, this is absolutely real – there are spirits that descend into human flesh. After doing a conjuration of the Devil, I had a vision of the Devil as a woman, and she sang a particular song. This was a time when I was looking into the use of sound as magic and consciousness alteration. What your mind projects is part of what you're thinking, too. And it was enough of a vision that you could form a whole religion around it. I didn't, but it became of great personal significance to me. So that changed everything. I thought I don't need to look any more at these ancient grimoires – apparently, this being has paid attention to me. I've graduated. And that was the point. It wasn't to be part of some group of others. I've never been a joiner and always looked at groups as being weak people coming together to feel some social warmth. I'm not good at being in Buddhist groups now. I'm not much of a sociable being.

So I thought now I'm in direct contact with this being – and you can interpret that in any way. You can think I'm a lunatic who had a hallucination, or it was an actual religious vision. Either way is fine with me. But it gave me a feeling of arrogance and maybe false confidence. At least I know it can be communicated with. I kept dialling the number, and now something answered. So I thought that now I have to do this in the world. That's what Radio Werewolf was – a black magical ritual. It was not even intended as a band – that was the front. By that time there was already the idea that music could be evil, rock music has sinister messages etc., and I played that up to the extreme.

Radio Werewolf's genesis was right after that in 1981, before it was really formed in 84. I'd been working with the musicians who became the first formation of it. My idea of it was to create a black magical ritual as an experiment, to see what would happen. If Mick Jagger can sing **Sympathy for the Devil** and Altamont happens, that was just a little episode. What if I'm doing it 24 hours a day? The world will turn into Altamont. That's how irresponsible and completely unethical I was. I didn't care about the consequences. I was very anti-social and not caring about what would happen.

So with Radio Werewolf, I took every cliché of what was already starting to get into pop culture – backward masking and so on – and I played it with a semi-straight face. We are the messengers of the Devil and we are going to brainwash teenagers to serve our cult.

You really were what everyone claimed the heavy metal bands were.

Yeah. Except I hated heavy metal music – in my usual arrogant elitist way I thought that was too proletarian.

And they were occult dilettantes – you were the real thing.

Right. And I was doing the real thing privately, but presenting it publicly, consciously, as a little bit of a joke. Is it a put-on? Is he serious? He can't really mean this nonsense. It was making fun of people's prejudices and clichés, incorporating them and also being them. It's a little bit like a criminal joking that he just robbed a bank, and he did. So that was the double bluff of the early Radio Werewolf. We've not just got backward masking, we've got the best backward masking in town – state of the art. And I learned very quickly that people don't get the joke. Some did. But immediately – to my advantage and disadvantage – in LA when I was a local phenomenon, people took it completely seriously. There's a demonic cult, this band is its representative, it's run by some other force behind it – which it wasn't, we had ten dollars. It was an interesting experiment in that I saw, OK, once you bring this symbolism into their mind, they will fill in the gaps. But like a Frankenstein's monster, it quickly got out of hand, to the point where the police were really harassing me. And getting death threats. And the concerts – well, as I said about Altamont, you unleash this energy permanently. It got to the point where we needed skinheads to be our security force, which is just like the Stones hiring Hell's Angels. It turned into idiotic disasters and confrontations, as you can imagine. It got way out of hand, very quickly. The theatrical nature of it became real. It became violent and, after a while, very stressful. I was blacklisted from practically going anywhere – in a way, that made the concerts more attractive, because it was like doing a forbidden thing. But I realised that this is no longer music or even art. It's like yelling fire in a movie theatre. And I do feel that whatever I was doing musically or artistically got lost in the shock value and provocation of it.

Nikolas Schreck as the Devil performing with Radio Werewolf at the Whisky A Go Go, 1986

Do you think that your work has suffered subsequently? Or still suffers because of that reputation?

Oh yeah, definitely. But there's no way I could've known it until I did it. I don't regret it, because I learned a lot about society and the way people work, but in retrospect, if I'd just said *"here's music"* and dropped everything around it, that would've been better for me as a creative artist. That's what I am, I'm an artist putting stuff out. But now it's always looked at through this prism. That becomes your karma. I created the monster, so I have to deal with it still wandering around.

I suppose in the end, you can try to fight it, which is impossible, or else embrace it.

You just have to accept it. So anyway, it all became very violent and unpleasant to the point that I've got serious police harassment, banned everywhere. The controversy wasn't fun anymore. It became like fighting a war. So I moved from Los Angeles, which is where it was all happening, to San Francisco to get away from it. The Satanic Panic was already beginning, but I wasn't really aware of it, because I wasn't looking at the media, and so I didn't know why I was getting such an extreme violent reaction.

At that point, it was after the first **Manson File** was finished, and I was going to write a book called **The Demonic Revolution**, about modern Satanism and occultism. At that time, I'd never joined any group, and never wanted to. I had read **The Satanic Bible** in the Seventies and didn't like it. It was saying there is no Devil, and was this rational critique of Christianity etc. I could agree with some of the social ideas but I didn't agree with the basic point that the Devil was just a symbol for carnality. I didn't hate it, but I didn't particularly like it either. But in the process of writing this book, I got in touch with every single occult leader there was. I was in touch with Richard Ramirez – the Night Stalker. Zeena spoke to Robert De Grimston, the founder of the Process – she's one of the few people who ever has since the organisation ended. The remaining people who knew Crowley.

Forrest J. Ackerman, the editor of **Famous Monsters of Filmland**, had known Anton LaVey since the Fifties – before he was Anton LaVey, or anything, just a colourful eccentric in his field of people. Ackerman had invited LaVey to his, I think, 70th birthday, and asked him if I could interview him for this book. He said yeah, and then didn't show. But he was already aware of me. Kenneth Anger was in LA when Radio Werewolf was starting and he sent Anton clippings and advertisements and reviews of Radio Werewolf, so he knew what it was. I had met Anger at Ackerman's birthday, and almost worked with him on a Radio Werewolf video. So through that, it was the first awareness that LaVey had of me. When I moved to San Francisco to get away from all the harassment, I literally went from the kettle to the deepest part of the pot. I got to know LaVey, and the reason I got to know him – I want to make this clear in your particular book – is not because I wanted to be part of the Church of Satan or had any interest in the organisation itself. It was to interview him to clarify all the rumours about his life – what was true, what was not true – and to put it in this book. So like with Manson and many of the other people I know, I didn't go as a follower, I went to find out the truth.

You went as a journalist.

Basically, yeah. From a weird, insider position and not being antagonistic. So we met in February 1988, when he came to my apartment when he heard it was completely decorated to the nines with Satanic paraphernalia and we became friends because we had mutual interests. Even though he didn't espouse any belief in supernatural beings, he didn't care that I really believed in the Devil at all – he didn't give a fuck about anything at all like that. He was a con man running his little business. So we talked about strippers, or organ music, or old films, or military history – that was the basis of our secular friendship. We didn't talk about Satanic philosophy, and I didn't have the least interest in the organisation. Innocently, I do a lot of research when I talk to someone. Most people had never done any when they talked to him, either as yes men saying

Nikolas and Zeena Schreck iinterviewed by Bob Larson in the documentary The First Family of Satanism

"yes Doctor, that's great" or those who called him a liar. I was saying *"OK, what really happened. You were in* ***Rosemary's Baby*** *– I don't find any evidence anywhere. Here's the video – show me"*. And that made him very uncomfortable. I was putting my foot in my mouth without realising it. I was trying to be helpful – show me where, tell me when and I'll confirm it. But it became obvious that you can't confirm it because it's clearly not true. On and on. For instance, I found **The Cloven Hoof**, which was the name of the Church of Satan's magazine at the time. I said *"in this Robert E. Howard story from the Thirties, there's a publication called* ***The Cloven Hoof*** *– did you take it from that?"* He didn't like that, even. I could look into his sources – he clearly read **Weird Tales** when he was a kid the way I read **Famous Monsters** when I was a kid, and took this stuff and put a spin on it.

And there's nothing wrong with that. There's great mythology to play with in those stories.

Well, that's the thing. I wasn't being confrontational at that point. The film **The Black Cat** is the only film I know of prior to the Sixties occult revival that has a guy – Boris Karloff – as a High Priest of Lucifer. I said, to Anton during an early interview for my book, *"You would've been a kid when that came out and it was a popular film. The Karloff character has a book that he opens called* ***The Rites of Lucifer*** *– did that in any way give you a role model?"* And that, strangely, he said *"yeah, that did."* So at this point I'm just a friend of his and an interviewer trying to give credentials to his reputation, not to destroy it. I liked him. I got along with him. He had a good sense of humour, but I realised I had to stay away from his career, because this is going to get very uncomfortable. I liked him and respected him for what he was – a colourful character, I liked his organ playing and so on, but thought why does he have to try to convince us of this transparent nonsense?

Do you think he believed the stories himself?

I don't know if he was a con man who believes his own bullshit eventually, or if there was an element of madness to it… I can't really speculate. But that night, I thought I had to back off from it for my own good. That was April. I went to London and I had not yet then met Zeena. I was just friends with Anton. When I went to London, everywhere I went – and I was there with my girlfriend – people would say *"I heard you're going to have a Satanic wedding to Zeena LaVey"*. Everywhere – like five or six different people had heard this rumour and I was laughing and saying *"that's ridiculous, I've never even met her"*. But it was strange – it would keep coming up. I went back to San Francisco to do a performance in May of 88 and I invited Zeena to come to it, via her father. She had seen me on a TV show called **A Current Affair**, and I had seen her on another TV show about the Satanic Panic. I thought she was beautiful and I had a huge crush on her, and she saw me on this TV show and liked me, so we knew each other in this very 20th century way, from our television image.

So she came to the concert and we met, and it was really like love at first sight. But... I fell in love with her, and she was the High Priestess of the Church of Satan. So at the very moment I fell in love with her, I was thinking I had to get away from Anton. I became deeply embroiled in her life, but I was never a member of the Church. I was given an honorary membership card, in the same way that Genesis P. Orridge, or Marilyn Manson or any other musician who he thought would be good as a member. I would defend him – I was on a lot of talk shows at the time, so if people would talk about the Satanic Panic and child sacrifice, and I would defend the Church of Satan. I would say *"no, they're not doing those things"*, and that was useful to them. So he said *"you could be a public representative for us"*, but that was for his benefit. He wasn't going out there to defend himself against all these insane accusations that were untrue – he wasn't committing those kind of crimes. So by falling in love with and then marrying the High Priestess in the Church of Satan, of course I was in the middle of all that. But it wasn't my personal beliefs.

People believe we were put together as some sort of Satanic elite, and I'm always referred to as Anton La Vey's son-in-law and designated heir. It's treated like some genealogical thing like the Windsors. So then it makes it all the more dramatic that we broke with him. But it wasn't that way. Zeena was already the de facto heiress of the whole thing, because it was a family business – it was a show business sort of thing. People say she wanted to take over – she *was* it. He was sitting in his Black House, she was doing all the dirty work. And she volunteered to do it because she saw that this Satanic Panic was a threat. She had to go out and defend it because this was a serious threat. She had other aspirations, but she did a magnificent job of quelling the stupidest of the Satanic Panic just by arguing with these people and being an obviously sane person disputing this nonsense. She almost single-handedly ended the Satanic Panic by just being there. He wouldn't go up there to defend it. And that created a lot of tension. I defended it and I explained what his beliefs were, but I was not promoting his beliefs.

*It's a little like being a publicist for a band. You're not actually a **member** of the band.*

He said *"you can be my official representative"*, but other people were too. During the Satanic Panic, everyone who was being attacked had to work together, even if you don't completely agree. There were pagans, witches, New Age people who were being accused of murder and molestation, so in a way it's like a wartime thing. You form alliances that you wouldn't necessarily form in peacetime. So that's how I came to know Tom Metzger, the white supremacist, because I was being attacked and we needed skinheads – the only people dangerous enough to fight our enemies. And then the Manson thing. All these things came together in this unholy alliance of everything extremist that was considered the enemy in America by the religious Right at that time. And if you marry into this family, then you are fully immersed into this thing. But from the beginning of my relationship with Zeena, she was already becoming very disenchanted with being the High Priestess of the Church of Satan. She was totally brought up to believe that this was a real religion, and slowly, systematically, she was disillusioned. As the public representative, it's like being Sean Spicer. And there is something very Trumpian in this narcissistic desire to be this mythic being, and if you said it's not true, it would be like 'fake news'. Zeena has said that she was in the position of Ivanka, being used as the pretty front.

The acceptable face.

Right. So eventually she couldn't defend it any more. I won't speak for her because she has a lot more to say for herself – I'm just saying I witnessed her doing her best to defend this thing and then it turned against her because she would no longer be defending lies.

So when did you both decide that enough was enough?

There were many things that led to her breaking with him. She wouldn't even speak to him. When I met her, she was telling me *"I'm not going to keep doing this, I'm going to gracefully bow out"* – the original plan was that she would just eventually say *"I'm done as public representative"*, but it didn't even go that far because it got so unpleasant. So we resigned officially, but it was not about religious issues. It had nothing to do with Satanism per se.

It was a break from him, not from the religion.

Right. She had very different religious ideas to the organisation - this was a challenge she had, in that her own spiritual beliefs and ideas of magic were very different from his. That was a difference too, but there were these very real dysfunctional family issues that could happen with anyone. At that same time, The Werewolf Order was a very different kind of black magical organisation that Zeena and I were running, and there was a lot of tension because the Church of Satan was more liberal humanist, and we were much more extremist. The two things really didn't gel.

The story we usually hear is that you both broke away to start your own religion, but -

It already existed. That's a good point. The Werewolf Order came out of the Radio Werewolf Youth Party – the circle around the original formation of the Werewolf Order, and it already existed.

And all the books on Satanism and cults will push the idea of continual breakaway factions.

Right, yeah. But they were concurrent things. We were in cooperation with LaVey and many other extremist things going on – more than I could even name - but in the same way the Process was involved with other groups. It's what often happens with very extreme groups – you form necessary alliances with other extremists. But it was an uneasy alliance, because we were talking about actual real spiritual beings and magic, not atheism and not just fun and games or being just against Christianity. So there were theological disputes.

Nikolas Schreck in ceremonial magic ritual chamber, 1981.

So how do you move from Satanism to Buddhism?

Even as a youth, growing up in the hippy counter culture environment, I was exposed to various Eastern mysticism, which was just as prevalent as the Devil stuff. In 1975, I had already learned to meditate in a hippy community called Coconut Grove. I was very young but that was normal. But I weirdly tried to combine it with Devil worship and Eastern techniques. But there was no ethics. No belief in karma. No belief in the consequences of your own actions. I just thought if I learn to meditate it will be a good superpower.

A way of focusing your energies.

Right. If a criminal learns to meditate, they'll be a better, more focused criminal. They won't be a better person, they're just be more disciplined. But learning to meditate does create consciousness-altering changes. I didn't accept the Hindu or Buddhist beliefs, but I would take their technique. And that is wrong, actually. That creates negative karma for me that I need to purify. So I was always meditating and knew about Eastern ideas, but I didn't accept the moral aspect of it – obviously, as a Devil worshipper I didn't believe in compassion for all beings, that everybody is suffering and so you should be kind to them. Not at all. It would be too detailed to explain, but Zeena and I have total, literally in every sense of the world, disenchantment with occultism of every kind. We were involved with the Temple of Set and there isn't anyone involved in the field of the occult that were alive then that we didn't know. I've talked to people who were part of the original Crowley circle. And every level of occultism – it's all bullshit. That's my personal experience. It's not something that leads to anything positive. It doesn't lead to spiritual awareness, it leads to infighting, spitefulness, power games and narcissism. Whatever

Nikolas Schreck in Werewolf Order insignia, 1988. Foto by Gisela Getty

there may be of value to it is diminished by what happens to the people who do it. Whatever value there may be to these people, it became clear to us in the early Nineties that organised occultists – and Zeena understood this before I did – are all phonies and bullshit artists. And I think people are in a lot of denial about it. They would like to romanticise that there is something good about it. We saw first hand that this doesn't lead anywhere productive. It's just people playing with spiritual symbolism.

Do you think that there is a way that occultism could lead to anything productive, maybe in a way that isn't being explored now?

No, I think even with the best intentions it can't lead to anything productive. If you use a symbol and you don't know exactly what that symbol means and take the spiritual world seriously, you're attracting bad energy. Let's take it away from the Devil. If you wear an amulet of Venus, then you're going to attract sexual and romantic energy, so don't be surprised that that's what your life will be. If you don't have any idea what the Devil really is, it's like inviting a stranger into your house and being surprised that they have their own personality, and their own wishes and desires. This being and these forces connected to it are independent agents. They want to come into the material world and cause trouble. And they do. I don't see any proof that it has led to anything productive. Jack Parsons, who is considered high occultism – look at his life and how it ended. Just the strife and the discord and the arguing between all these groups. I can't see anything positive that comes from it. It's people who look at it from the outside and see the aesthetics of it and the artistic beauty of it, but they're not seeing it from back stage. You could see a magnificent opera and then go back stage and see the actors quibbling with each other. That's what it's like. And I know I can't convince people. I've been behind the scenes of all of these things and I can't see the glamour of it.

You're seeing the wizard behind the curtain.

Exactly. But I don't blame people for doubting me because they haven't seen it.

The in-fighting between Satanic groups is still happening.

That's true of organised religion as well. Every religion has schisms. But it doesn't even get to the point where the religion becomes anything before they start stabbing each other over who is the Great Magus and so on. This produces nothing of any value. Artists fight with each other too, but they do produce creative work. Richard Wagner, to know him as a person he was a complete asshole, but the music is beautiful. But what has Western occultism created that is a positive thing? I can't honestly tell you. When it comes down to it, does it make your life better? Has it increased the measure of human satisfaction? But to come back to your original question: we had come to a dead end in the early Nineties. We'd ended the Werewolf Order's magical ritual – the whole thing was, as I said, not a band but a public ritual. We'd learned what we could learn from it. Like a scientist, we were done with it. Now we have to retreat from all this public spectacle, which we did, completely. We didn't do any interviews, we didn't answer any questions, and we created a lot of problems that way, because we let a lot of nonsense grow up in our wake. Good and bad. But we ignored the world, and we began our own personal spiritual search. What can we make of what we've learned? We rejected completely Western occultism, and both slowly moved into the Hindu left hand path – tantra of the Hindu variety to put it in the simplest way is the real left hand path. That phrase is very misused by Satanists and black magicians. It doesn't mean Satanism. The left hand path is a particular spiritual tradition in tantra. There's the Hindu left hand path and the Buddhist left hand path, which is the Tibetan tantra. That is the form that we eventually went to, but it was a slow learning process of weaning towards a durable spiritual tradition with a lineage that you can prove: this teacher taught that teacher. After all the nonsense and mythifying and bullshit of occultism, with people making up their pedigrees – all of those things are false, fantasy religions. We needed to connect to the real thing. I had also in 1981 started doing Zen meditation, although still wrongly because not for the right reasons. Eventually through meditation – and I speak only personally – I had a meditative experience and saw that the tenets of Buddhism are true. Meditation itself showed me that karma is real. There are consequences to our thoughts, to our actions. We wrote this book **Demons of the Flesh**, which came out almost twenty years ago – that gets into what the left hand path is really all about. Our spiritual experience – not theoretical or intellectual – showed us that this is the truth. We converted to Buddhism. A lot of Westerners say *"I'm a Buddhist"*, but we have taken vows and oaths that come with tantric Buddhism and we follow it very diligently.

Do you see a connecting line between where you were in the 1970s and 80s to where you are now?

Taylor Swift's a clone of Zeena according to the internet. In a world where people really believe that, I don't care what people think any more. But I think within the context of your book, it's useful to say that the common thread is that even as a child I was on a spiritual search. I had metaphysical experiences that told me there were past lives. There are spiritual forces well above the human realm of existence, and I wanted to understand them. The first thing that comes to you is the dark side. When Jesus went to the desert, it was not God who came to him, it was the Devil. When the Buddha was trying to become liberated under the Bodhi tree, it was Mara, which is the Devil of Eastern tradition. But when you are a child or an adolescent or even a rebellious middle aged person, the temptation of the dark side is very attractive. People don't realise, I've been a Buddhist much longer than I was ever involved with any of these other things that I'm known for.

But it's very boring for people. They don't want to know about meditation, it's not exciting.

To use the rock band analogy again, people will always want to talk about the original line up even if the current line up has been together much longer.

True. That's something that I've learned about show business – you better be careful about your first song. If you do a reggae song, you're a reggae band. You can't then decide to be a country and western group. In my musical career too, I've never picked a style to stick with. I've done things in every kind of genre, to the point where people have no idea what I'm doing. But they don't see that. But that's human nature. They take your work and they put a preconceived label on it to try and fit it into their own idea.

Given that I'm here talking to you for **Satan Superstar**, *I'm probably answering my own question, but do you find that the occult still follows you around?*

Oh yeah, every day.

How do you feel about that?

I feel like it's my own fault. I put myself out there. I can't blame anyone. I did these things in a very provocative, over the top, extreme manner. I can hardly be surprised that it had an effect. It was intended to, and it did. But it's like the Sorcerer's Apprentice or Frankenstein's Monster – you do it and it takes on a life of its own. I can live with that and accept it, and I've learned a lesson from it. But there's nothing you can do to change it. And I don't know that I would, because I learned many valuable lessons from it. I was very good friends with Richard Ramirez – we understood each other because we were connected to the same force. I saw it in his eyes. We were united by that. Many people would be appalled to even admit that. It goes much deeper than I can talk about in one interview. So I don't regret it. It was lessons I learned.

In the Buddhist tradition, there's someone that I relate to particularly, in Tibetan Buddhism - Milarepa is a great master, and he was a black magician in Tibet, who used black magic and actually killed people with it and went under the tutelage of another master named Marpa, and renounced black magic. That is my role model and inspiration. I think because I have seen evil and the dark side, I can be a much more effective teacher, because I'm not just talking about it abstractly. And I can speak about it without morality, I'm not wagging my finger at people and telling you to be a good citizen, I'm saying that there are consequences to fucking around with spiritual things that you don't fully understand.

The final thing I wanted to stress – the main reason, if you were a Satanist reading this, to reject it – and I don't care if anyone does or doesn't, I'm not trying to convert people in the same way that I'm a vegan but I don't go out and tell people not to eat meat. It's their business. But from all the research I've done and first hand dealings with this actual being, as crazy as that sounds, I know who the Devil is. And it is not what Satanists or people attracted to occultism think it is. This being is the messenger of Yahweh. Of Jehovah. Like Marlon Brando as Colonel Kurtz in **Apocalypse Now** says to Martin Sheen, Satan is just the errand boy for the supermarket. If these people could detach themselves from their own emotional and aesthetic interest in the symbolism of goats and heavy metal music and whatever they think is attractive about the Satanic milieu, they should know that they are working for the wrong side.

Satan, Lucifer, the Devil is not the adversary of God. This is a very important point if you care about the fine points. The word adversary – Sa-Tan in Hebrew – means he is the attorney for God against humanity. He's like the District Attorney who comes and says *"you haven't been worshipping God enough, I'm here to punish you"*. Or to tempt you – to test you. He's like the KGB saying do you really believe in Marxist Leninism. If you say you don't, he reports back to God. So you shouldn't trust this being if you don't like the Abrahamic religions. If you look deeply into what this being is, he's not what popular culture and Dennis Wheatley and whatever the latest black metal song says. The real thing is an agent of Jehovah, who comes to tempt people and to punish them, as in the story of Job in the Bible. The idea that Lucifer is the rebel angel is a misreading of the actual scriptures. The word 'lightbringer' is also used in the Bible to describe Jesus – in the Catholic version of the Bible, Jesus is referred to as Lucifer. So it's a mistranslation of the star Venus.

I know nobody wants to hear me – especially me – say these things, but I've looked into it and researched it, and it's all myth and hot air and illusion. If you wanted to find the Devil, you would find a servant of Jehovah. So if that's what you are looking for, you would have to consider Satanism to be a sub-sect of Christianity. I'm not saying that to insult people or make them feel like an idiot, I'm just saying think about it seriously before you call yourself this, if you don't know what this is.

THE WITCHES

PULP FICTION FOLK HORROR FROM THE 1980S

DAVID FLINT

"A thread of bright blood trickled across the woman's naked body."

Starting as it meant to go on, the opening line from the first volume of James Darke's eight-volume series of 'adult horror' novels that were published under the umbrella title of **The Witches** sets the scene for a collection of entertainingly sordid pulp horror novels - inspired by films like Michael Reeves' **Witchfinder General** - that are mostly forgotten today, and yet which have the same delirious sense of bad taste and verve that can be found in many of the more beloved paperback atrocities of the 1970s.

Ground out with unseemly haste – all eight books were published between 1983 and 1986 – these novels were a last gasp of the pulp horror and exploitation boom that had run throughout the 1970s, but was now feeling the squeeze as shelf space was reduced and the audience for such stuff was being tempted by the more immediately visceral and visual thrills of home video. The Video Nasty era – and the media-driven backlash against it – also meant that horror - particularly grubby, sex 'n' violence driven horror - was seen as something of a pariah, and there was less chance that branches of WH Smith would find the shelf space for a series of novels that featured scantily-clad glamour models on the covers and were being sold on the basis of explicit sex, graphic violence and torture.

The series was published by Sphere, then in their last days as an independent publisher of books that ranged from the respectable to the disreputable. Sphere had scored big in 1976 when they snapped up the rights to the **Star Wars** novelisation (and the subsequent sequels); they had also published the **Conan the Barbarian** collection and - in their final days - Clive Barker's **Books of Blood**. But Sphere were happy to publish lurid modern exploitation as well. Amusingly, the first couple of novels in **The Witches** series have back page advertisements for the hysterical recovered memory Satanic Panic firestarter **Michelle Remembers** – a inspired move to pitch both books at the same readership, you might think. Sphere was sold in 1985, the year that the final book in **The Witches** series was published, marking a symbolic end to the Golden Age of British pulp fiction.

But if the paperback nasties that Sphere, New English Library and others made their name with were on their last legs, then **The Witches** was an impressive final stand. Imagine, if you would, the plot of **Witchfinder General** strung out across eight novels – admittedly, each just under 150 pages of not exactly tiny type, and so the sort of thing that you could plough through in a couple of hours should that be your want. While the notorious Matthew Hopkins makes an introductory cameo in the first edition, the witchfinding here is effectively a franchise operation run by one Robert Monk, who has seen the profits and pleasures to be had from rolling into a town and being paid to torture confessions from old crones and nubile young hotties, men and women (author Darke cheerfully writing up lecherously explicit sex scenes involving all ages and genders, proving himself not to be an equal opportunities exploiter, at least) in the lawless days of the English Civil War.

With an eye on the probability of new readers skimming through the first few pages before making a purchase, each book begins with a chapter in which Monk and his associates – starting with the three gypsy brothers the Mendozas and the 'slattern' Liza Hall (a cartoonish grotesque with a voracious sexual appetite and a fine line in the torturous rape of victims); later, as characters were killed off, changing in number and character – torture a hapless soul accused of witchcraft. Over the first six novels, Monk is relentlessly pursued – or pursues – former Roundhead soldier John Ferris, who is sworn to vengeance after the witchfinder has killed his parents, a doctor and his wife both falsely accused of witchcraft. Each book allows Ferris a small victory, while keeping Monk alive to allow the story to continue. Along the way, he makes new friends and enemies, has various scrapes with death (not just at the hands of Monk) and finds and loses lovers. It's quite a ride, admittedly one that is sometimes over-stretched as Darke establishes character/pads out the thin narrative.

The series title is a touch disingenuous, but the title **Witchfinder** had already been taken for a two-book series by Brian Ball in 1977, another sexy occult story that pitted a modern day witchfinder/exorcist against the supernatural. In fact, the 'sexy witchfinder'

horror novel dates back to 1967, when Robert Neill's **Witch Bane** – *"witchcraft in Cromwell's England"* – was published, actually pre-dating **Witchfinder General** (though not the historical novel that it was loosely based on) by a year.

In **The Witches**, as with Reeves' film, there is little initially to suggest that the accusations of witchcraft are in any way true, though as the series progresses, some characters – a travelling fortune teller, a pair of gypsy women - do show magical qualities. Admirably though, Darke ensures that his 'genuine' witches are shown to be decent, heroic characters and the villain of the piece remains the cynical opportunist Monk. Or at least, he does until the sixth novel, when – in a sudden and rather jarring switch - the witches become genuine, child-sacrificing nobles and Monk finally meets his doom (in a somewhat weak and unsatisfactory way). This sudden switch signals a change in direction for the series that might have been necessary – there's only so long that you can realistically have the hero chasing the same villain before it becomes tedious – but it somewhat throws the direction off for the last two books, which feel like grafted-on extensions to the main story, as Ferris battles both a coven of witches and the Black Death.

A weak finale aside, this series suggests that Darke was an author to watch – a new talent emerging with a series of pulpy exploitation novels who could either progress to bigger and better things, or establish a career – like Guy N. Smith before him – as a cult writer, cranking out a string of outrageous horror novels if only the timing hadn't been against him. But James Darke is not a household name among horror fans, and his career doesn't exist beyond these novels.

There is a good reason for that. James Darke does not exist.

The pulp writers of the 1970s – the hacks (in the best, most respectful meaning of the word) who ground out book after book across a variety of genres, depending on what was selling at the time – tended to use a variety of pseudonyms for their work, and James Darke was in fact Laurence James. James had been an editor at New English Library in 1970 – the year that the first **Skinhead** novel by Richard Allen (real name James Moffatt) was published, and the whole youth cult fiction cycle really kicked into gear in the UK. As Mick Norman, James wrote a quartet of **Hell's Angels** novels that remain much admired by fans of the genre. He took over the **Confessions...** novels from Timothy Lea (real name Christopher Wood), writing as Jonathan May. Under the name Mary Fraser, he wrote romances. And under his own name, he authored a number of science fiction stories, before ending his career in the 1990s as James Axler, author of the **Darklands** series (which, in a move that he doubtless would have approved of, continued after his death with other writers using the Axler name). He was, clearly, a man who could turn his hand to anything.

James cunningly kept his different pseudonyms separate – each name had his or her own literary field to plough. But inevitably, there was a certain similarity of style throughout his books – at least those that were cranked out within a couple of weeks. He would typically write a novel a month – sometimes more – and had authored 160 novels by the time of his death in 2000. He was only 56, and so if cancer hadn't taken him and the market hadn't dwindled, it's easy to believe that he might have comfortably doubled that number. It's claimed that his work has sold over 12 million copies, though of course most people – even those who read his books voraciously in the 1970s and 1980s – have probably never heard of him.

It's probably fair to say that **The Witches** is not his best loved work. That it ran for eight volumes is impressive, admittedly, at a time when the market for such stuff was drying up, but these are not books that are especially sought after on the collectors market, and no one seems to be lining up to reprint them. That's a pity – while not his finest writing by some way, they deserve to be better remembered than they are. How interested James was in the project is open to debate, but that hardly matters – while he was clearly grinding out books of all descriptions for financial reasons rather than artistic ones, almost all the James pulps have a verve and a page-turning compulsiveness that suggests a writer who at the very least was entertained by what he was doing. The **Hell's Angels** novels have a gut-punch attitude and a driving sense of action that is infectious. His **Confessions...** novels are chirpy, amusing and lacking the mean-spirited style of the Timothy Lea stories. Both series rise above their apparent limitations. **The Witches** also manages to rise above its limitations, but it takes the series a few volumes to eventually reach the point where the reader starts to think that this is something more than just a salacious pot-boiler (not that there's anything wrong with that, of course).

The books clearly sold enough to last for as long as they did – the first three books were published almost back-to-back in 1983, and volume three, **The Torture**, claims to be *"the terrifying climax to the witchfinder's reign of terror"*, suggesting that the series might have remained a trilogy is sales hadn't warranted its continuation the next year – though James, smartly, offers no such climax in the story, with Monk surviving to carry on his atrocities, and Ferris still thirsting for vengeance. Indeed, the 1984 fourth book, **The Escape**, where Monk apparently meets his fate at the hand of a camp of gypsies while Ferris' former lover turned witchfinder's mistress and torturer Mary Villers is dispatched in a gory, if rather blunt manner, feels like the natural conclusion to the story.

When the series returned in 1985 with **The Meeting** - with Ferris and his new gypsy wife Sarah having travelled to 'the New World' and now in Virginia where, rather unfortunately, a very much alive Monk also turns up – it feels like the start of a second adventure, taking place over a year after the last and essentially rebooting the action with a new set of supporting characters, a fresh location and a new thirst for vengeance from Ferris after the now-mutilated Monk kills his wife and unborn child. By book six, **The Killing**, both Monk and Ferris are back in England, and it is here where the story switches; Monk finally meets his end and the coven of genuine Satanists appear, managing – in a particularly sordid sex scene where our previously noble hero becomes a vengeful rapist at one point – to make an enemy of the increasingly disturbed and ruthless Ferris. This new set of enemies continue the story over the last two books, with the final volume – **The Plague** – managing to throw Arabic Satanists and the bubonic plague into the mix, as Ferris and his albino companion Andrew Turlough track down the former soldier's new mortal enemies for a final reckoning. The story ends with hints that witchfinder Monk might have a brother who is carry on in the family trade, thus opening the door for further instalments should they have been required. But Sphere's new owners seemed disinterested in salacious horror, and so Ferris was left to live the rest of his life in peace.

While not what you might call great literature, **The Witches** novels are solid examples of pulp fiction, deftly mixing horror, splatter, sex and action – if **Witchfinder General** has the feel of a British western, then that is ramped up here, and the swashbuckling and battle scenes are certainly as significant as the more outrageous content. The writing is tight and efficient, and James provides more of a narrative than you might expect, given the 'adult horror' tag and the fact that he is essentially stretching the story to breaking point. There's the odd turn of phrase, some amusingly florid descriptions during the frequent sex scenes (*"Mary's passion for making the beast with two backs between the blankets almost frightened him"*), entertaining attempts at period language ('swiving' in place of fucking, time periods like 'sennight', references to hedgepigs and the like), and some humorous references for those inclined to find them – three characters called Hawks, Ford and Hathaway in the first book, and a 'Captain Cimino' of the ship *Gate of Heaven*. At one point in book five, **The Meeting**, a character even starts quoting lines from The Beatles' **Let It Be**. Clearly, James is having fun with these novels, regardless of how much of a hack job they might seem to be.

Ultimately, it's the simple sense of professionalism that comes from having written so many books that ensures these stories are eminently readable. And in truth, the books get better as they go along – whether that is down to the author getting more into his story or the reader being pulled into the developing narrative arc is hard to tell – it's possibly a combination of the two. While it's hard to imagine that many people would have been so invested in the story to keep buying the novels over a three year period, when read as one long tale – rather like binging on a TV box set – the novels never become dull, even if there is obvious padding and repetition throughout and things rather loose direction with the final two books. You find yourself pulled into Ferris's world and at times, James manages to bring a real sense of tragedy and passion to the stories. When Monk kills his adversary's pregnant bride Sarah in **The Meeting**, it's a surprisingly powerful moment, if not exactly unexpected given the fate of many of our hero's friends and loved ones. Ferris is not, it must be said, a lucky man.

These books were hyped as 'a Sphere adult series' – which of course translates as 'erotic' to most readers, a suggestion reinforced by the low rent glamour girl photo covers that are rather more basic and unimpressive than the paintings that graced the covers of many a Seventies horror pulp, while lacking the nudity that was commonplace on book covers in the previous decade but was now of a legally questionable nature thanks to the Tory government's Indecent Displays Act passed a couple of years earlier. And the sex scenes are certainly explicit and extravagant enough (*"it is so hard, my hero…*

I want to feel it between my legs. Deep within me, driving me to the bed like a mighty hammer of Thor"). But what's really notable about this series is the almost gleeful lack of restraint when it comes to the violence and grotesquery. This is where the books really come alive and throw all sense of human decency and good taste aside. Many of the sex scenes are deliberately gross, involving genuinely revolting sounding characters that it's hard imagining even the most eagerly onanistic reader gaining satisfaction from, and the violence is lovingly described. The description of 'the black' Brutus York's burning at the stake in **The Trial**, for example, is spectacular in its vivid detail, with startling descriptions of seared flesh, burnt genitals and collapsing bowels. Lack of even the slightest human decency does not diminish as the series progresses – in fact, the sixth book has quite the most outrageous opening chapter you could ever hope for, with Monk's new female assistants – Beth and Sheba! – anally fisting a hapless male victim (*"'you ride his cock' cackled Sheba, her chins wobbling with obscene merriment. 'I'll ride his tongue for a pommel. Settle on his witch's lips for a fine saddle'"*) and torturing a dog, while the final book reaches new heights – or depths, depending on your point of view – of offensiveness, with a priapic dwarf sodomising a priest before carrying out a re-enactment of Christ's crucifixion on the unfortunate fellow, all loving described in minute detail. Subtle it is not.

Fans of British pulp classics like James Herbert's **The Fog** or just about anything by Guy N. Smith will be thrilled by this sheer lack of restraint. Indeed, we have to assume that the 'adult' label on the cover was as much due to the censorial attitudes of the era as to the content, which is certainly no more graphic in terms of sex or violence than those earlier pulps that were keenly gobbled up by schoolboys (it's said that most second-hand copies of Herbert's **The Fog** would automatically fall open at the most explicit sex scenes, those being the most eagerly read and re-read by teenagers). By the early Eighties, with the Video Nasty hysteria in full flow, it was probably circumspect to at least make a token gesture towards preventing such tales from being sold to children.

This censorial atmosphere probably made **The Witches** a harder sell than it might have been in the past, and the declining market and shrinking outlets for deliriously trashy pulp fiction ensured that there would be no more adventures for Ferris, even if James had felt inclined to continue. The books quickly faded from memory and are now a minor footnote in the history of British pulp writing – a fifteen year period of fevered imagination and outrageousness that seems barely imaginable today. While some publishers have tried to revive the spirit of the British pulps over the years – Creation Books published a collection of James' **Hells Angels** novels in the 1990s, while others have reprinted the **Skinhead** books or attempted to recapture the thrills of that era with new novels that emphasise youth cults, violence and 'torn from today's headlines' sensationalism – none have really succeeded, and the outlets for such books tend to be mail order and specialist book shops… far removed from the newsagents, high street retailers and chemists where teenagers would eagerly snap up these affordable, accessible and disreputable publications. And the audience for such revivals is strictly a nostalgic one. The kids, unfortunately, have moved on.

"The Devil's Train will take you
To a land of groans and pain
You'll spend your days in sorrow
If you ride that Devil's Train"
Hank Williams – **The Devil's Train**

Warnings and parables, but nothing that would cause you to believe that there was a genuine fear of evil incarnate, a fact compounded by the likes of Hank's own grandson, Hank Williams III, whose metal/country outrages have made more of a cartoon of the Devil than any twanging and twee couplets. Yet, there is one country album that drives home the existence of the Devil as clearly as any black metal act ever did.

The Louvin Brothers' **Satan is Real** gives any Deicide album a run for its money in terms of Devil name-checks. No Ramones or Righteous fripperies at play, the Louvin Brothers really were siblings, though their given names were, magnificently, Ira and Charlie Loudermilk, the latter being born in 1927 and the younger by three years. Two of seven brothers born into a household nestled unassumingly in the small city of Henagar in North Eastern Alabama, their upbringing was a Southern cliché, right down to the Depression-era timing.

Working on the family cotton farm, their future was somewhere between bleak and broken, leading to an exhausted Ira reaching a moment of revelation. *"We ain't got no choice, Charlie. You know that,"* Charlie recalled in his autobiography, *"No choice about whether or not we make it as singers; I can't do this for the rest of my life."*

Regularly beaten by their father, Ira (who received the worst of it) and Charlie fell back on the songs taught to them by their mother, fiercely religious songs sung in a style developed over the previous 150 years. The Sacred Harp style involved no instruments but, instead, the entwined harmonies of a gathering's voices. More particularly, and in common with some Medieval styles of choral work, they leaned heavily on 'unwritten incidentals' – inflections and peculiarities which would not be written down on any sheet music but would come with the musician or singer themselves as part of their inherited understanding. Ira and Charlie would be taught songs by their mother that were taught to her by her mother and so on ever after – the emphasis and delivery of songs was understood as part of the family's very essence, but was not to be found as printed lore. They sang it at they had it sung to them – always pure voices, shorn of vibrato or flourishes and with emphasis on harmony and Godly teachings.

They began to perform in earnest in their early twenties, now renamed as the Louvin Brothers, fleshing out their secular gospel sound with a mandolin or guitar. It wasn't long before Ira began to go off the rails – hitting the drink to fade the memories of his harsh upbringing, he regularly got into fights with both fellow performers and audience members. Even well-wishers were victim to his inebriated caustic tongue, Elvis Presley, though a huge fan of their music and a support act for them early in his career, vowed never to perform one of their songs after receiving a suitably foul-mouthed assault from Ira – it was a move which potentially cost the brothers millions of dollars in royalties.

Despite Ira's Mr Hyde personae becoming ever more the more dominant side on show, the brothers were highly regarded by the country fraternity, their pious, gospel songs marrying with their rounded tones to create an entirely unintentionally sinister experience. Their recoding output began in earnest at the start of the 1950s, an early B-side attracting passing attention more due to a Chet Atkins appearance than anything else. Another single was an early sign that their preaching extended beyond mere praise of God to overt declaration of the doom that would befall us if not.

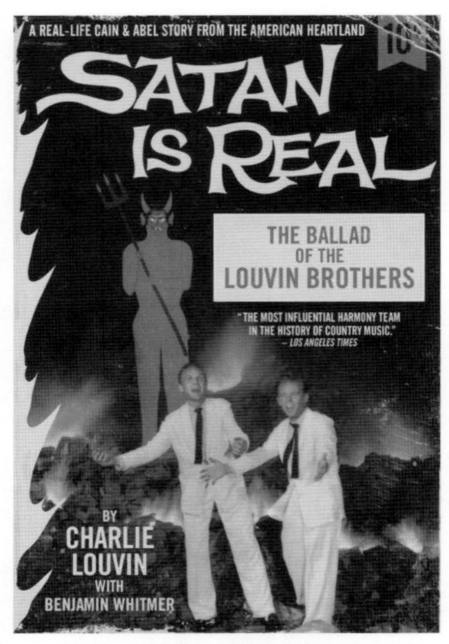

The double-header of **The Great Atomic Power** and **Insured Beyond the Grave** saw warnings of both the physical (*"A terrible explosion will ring down upon our land/Bringing horror and destruction, blotting out the works of man"*) and the spiritual (*"Insured beyond the grave, protection on your soul /When this old house you're living in, the hand of death will close"*). Neither song ended with peals of laughter, suffice to say. Further singles nodded politely at success but by the release of the three-part EP, **Tragic Songs of Life**, in 1955, they had joined the Grand Ole Opry, where they would stay until the end of their joint careers.

By the turn of the decade, they were firmly part of Capitol Records' roster, with a steady release of records which, though now creeping away a little from their gospel roots, only toyed with bluegrass, pop, and more contemporary sounds. The brothers were now so in tune with each other that the higher-range of notes usually covered by Ira was effortlessly exchanged with the lower tones of Charlie; it becoming impossible to tell which part was being performed by which brother. It was at the height of their powers then that they released one of the oddest albums in the whole of country music's history – perhaps even music as a whole

Satan is Real, recorded in seven days in 1958 and released on November 16th 1959, is the absolute summit of their fire and brimstone recordings, an album so completely out of step with the rock 'n' roll revolution - and, indeed, the fact that the 19th Century had ended - as to make one wonder exactly who at Capitol was keeping an eye on them.

The cover itself is extraordinary. Featuring the brothers decked out in heavenly white suits and square-ended black ties, there's a sense that you've just peeked behind the house pictured in Grant Wood's **American Gothic**. Their strange posture is less religious fervour and more to do with the rainstorm which had just threatened to ruin their pristine outfits. Behind the brothers is a quarry they had filled with car tyres, then set light to, though in case you were still wondering if this was Hell, there's the 12 foot high plywood devil painted by Ira overlooking proceedings.

The songs on the album don't fail to deliver, featuring some of their most intoxicating warnings of an eternity in the fiery depths lest you surrender your life to God. Launching the album with the title track, you're immediately assured that Satan is indeed real and the chances of avoiding him slight. Even songs like **The Christian Life** (later covered by The Byrds) have a strangely dark quality, the mandolin and freakishly pure voice escaping a two-branched throat suggesting a life controlled by other forces is the best you can expect. Now something of a standard, their reading of **The Kneeling Drunkard's Plea** has never been matched for its churchy doom – so angelic are the Louvin's voices that they sound like they're mocking the Drunkard rather than offering any comfort.

The album takes delight in the inevitability of death; a mournful, creaking church organ appearing on many of the songs, a wheezing last breath on **He Can Be Found**, though even the jauntiest of their numbers, **The Drunkard's Doom**, seems almost sarcastic considering Ira's daily booze intake. Later covered by Emmylou Harris, **Satan's Jeweled Crown** is, appropriately, a majestic battlefield pitting God against Satan, a matter-of-fact duel which sees you wearing the Devil's crown from the off, demanding you make an effort to rid yourself of it the only way possible.

When I lived my life, so reckless and evil
Drinking and running around
The things I would do were the will of the devil
I was giving my soul for Satan's jeweled crown

In fact, after the album's release, the drinking and running around only got more prolific. By 1963, Charlie could stand Ira's violent outbursts no longer and he dissolved their partnership, leaving his brother to pursue his destructive lifestyle. Later that year, Ira attempted to kill his (third) wife by strangling her with a telephone cord – she responded impressively, shooting him six times in the chest, though failing to finish him off. In fact, it was two years later, with his fourth wife, that Ira was killed, drunk at the wheel of his car with a warrant for his arrest hanging over him. Ironically, it was whilst they were static in traffic that another drunk driver hit them head-on, killing both of them instantly.

The legacy of the Louvin Brothers mirrors that of many of country music's acts who have dug a little deeper into the pit. Their vocal harmonies would influence everyone from The Everly Brothers to the Beatles; their lyrics would echo in the work of Nick Cave and Beck; but the unspoken undercurrent declaring the ever-present horned god of the underworld would remain a particularly country and western trope. True believers of both an upstairs and a downstairs, with real life tales wrapped up in myths, salvation and damnation, it was and remains a mystery as to where Satan and country music start their relationship and end it.

SOME VERY BRITISH SATANISTS

AN INTERVIEW WITH JOHN WAIT FROM THE CHURCH OF RATIONAL SATANISM

SARAH APPLETON

Satanism would all too often be considered a preoccupation of the most devilish reprobates, sacrificing virgins, worshipping demented goats and generally being evil and frightening people. However, this widespread misconception distracts from the real Satanists' core beliefs and less-than-wayward ways. **The Satanic Bible** was written by Anton LeVay in 1969 and comprises of four books: *The Book of Satan*, *The Book of Lucifer*, *The Book of Belial* and *The Book of Leviathan*. **The Satanic Bible** is followed by Satanists to this day, although some revellers have moved into a new realm of Satanism. The rational kind.

The Church of Rational Satanism was formed in the UK in 2009 by Lee Banks, a 36-year-old from Wolverhampton. Banks had a stroke in 2005, which opened his eyes to a new direction for his 'Satanic' views and led him down the path to creating a 'rational' Church of Satan, reaching out to members across the country and even around the globe.

John Wait is the Devon and Cornwall representative for the church, and we investigated what it was all about in the following interview:

First of all, can you tell us exactly what you're about and give us some context? What is the CoRS and the core beliefs held?

Rational Satanism is one of the most adaptable and progressive philosophical systems out there that all can connect to. It holds onto logic and rationality, being able to see past delusional doctrines and religious propaganda and harness the 'self' to our personal advantage. We do not deny humanity's need for gods, but we keep it rational and internalise one instead of worshiping an external being.

How did the Church of Rational Satanism come about?

I think it was born of Lee Banks' dissatisfaction at the direction Satanism was taking at the time. With the Satanic Panic over and LaVey dead, it was a time of malaise and discontent. Following a stroke at the age of twenty-five, Banks decided to put down his ideas onto paper and used it as a tool to aid his recovery.

Are you connected with the founder Lee Banks? How does he feature within the CoRS?

Sadly yes, we talk every day, sometimes all day. It's distressing and I should really get a life. He'll be grinning at the thought of me having to blow smoke up his ass here, but he's a truly unique individual. He has an ability to apply inspiration in a way I've never seen anyone else come close to. He's also incredibly down-to-earth and shuns any type of hierarchy outside which is necessary to run the organisation on a day to day basis.

How do your practices differ from that of the Church of Satan itself?

I guess we're based on LaVeyian Satanism but with added concepts. A more modern approach; less of the carnal - a product of the Sixties - more self-empowerment through personal development and awareness.

So do you reject Anton LaVey's ideas about Satanism, or do you follow a similar way of thinking? And do you follow his Satanic Bible?

I don't reject it, I also don't follow him. He had ideas that resonate within me, but he was a product of his time and the world has moved on. Rational Satanism uses his ideas as a platform to build from with new modern concepts that move the focus toward self attainment. I respect him and his concepts and the way he projected them, but also he was very much a real fallible person. I also believe he would turn in his grave at the idea he should be followed.

The website talks about Satan as in the mirror when you look at yourself, do you believe Satan is in everybody?

No. Satan represents a quality that I personally feel is a basic requirement. The adversarial; the critically aware, self-responsible individual.

Do you believe in a Satan/Devil figure who lives in Hell? Do you believe in a Heaven or a Hell?

No. However CoRS doesn't dogmatically require adherence in any way, so what you believe is up to you. We provide the tools to become a better person, so these questions are only my subjective interpretation of my reality not those of all members. It is up to the individual to fashion their own 'Model Dependant Reality'.

How does God, or people's perception of God, come into your rational Satanic beliefs? Do you believe in a God/deity of some sort as an opposition to Satan? Is Satan, God?

No I don't personally. For me it's about utilising an archetype, or communicating a personal ideal. Satan represents something to me. Lucifer represents something different but they are, to me, two sides of the same coin. There's so much historical and literary background as to why we use Satan as an archetype that gives far better insight than

I can here. We view these characters as archetypes with traits we find admirable, advantageous or desirable. I'm essentially an atheist. We might refer to the attainment of the godhead through the eight cognitive realms but that's not to say we desire to be omniscient beings. We aspire to be the best we can be. Many members are shedding religious dogma from previously inculcated lifestyles.

Your motto is 'Satan regnat, et virtus rationi interius' or 'Satan reigns to reason and the power of the inner'. What does this mean to you personally?

I know it means a lot to Lee. The Motto was created in that time of physical and mental hardship after his stroke. So I think some of that has rubbed off on me, it means a lot to me because it means a lot to him and also because it describes succinctly the essence of Satanic self-responsibility.

Why do you think that being a Satanist is often linked with being a 'bad' person?

Ignorance I guess. The traditional interpretation of Satan is evil, but with a little thought it's clear that biblically God was the aggressor in most fables. People on the whole believe what they want to believe or indeed told to believe. If you think a Satanist is automatically a bad person you're ignorant. However if you think all Satanists are good people you're equally so, and know nothing about human nature.

I think Satan is and always will be the scapegoat of the self righteous. And let's be honest - if it was a problem we'd choose another name, but it eloquently describes my personality type and communicates that effectively. The way I see it, there are three types of people.

1. Those that fear it - I'm not really interested in discussing it with them, I'm not out to convert anyone and unless challenged, see no reason for them to know my path.

2. Those that are genuinely curious - I'm more than happy to discuss concepts, and basic philosophy and why I think the Satanist is actually a morally superior member of society.

3. Those that resonate with Satanism - Guiding these folk onto the beginnings of their path is always satisfying.

What services and help do you offer to members of the Church of Rational Satanism?

CoRS is a group of friends, like minded in a way but also strongly individual with varied and diverse paths, careers and outlooks. Members benefit from our collective experiences, willingness to share them and the many sub support groups we have. For example, parenting and mental health groups where support and a non judgmental atmosphere is encouraged in full confidence.

What is your daily routine with regards to being a Rational Satanist? Do you do anything particularly interesting?

My daily routine is much the same as any other husband and father who works full time. I don't drink or smoke but try to enjoy life as much as I can, as I believe this is the only life I'll have. Satanism is who I am not what I do.

The website talks of 90% logical thinking and 10% fantasy and psychodrama. Can you tell us much about the 10%? What do you do? Do you take part in rituals often? What do these rituals consist of?

Some of the members are very much into the 10% in a classical sense, with rituals etc. Me, not so much, but that's not to say I don't enjoy types of decompression. For some that's utilising ritual in a decompressed state to help focus the will. A therapeutic, cathartic use of the senses and imagination in an appropriate setting to achieve wellbeing. The percentage or fraction is moveable and entirely up to the individual. Some might like to immerse themselves in the spiritual more so they'd up their lower fraction.

Can you explain more about the 90% thinking?

This is about acknowledging that the majority of our time is spent performing mundane tasks, working and other everyday things that are necessary. As the lower fraction is adjustable so will the higher. If they switch you may want to re-evaluate your mental state and progression in life.

Is the church based on similar thinking to other religions such as Catholicism that relies on fearing God? Do you fear Satan, is that why the philosophy involves being honest and well behaved?

The archetypes are drawn from religions as they're already communicable attributes. I don't fear what doesn't exist. I embrace an interpretation of his character I don't acknowledge a real being only the idea. My morality comes from being an educated well-rounded individual, not from some archaic moral code with political and patriarchal agendas.

What does being a Rational Satanist bring to your life?

It's who I am, so everything I guess. In my position I'm incredibly proud of where we are as an organisation and the quality of its members. I enjoy contributing and learning every day. From the books to the university tours and the many original concepts it's a great time to be a Rational Satanist in a world that is largely floundering.

What is Satanic S Theory mentioned in the fourth book?

It's a psychological tool used to form your model dependant reality. It's probably too intricate a concept to explain in detail properly on this platform.
There is talk of an S-type personality. How would one know if they had this type of personality themselves? Also what does this directly mean in relation to Rational Satanism?

Quite often it's pointed out to you, sometimes the chance discovering of Satanic literature resonates within you. Essentially, and some still argue this, we are born not made. The S-Type personality denotes the requisite markers of the Satanist.

Do you think there is something uniquely British about the idea of Rational Satanism? If so, what do you think the differences are?

I think our down-to-earth, humorous and non hierarchical ways are very British. But we are well renowned globally and have members from all over the world. It's easier with our focus on the self to incorporate other cultures into our concepts as the systems developed can be as easily based on other histories and aesthetics if needed.

What is the Satanic third side, mentioned in one of your Facebook live videos?

Basically a critical view of the world that seeks to find the closest thing to a personal truth among the conflicting and biased information streams. It describes an ability to see through bullshit essentially and see the machinations of the world for what they are without venturing down rabbit holes or wearing tin foil hats.

Lastly, would you consider yourself a reprobate?

I would consider myself highly principled but I'll concede to the Calvinist definition and accept I'm a sinner to some!

SATAN SUPERSTAR - A PERSONAL VIEW

BILLY CHAINSAW

To me, Satan doesn't represent evil.

Satan symbolizes a force of freedom, a force of fun, the great prankster.

I don't believe Satan's doing all this evil, it's man who does the evil.

Photo: Manko Sebastian

'Satan Superstar - A Personal View' curated by Billy Chainsaw.

FROM WITCHCRAFT TO CHRIST

DOREEN IRVINE AND THE BIRTH OF THE BRITISH SATANIC PANIC

DAVID FLINT

"I managed to get away with the biggest lies. No one doubted them in the least. In fact, I often felt that if I were to tell the truth, no one would believe it. Lies were more readily accepted."
Doreen Irvine, **From Witchcraft to Christ** p.106

The Reverend Arthur Neil's introduction to Doreen Irvine's 1973 'true life story' **From Witchcraft to Christ** calls her account of a life of Satanism, witchcraft and Christian salvation *"incredible"* - and indeed, it is beyond the bounds of sensible credibility. Over 188 pages, the book tells a story that reads like a collision of Dennis Wheatley, the pop occult documentaries of the early 1970s, Catherine Cookson's Victorian squalor stories and holy rolling propaganda. It's the sort of hysterical, badly written nonsense that ought to have been laughed out of print and consigned to the dustbin of Christian publishing history. Instead, the book became an instant best seller, and helped pave the way for the Satanic Panic of the next decade - and it continues to be a key text for both fundamentalist Christian extremists and conspiracy theorists to this day.

Irvine's book was part of a publishing boom that proved popular in the 1970s, as traditional religious belief went into decline and the believers who kept the faith became ever more devout in the face of a growing interest in occultism, paganism and New Age religion, as well as the wider 'permissive society'. Religious publishers did a roaring trade in books that purported to tell the story of lost sheep brought back to the flock, whether it was 'crime to Christ' tales like **The Cross and the Switchblade**, or books like this, which claimed to be the story of a Satanic witch who was saved from her dreadful, sinful life by the love of Christ and His followers. As with many of these books, **From Witchcraft to Christ** is a knowing, melodramatic tale that only those already primed to believe could ever take seriously, and delivers just enough sinful sensation to give moralising readers a secret thrill.

The book opens in 1939, as war breaks out. Irvine is leading a life of Dickensian squalor in the East End of London. There is some hilariously unlikely poverty porn at play here – as well as a table cloth made of newspapers, Irvine also had a bed that *"wasn't a bed at all, only a makeshift pile of dirty coats on the floor"* (of course they *would* be dirty!). Dad is a drunken sot and wife beater, of course, while mum is too proud to as for credit at the local shop when her money runs out (though not *so* proud that she won't send her small daughter down with a begging note).Eventually, when Dad gets a new 'fancy woman', Doreen's mum tries suicide and then leaves the family. At thirteen, the worldly-wise Doreen runs away to London, where she is picked up by a man on the street – but fear not reader, he's a kindly sort who takes her home to his mother. The market for child abuse memoirs hadn't been developed yet.

Much of Irvine's book, even before she gets to the Satanism and witchcraft, beggars belief and reads like cheap fiction. Doreen is the clichéd Cockney urchin – a naughty but essentially caring and decent kid, given to cheeky comments that no child would ever say (*"oh I see now, yer in the club"*). Her time as a fourteen-year-old maid is frankly unbelievable – anyone as mouthy and incompetent as her would have been fired in days, not allowed to stay for nine months. And her descriptions of her time as a prostitute are awash with cliché – *"women of twilight"* and *"the most shameful profession"* are used in one sentence, while shortly afterwards, she actually refers to her sex worker friends as having *"hearts of gold"*.

Doreen becomes a stripper soon after becoming a prostitute, which means that she would've been around fifteen or sixteen – which places the time in the late 1940s. But there were no strip clubs in Soho in the 1940s. Even the Windmill Theatre was still restricted to non-moving nude tableaus. Perhaps a decade had gone by between the two career moves – like many books of this sort, the story is tellingly vague about dates, for reasons that I'll discuss shortly. The most likely scenario is that Irvine's story is entirely fictional, even at this point. Certainly, 'Daring Diana' – the name she allegedly stripped under – doesn't crop up in any strip club advertising or records, despite her alleged fame.

Everything in the book sounds like it has been lifted from pulp novels or movies. Her immediate addiction to heroin – mere weeks after her first 'reefer' - smacks (no pun intended) of hysterical drug fiction. Even the terminology is lifted from bad drug movies. Similarly, her descriptions of the Satanic cult seem to be dragged from the fevered fantasies of Christians. Her initiation into the Satanic cult – which is a top secret organisation, yet manages to hold meetings in a dedicated Satanic Temple in the centre of London where several hundred people (and, it seems, whichever unvetted guests they choose to bring along) gather, something that you might think couldn't go unnoticed – is laughably easy, and before you know it (again, no time scale is given), she is the lover of 'the chief Satanist'. That's the only name he is given throughout the book, and sounds like the sort of thing a ten year old might invent – what's wrong with High Priest? Had Irvine's researches not introduced her to that title?

The chief Satanist is laughably dedicated to the sort of evil that would only scandalise the most repressed religious believers, and the rules of Satanism are a hilarious collection of theist, anti-Christian nonsense, including "*all must love, honour and obey without question the chief Satanist*" and "*prayers to Lucifer must be made daily*". There's also a rule that states that anyone arriving late to the temple will be whipped, suggesting a devotion to the rigid discipline that might make sense to a Christian making up a Satanic cult, but hardly fits with the hedonistic, evil-worshipping cult that Irvine wants us to believe in.

The descriptions of the Satanic rites are a heady mix of Wheatley, horror movies and, frankly, the sort of lurid fantasies that many Christians seem to have about Devil worshippers. They are described with just enough detail – hints about sex orgies, homosexuality and lesbianism, and other things that we are told are too shocking to describe doubtless sent a shiver of judgemental excitement through many a reader. Irvine is in no doubt as to the seriousness of it all – this isn't symbolic evil, but the real thing, with Lucifer actually manifesting himself to the worshippers more than once. Yet despite all this, she is still startled to her that her lover is also a Black Witch. Surely a Satanist practicing black magic wouldn't have seemed that ludicrous to her after all she claims to have seen? If the clued-up reader wasn't already convinced that this story was primarily nonsense, this chapter should do the trick. Irvine makes frankly insane claims - that she could levitate five feet in the air, aided by demons, walk through bonfires and make herself invisible. Even the most gullible readers might start to raise an eyebrow at this point.

In no time at all, Irvine has become the Queen of the Black Witches, crowned at a ceremony on Dartmoor where, again, over a thousand witches from around the world gather for open-air Bacchanalian orgies without anyone else noticing. Spooky! Why Irvine would be hailed as the Queen is anyone's guess – but doubtless her story would be less dramatic if she had simply been a mid-ranking witch and C-list Satanist. Yet after a year, she has stepped down from her position, split with the chief Satanist – though she's still a follower of Lucifer - and is back as a common prostitute, scrabbling for money. So much for the power granted by Satan to his followers.

Readers searching for salacious stories of naked witches and sexually charged Satanists might feel a bit short-changed, as after just two chapters dealing with Satanism and witchcraft, Irvine is converted to Christianity – will all the speed and ease, but rather more hallelujahs, as her conversions to Satanism and witchcraft – by visiting evangelical preacher Eric Hutchings, initially with the intention of punching him on the nose, as you do. Hutchings was a real person, who was referred to as 'Britain's Billy Graham' in the early 1960s. There's no doubt that Irvine knew him. Perhaps she really *was* converted by him. But that hardly validates the rest of her story. Even if we believe that she was a sinner who found Christ, the rest of her story is clearly nonsense. And even her salvation is the stuff of fantasy, as she literally lives out the cliché of someone with Satan (an actual, living, breathing Satan) whispering in one ear, Christ in the other as they battle for possession of her soul. Frankly, I doubt either would care that much.

Interestingly, Irvine is dismissive of regular Church of England churches and vicars, in the way that only a true fundamentalist can be. The CoE is a bit too bland for the likes of her - only the fire and brimstone approach of the evangelical church could save her, and by inference, you. Of course. It's hard, after all, to imagine a regular CoE worshipper coming out with a book like this - but evangelicals feel it is their duty to convert at any cost, even if it involves deliberately presenting hysterical nonsense as fact. The hysterical nonsense here includes her lengthy exorcism at the hands of the Reverend Arthur Neil. Neil was a Baptist minister who died in 2013, and his (and Irvine's) malicious influence continues today. One person, on his online obituary page, comments *"I read of your work in Doreen Irvenes book from witchcraft to christ.i was born in Brixham and have sufferd with demons ive searched for you only to find you have passed to the kingdom of Heaven Blessings be to you look down on me Farther and guide me.God Bless you i wish i could have known you we meet in Heaven one day .You are a good good man and a true servant of the Lord"* (spelling and punctuation as originally posted). Perhaps we should be grateful that this person couldn't be 'exorcised' by Neil – hopefully, he received the psychiatric care he clearly needed, though it seems more probable that he might have simply been delivered into the hands of other exorcists.

Exorcism, of course, consists of the mentally ill - or those who dare to be different in conformist, religious communities - being abused by the religiously deranged… often damaged people being further damaged by dangerously unqualified lunatics who, like therapists who dig false memories of Satanic Ritual Abuse from troubled individuals, convince them that the root of their problems lies with demonic possession. The 'saved' often become religious fanatics themselves – after all, they are effectively swapping one life crutch (be it drugs, drink, sex or whatever 'sin' they have clung to) for another. Religion is often more damaging than their previous addictions, if only because the 'saved' like Irvine will invariably become fundamentalists and seek to impose their twisted world view and fantasies on others.

The exorcism - or more accurately, *thirty* exorcisms - of Irvine, which includes encounters with some forty-seven demons, took over seven months. Seven months of being told, without respite, that you are possessed might be seen as a form of abuse in itself – and certainly qualifies as brainwashing. Perhaps we shouldn't be surprised that she came out of it as an evangelical fanatic.

Throughout, there's a frustrating lack of dates in Irvine's story – now and again, she'll mention her age, but not very often. She explains this at the start of the book:

Author's Note: I have of necessity omitted many details of my former life, the people I was associated with at this time and other personal details. I should also point out that the time and sequence of events described in my book covers a very wide period in my life and so it is advisable that they do not be read as a continuing sequence with an assumed time span. The reason for this was to present a readable account of part of my life and to avoid having to relate definite dates and situations with known persons living or dead.

This lack of markers in time is, of course, very convenient. It means that her claims are harder to demolish, for one thing, being so vaguely placed in her life. If she had stated specific dates, named names and so on, researchers might have been able to check her story. More to the point though,if she knew who the chief Satanist was, and where the Satanic Temple was located, surely it was her duty to expose this evil? But let's read that disclaimer again – surely *"avoiding having to relate definite dates and situations with known persons living or dead"* is simply another way of saying *"I don't have to provide any evidence or any facts for my wild claims"*.

In the case of Doreen Irvine, the only real question is: did she actually believe her wild stories – a case of false memory syndrome run rampant, which would be understandable after such abusive treatment from Neil and his followers – or did she just make up the whole thing for the greater Christian good (or, more cynically, personal aggrandisement)? If the latter sounds unlikely, we only have to look at the case of fellow satanic fraudster Mike Warnke, who's book **The Satan Seller** appeared around the same time as Irvine's 'true life story' and shares many of the same traits. Warnke's claims – which included being the High Priest of a satanic cult that kidnapped, murdered and raped before being 'saved' after joining the military - were proven to be entirely false in a 1992 investigation by Christian magazine **Cornerstone**. Warnke had never been a Satanist. His claims were entirely fictional.

But by then, the damage had been done. Books like **The Satan Seller** and **From Witchcraft to Christ** helped pave the way for the Satanic Panic that took hold in the 1980s. It's true that Irvine's book, at least, does not portray a Satanism that is a suburban, child abusing, baby eating cult – that is an idea that would develop primarily from the equally hysterical **Michelle Remembers**, written by Michelle Smith and therapist/husband Lawrence Pazder, a book of 'recovered memory' that set the scene for delusional beliefs that continue today, despite being widely debunked by researchers.

But Irvine would, in fact, become a leading light of the Satanic Panic, and her activities had real world consequences. She appeared in the delirious documentary **Devil Worship: The Rise of Satanism**, produced by evangelical producers Jeremiah Films (makers of such other classics as **AIDS: What You Haven't Been Told**, **The Mormon Dilemma** and **The Evolution Conspiracy**) and, more damagingly, she was part of the Investigation Committee of the Evangelical Alliance, a fanatical group that had the ear of politicians like lay preacher Geoffrey Dickens – a man who conspiracy theorists hold in great esteem due to his alleged dossier on high-ranking paedophiles that was supposedly buried by the government; people are less vocal about his campaigns in the 1980s to have homosexuality recriminalized, the return of hanging, a ban on both witchcraft and teddy bears and general demands for censorship of video nasties and pornography. Irvine's fantasies had managed to seep out into the mainstream, and she was only too willing to adapt them for the current moral panic. You might think that if Satanists had been impregnating 'brood mares', forcing abortions and then eating the foetuses, this would have been something that she would've mentioned in her book - as a case for outlawing occult practices, it would certainly be more compelling than a bunch of people holding theatrical rituals where the only things that are sacrificed are goats, chickens and clothing. But nothing like this is mentioned in her book.

Nevertheless, when the Satanic Panic took hold, she was happy to go along with these new claims, and started to act as a counsellor for people who believed themselves to be former members of satanic cults. These people were almost exclusively disturbed individuals who fell under the influence of evangelical groups. One such person was Caroline Marchant, who claimed an almost textbook series of Satanic atrocities that she had been subjected to – abortion, the ritual murder of her boyfriend, baby sacrifice, forced prostitution and drug addiction. Other than the more sensational, very 1980s elements of her unfinished and unpublished biography, the story feels like it has been lifted wholesale from Irvine's book – some of her writing that has been released is effectively plagiarism.

Marchant's tale of Satanic abuse emerged slowly – in 1985, she joined a Baptist church, and in giving her testimony to the congregation, claimed that she was a rape victim. She didn't mention Satanism at this point. By 1989, she was living in the care of evangelical Christians Peter and Mary Cole, who quickly became frustrated with her and insisted that she confessed the truth about her Satanic past or be cast out. She chose to confess – but by now, she'd already admitted being a Satanic witch in the Irvine tradition; what else could she come up with? She was put in touch with Maureen Davies, who ran the Reachout Trust, an evangelical group that preaches the dangers of the occult, New Age beliefs, Jehovah's Witnesses, Freemasons and **Harry Potter** films. Davies introduced her to solicitor Marshall Ronald, and to him Marchant claimed that that she had knowledge of arms deals involving the IRA and Baader-Meinhof gang, snuff movies and more - suitably upping the ante of Satanic horrors without actually providing *any*

evidence to back up these wild claims. Marchant was then passed on to the Reverend Kevin Logan, the author of **Paganism and the Occult**, who ran a halfway house at St. John's Vicarage near Blackburn for ex-Satanists and witches - and also performed exorcisms. She moved in. We can only imagine what the atmosphere of that place was like.

In February 1990, the morning after sitting up late talking to Logan, Marchant handed an envelope, for the attention of Logan and containing a suicide note, to another house 'guest'. She then went back upstairs and took an overdose of anti-depressants; she died 19 days later in hospital. Davies and Logan immediately claimed that she had been hounded to death by Satanists, a claim shamefully and unquestioningly repeated in a salacious story in the **Sunday Mirror** (both the **Daily** and **Sunday Mirror** have a shameful history of promoting Satanic Panic stories), with the headline *"I SACRIFICED MY BABIES TO SATAN – FROM SEX ORGY TO DEATH AT THE HANDS OF THE DEVIL'S DISCIPLES."* The story was based on second hand accounts of Marchant's claims, taken from her incomplete autobiography and filtered through the belief system of Davies and Logan, and it failed to mention the significant fact that when she died, she was under the 'care' of evangelicals.

Marchant's real story would emerge some time later, and predictably contradicts her claims. There is evidence of a troubled childhood that was, nevertheless, well monitored by the authorities when she entered foster care after her single parent father found looking after two children and working full time to be too much to deal with. She then led a very ordinary life that slowly came to depend on fellow Christians for support after being born-again in 1985. Over the years, as her religious obsession grew, she began to make increasing erratic and conflicting claims about her involvement in Satanism. The dates and details would change as her story developed.

After her death, a second post-mortem – paid for by her father after Ronald persuaded him that it was necessary - found no evidence that she had ever give birth or been sexually abused, and the Satanic symbols that she claimed had been carved on the inside of her vagina were nowhere to be seen. However, the pathologist Michael Green did comment that she had scars *"in sites which are sometimes associated with Satanic practices. They could be self-inflicted"* as well as evidence of anal intercourse. We should note that Green was not an expert in Satanic rituals – he had been told what to look out for as signs of Satanic ritual by Roland. Who of course had met Marchant while she was alive. Friends of Marchant who knew her while she was growing up have a more prosaic, less sensational explanation for the scars – she was, like many an unhappy teen, a self-harmer. Green would later withdraw his comments about her injuries, saying that he had been unduly influenced by Roland. He told David Hebditch and Nick Anning – who wrote a thorough piece about the case for **The Independent on Sunday** in 1990 – that *"pathology is like a computer. If you put garbage in, you get garbage out."* The police bluntly stated that *"we found no evidence to support the allegations. In fact, we found evidence to the contrary."*

In the end, the only real proof that we have about Marchant's involvement with dangerous cults is that she killed herself while under the influence of evangelical fundamentalists – and perhaps that tells us everything that we need to know. Here was a troubled young woman who had delusional fantasies, who was indulged and encouraged by those around her. But where did these delusions come from to begin with? Well, we know that she had read Irvine's book – the first of many books that later included the provenly fraudulent Satanic abuse memoir **Satan's Underground** and **Michelle Remembers** – both sold by The Reachout Trust. Hebditch and Anning interviewed her schoolfriend Sarah Pollard, who started that *"Caroline first claimed to have been involved in Satanism some time after she read a book called **From Witchcraft to Christ**. I loaned her my copy of it while we were on a visit to Cirencester in the summer of 1986. She began to hear voices and believe she was possessed by demons."* In 1987, Marchant met Irvine, when the former Queen of the Black Witches counselled her at the Zion Christian temple, near Bristol. It's not hard to imagine that Irvine encouraged her fantasies. Perhaps – if we are to be kind – she did so in all innocence, genuinely believing that this clearly disturbed and unhappy girl was in need of exorcism rather than psychiatric help. Perhaps there were more cynical and self-serving motives at play.

In the end, it hardly matters – the result was the death of a young woman who needed help and instead found superstitious furtherance of her delusional beliefs. Knowing this, it's hard to simply see Irvine's book – which went through six printings in its first year and is still in print today – as harmless, rather kitsch Christian propaganda. Irvine, who died June 2011 aged 87, made a lot of money from her nonsense, and ruined a lot of lives in the process. Even if her book is not exactly the template for the fictional works of the Satanic Panic that would come a decade later, it's certainly a gateway drug that can be directly traced to the obsessive beliefs that allow lunatics to make insane accusations about Satanic Ritual Abuse to this day. Irvine pushed the door open and encouraged the psychopaths, the unbalanced and the malicious to charge into the room.

References: **From Witchcraft to Christ** - Doreen Irvine, Concordia Press 1973
A Ritual Fabrication – David Hebditch, Nick Anning, The Independent on Sunday, 30.12.1990
Satanic Panic -Kier-La Janisse, Paul Corupe, eds, Spectacular Optical 2015 / FAB Press 2016 (***"Confessions of a Creature Feature Preacher: Or, How I Learned To Stop Worrying About Satanism and Love Mike Warnke"*** by David Canfield)

THEY SOLD THEIR SOULS FOR ROCK 'N' ROLL

A SATANIC ROCK TOP TEN

DARIUS DREWE

So, just what *is* Satanic rock? And what is occult rock? Is it black metal, traditional heavy metal, wyrd folk, ritual blues, industrial music, esoteric exotica and electronica? The truth is it's all of those things and more. Much much more.

Whether one even believes in the supernatural, God, the Devil, Christ or any demonic entity is, to be honest, entirely unimportant in this, the second decade of the 21st century: the principal point is that these influences (by whatever name we know them) have been for years a motivational force in all popular culture, and as such are all around us wherever we go.

From the moment Robert Johnson wrote of having a *"hellhound on his trail"* and meeting the Devil at the Crossroads, the die was cast: even in the 1950s, Sinatra was crooning songs with titles like **Witchcraft** and **That Old Black Magic**. And why not? They do say the Devil has all the best tunes.

Here, then, in chronological order, are ten of what I perceive to be the most important albums in any diabolist's collection- over a fifty year period, from Coven to Ghost via all points in between, they're all there. You may agree or disagree with the choices – and if room allowed, we would certainly be mentioning all the performers that you are probably even now complaining have been omitted. This is just a sampler.

COVEN - Witchcraft Destroys Minds And Reaps Souls (1969)

Was this the first 'truly' Satanic (or at the very least witchcraft-based) rock album? Maybe. Released in 1969, it definitely predates almost everything else in the genre: yet the most distinct difference between Coven and the plethora of similar bands professing such associations was that they were, and to this day still are, the real deal. Lead singer and sole remaining founder member Jinx Dawson has never made any secret of her lineage as a seventh generation witch: thus, the numerous lyrical references to the Craft that pepper virtually every song on this record come from a far less sensationalist and more informed perspective than those adopted by many of her contemporaries. And, as if

that weren't enough in itself, the final track is not a song, but a recorded transcript of a spoken Satanic ritual. Sure, fifty years on, the actual music (bearing more relation to a quaint witchy version of Jefferson Airplane than anything remotely heavy) may seem less threatening than it once did, but in their desert eeriness, tunes like **Coven In Charing Cross**, **Choke, Thirst, Die** and **Wicked Woman** still pack a punch today. Best of all, however, they boasted a bass player called Oz Osborne *and* an opening number entitled **Black Sabbath** a year before the other one was even recorded...

BLACK WIDOW - Sacrifice (1970)

Often mistaken for fellow Midlanders Black Sabbath (and thus partially responsible for the latter's undeserving reputation as a Satanic band) this Leicester-based blues/soul/prog combo were formed out of the ashes of Mod act Pesky Gee! (spelt like that) in 1968, and were probably the first British band to openly declare not just an interest in, but a full-blown allegiance to, the principles of Satanism. Sure, in retrospect, their overtly theatrical, mock-ritual stage act seems a little dated, schmaltzy and faux-Hammeresque now - but in 1970, with such incendiary weapons as **Sacrifice**, **In Ancient Days**, **Will To Power**, **Conjuration** and ultimate occult-rock anthem **Come To The Sabbat** (all featured on this astonishing debut) in their armoury, they were capable inciting ritualistic frenzy in audiences, and more often than not, that's precisely what they did.

After their first split in the mid-Seventies, saxophonist Clive Jones switched to lead vocals, came out as a gay man, and formed the incredible, criminally neglected transgender glam-punk outfit Agony Bag (check out **Rabies Is A Killer** and **Golden Shower Passer**): some three decades later, he finally regrouped a 'new' Black Widow with second guitarist Geoff Griffith and original female vocalist Kay Garrett, but sadly, the deaths of two-thirds of that trio from cancer not long after the release of the admittedly excellent if slightly daft **Sleeping With Demons** album meant it never saw any live action. Nonetheless, at time of writing, we firmly believe there's at least one more chance for Trevor, Garrett, Zoot Taylor and Jim Gannon - that's four originals, should, they be in fine enough fettle - to return the Horned Beast to His rightful place on the rock n roll stage. Join us in our quest for knowledge!

GRAHAM BOND & HOLY MAGICK - Holy Magick (1970)

Though undoubtedly a pioneer in the fields of British jazz, blues and RnB, Graham Bond (1937-74) looks sadly destined - much like Paul Kossoff, Nick Drake or Brian Jones - to forever remain one of 'those' musicians whose reputation hinges more upon their untimely demise than their transcendent

musical ability. Like at least two of the above, the organist's mysterious death has never been satisfactorily explained: granted, the prosaic answer would almost certainly be 'suicide brought on by recurrent depression, alcoholism and drug addiction' (all of which he suffered heavily throughout his short life) but nonetheless, there have been numerous other explanations offered, several of which pertain to his fanatical interest in the occult.

To a certain extent, Bond had always cut an eccentric, sinister figure even before discovering the esoteric arts: his loud apparel, bear-like build and jive-talk hardly made him easy to miss. Somehow, though, despite influencing the likes of Jon Lord and Keith Emerson *and* providing both Ginger Baker and Jack Bruce with their first big breaks, commercial success on the level attained by his protégés always seemed to elude him - so maybe it's no surprise that in his quest for something beyond the mundane, and having already disbanded his best-known combo The Organisation, he and his then-wife Diane formed instead this controversially progressive lineup. Rather than being 'just' a band, the 'dual aim' of Holy Magick was initially to provide a legitimate forum for the keyboardist's idiosyncratic compositions that dwelt comfortably in neither the rock nor the jazz idiom, and bring his newfound beliefs further into public focus: for a while it almost worked too, with several key tracks on this album, tracks such as **Qabalistic Cross**, **Abrahadabra** and **Pentagram Ritual** seeming full of power, conviction and intent. Unfortunately, its rush-released followup **We Put Our Magick On You** (1971) didn't, with the exception of the bouncing title track, possess quite the same urgency, and soon the band were no more: an attempt to form a folk trio called Magus with Carolanne Pegg came to nothing, and soon, Bond was hitting the heavy substances again, spending time in and out of mental hospitals and becoming increasingly dishevelled in his appearance. By the early Seventies, rumours widely abounded that he believed himself to be the illegitimate son of Aleister Crowley (which, as he was born in 1937, would have been possible, though unlikely) and had taken to hanging around the Great Beast's former residence of Boleskine House in Invernesshire, at that time owned by Jimmy Page: by early 1974, however, he was allegedly clean of all substances and adopting a far more positive outlook, something that therefore rendered his sudden and mysterious death under the wheels of a mainline train at Finsbury Park station all the more shocking. An open verdict was recorded, though obviously, many conspiracists have since ascribed their own interpretations: what cannot be denied, however, is the importance of this record, which raised the profile of the Black Arts in rock'n'roll to a hitherto unprecedented level and took the *full* quantum jump - iconic cover included - into the darkness that its precursor **Love Is The Law** had merely dabbled with. Perhaps, on some level, it ultimately proved for its maker to be one jump too far.

COMUS - First Utterance (1971)

Believe it or not, none of the brains behind this shuddering, juddering demonic folk-rock incantation were members of any actual coven or organisation at the time of the album's recording: however, as guitarist, male vocalist and principal songwriter Roger Wootton freely admits, he did become a practitioner of some unspecified discipline later on, and as the material has clearly been written by someone who's at the very least studied their subject matter closely, **First Utterance** definitely qualifies for this list.

Although the true inspiration behind the concept was actually an impossibly-lengthily-titled Milton play, the word 'dark' still doesn't even begin to hint at the lyrical content on offer here: with its references to broken Christians, deadly pathways, hearses, raped virgins, mudded bodies, 'clitoris clutchers' and asylums for the mentally sick, tracks like **Diana**, **The Bite**, **Drip Drip** and **The Prisoner**, are, upon first hearing, utterly terrifying, and it's from these foundations that the Kent sextet's unholy legend has stealthily sprung. To someone who hasn't heard it, it's a hard album to describe: imagine Family trapped in a forest of Sam Raimi-style killer trees, Tyrannosaurus Rex twergled through some form of industrial mangle or The Incredible String Band after ingesting some seriously brown acid, and you might get halfway towards hinting at the extreme mood of this 1971 classic, but even those comparisons don't really do it justice.

Despite being infinitely more diable, the 1974 sequel **To Keep From Crying** is also far poppier and less interesting: however, given all the repeated plaudits heaped upon them by crate-digging arbiters like Lee Dorrian, Mikael Akerfeldt, Steve Wilson, Thurston Moore, Steve Stapleton and David Tibet, they were bound to reform eventually, and in 2011, they did precisely that, releasing the superb **Out Of The Coma** album and playing several astonishing gigs attended by such luminaries as prog-collecting snooker ace Steve Davis. Sadly, because of a number of varying personal differences between members (not to mention geographical distance from one another) all seems to have gone disappointingly quiet since: yet we still hold out hope that one day, they will return again to terrorise us with their wyrd hymns of apocalypse and dismemberment, and who knows, if we turn our cowled heads to the ground and chant loudly backwards, maybe

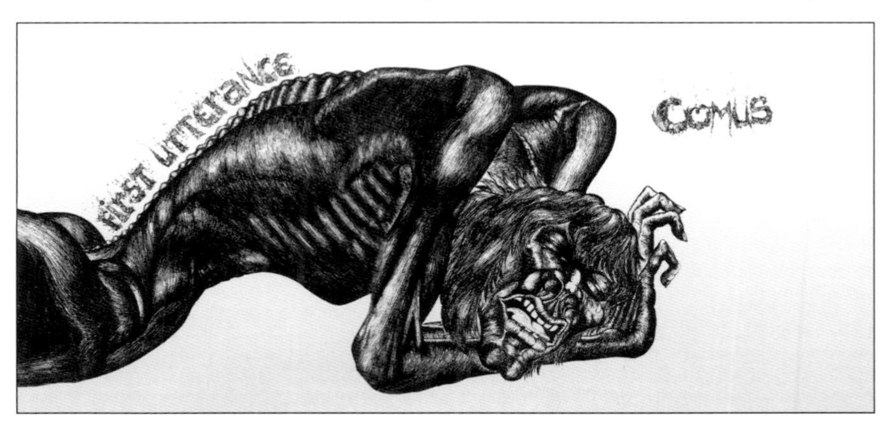

they will. For further reference, seek out Lindsay Shonteff's classic 'groupiesploitation' flick **Permissive** (1972) in which the band appear alongside fellow psych-heads Forever More and Titus Groan: true anoraks, meanwhile, should also hunt down the same director's **Big Zapper**, **Zapper's Blade Of Vengeance** and **Spy Story**, all featuring incidental music by the group.

ZIOR - Every Inch A Man (1972)

Boasting practically the same lineup as infamous mumbo-jumbo-jam band Monument (whose sole release **First Monument** almost out-Arthur Browns Arthur Brown for overblown theatrical doom-rock) and a link or two to the *original* Iron Maiden (no, not that one) Zior were formed in South Essex in 1970.

Reputedly far wilder in a live setting than on record (though I guess we'll never really know) and with a notoriety for indulging in onstage ritual acts, this proto-metal, heavy psych/RnB combo allegedly took their name from the 'Desire Foundation' (the coven to which several members supposedly belonged) and played what might with retrospect be termed a 'library music' or British horror soundtrack take on the pioneering sounds of Cream, Hendrix and Deep Purple: ersatz, basic, organ-driven and not amazingly heavy, but all the more fascinating because of its limitations rather than in spite of them. Standout tracks across their brace of releases include **Love's Desire**, **Angel Of The Highway**, **Quabala** and the incredible **Entrance Of The Devil** - whilst on the Monument LP, one should look to **Dogman**, **Give Me Life** and the spookily minimalistic **Overture For Limp Piano In C** for a hint at the more 'evil' end of their oeuvre.

The full extent of the band's esoteric involvement has never been precisely corroborated one way or the other: however, what I can attest beyond all shadow of a doubt that is that the story printed inside the Audio Archives reissue of First Monument, concerning a *"Satanic debauch after which vocalist Steve Lowe was found hanging from a nearby tree"*, is utter bollocks. For a start, there was no vocalist called Steve Lowe in the band, it was merely a pseudonym invented to avoid contractual infringement from the 'other' band's label: moreover, as one of them recently told me personally online, all former members were still alive and well (one even running a popular Southend nightclub) at the time of said CD's release. In fact, as recently as 2017, a new album was rumoured to be in the pipeline: at time of writing, we're still waiting, but my hopes remain undiminished nonetheless.

VENOM - Black Metal (1982)

Venom

In 1981, almost everyone regarded tthis pioneering Geordie power trio as a joke, but 37 years later, and with an entire genre since having grown in and around appreciation of this album's title, people can see Venom - or, to give them their full names, Cronos, Abbadon and Mantas - as the visionaries they truly were.

Rising from the ashes of several earlier, Tyneside-based metal, prog and even folk bands, Venom (originally a quartet fronted by the ironically named 'Jesus Christ') officially came into being sometime around 1980: yet, it was only after the vocalist's departure in 1981, placing bassist Conrad 'Cronos' Lant into the role of frontman and trimming the group down to its classic triple-pronged format, that the likes of **Sounds** (and, subsequently, the newly inaugurated **Kerrang!**) began to sit up and take notice. Even then, mind you, the country's 'metal press' seemed bemused and befuddled by the Toon Army terrors: perhaps shockingly with hindsight, the description most often used was *"that bunch of buffoons"*. Yet for every Brit that didn't get it, another ten dozen listeners in America, Germany, Sweden and (in particular) Norway understood only too well - and soon, the genres we all came to know and love as Thrash, Speed, Death and (obviously) Black Metal were no longer mere abstracts but facts of life.

Admittedly, they did seem to run out of ideas as quickly as they came up with them: after the confusingly-titled, prog-influenced **At War With Satan** album (only a year before, they'd been *"in league"* with him) a drastic lineup change pushed them into more commercial waters, and it wasn't until the early 00s, by which time a younger audience had assimilated their influence, that they (a) gained the full respect due to them and (b) regrouped in classic mode to record anything of similar value. Always your go-to-guy for a ready quip, Cronos would later admit that the band's Satanic lyrics (as displayed here on such unsubtle slices of bludgeon as **To Hell And Back**, **Don't Burn The Witch**, **Sacrifice**, **Countess Bathory** and **Black Metal** itself) were always written with tongue planted firmly in cheek: yet they still sounded for a while like the most singularly evil thing to have ever picked up an electric guitar, and if the likes of Tom G Warrior, Quorthon, Atilha Czihar and Nocturno Culto didn't crib practically their entire vocal styles from Lant's dirge-like groanings, then I'm a Dutchman.

CURRENT 93 - Dogs Blood Rising
(1984)

Since leaving Psychic TV in 1982, the impossibly prolific, eccentric and (there's no easy way to say this) downright strange David Tibet has more or less made Current 93 his life's work: following the release of the **LashTAL** EP in 1983, over a hundred more albums, mini-albums and EPs - their styles ranging from industrial drone to mediaeval folk to gothy electro to lounge piano to acid rock to doom metal - have ensued, spawning not only one of rock's only truly independent cottage industries but one of the most singular visions in all recorded music. Having first became a fan sometime around the release of 1994's **Lucifer Over London**, I slavishly collected everything released by the group (as well as their 'sister' band, Nurse With Wound) for years afterwards, and **Dogs Blood Rising** remains one of *the* most terrifying of all his early works.

Ironically these days, Tibet - having already chewed his way through Satanism, Thelema, Buddhism and Gnosticism - is now a fully confirmed Roman Catholic, and has almost completely disowned the 'demonic' period of his career: however, he's also allegedly still 'OHO of OTO' so what that says about the Church Of Rome is anyone's guess. Nonetheless, I still defy anyone, regardless of their denomination, to sit in the dark, either alone or accompanied, and listen to the blood-curdling, mucus-dripping reverb dronescapes of **Falling Back In Fields Of Rape**, **Christus Christus** and **From Broken Cross, Locusts** – all literally designed to invoke the Horned One himself, although the first-named, with guest vocals from Crass frontman Steve Ignorant, also touches heavily on the effects of the Holocaust - without feeling extremely perturbed.

MAYHEM - De Mysteriis Dom Sathanas (1994)

Quite possibly *the* most infamous, notorious and torturously-recorded album on this list (not to mention being possibly the only record *ever* to feature a murderer and their victim playing alongside one another) and to this day, the definitive release by Metal's most controversial band, the story of **De Mysteriis** is the stuff of which even the heaviest of Metallers' nightmares are made. In fact, if we the cash, we'd be turning it into a movie ourselves. But for those of you who don't know the story already…

The first sessions for this titanic trove of terribleness actually date as far back as 1987, when Pelle Ohlin ('Dead') replaced second frontman Sven 'Maniac' Kristiansen and began writing new material with guitarist, self-publicist and all-round braggard Osytein

'Euronymous' Aarseth. To say that Dead was 'a bit odd', even by Black Metal standards, would be an understatement: he frequently cut himself onstage (OK, Iggy did that in '69 and Wendy O Williams in '79, but this was different) wore dead animals round his neck, carried actual carrion around with him, buried his clothes in the ground before performing, often starved himself for days to get malnutrition scars, designed and wore t-shirts announcing the funeral arrangements (cut from local newspapers) of local residents, slept with dead crows under his bed, and eventually took his own life at 22 by cutting *and* shooting (writing the most elaborate suicide note ever in the process) leaving only two live albums and a near-unlistenable demo, the latter recorded with his old band Morbid, by way of legacy. His death immediately split the still-nascent Norwegian black metal scene, mainly based around Aarseth's record shop Helvete, in two: after discovering that the guitarist (who lived with the vocalist and also found his body) had removed parts of Ohlin's skull before calling the police and made them into a necklace, fewer people in Oslo wanted anything to do with him, and this in turn may well have been a major part of the reason why he eventually enlisted Hungarian vocalist Csihar (ex-Tormentor) as a replacement. However, line-up changes would soon prove to be the very least of his problems…

In August 1993, bassist Varg 'Grisnackh' Vikernes, also known for his own work under the name of Burzum, travelled across suburban Oslo to Aarseth's flat, where he subsequently stabbed him to death: though a variety of explanations, ranging from rivalry and religious differences to self-defence, money and even homophobia, have been offered over the years, no cast-iron reason for this killing has ever been fully given, and even now, some ten years after Vikernes' parole, it's unlikely they ever will be. What is certain, however, is that it looked for a while likely to indefinitely hold up the release of the (by now thrice re-recorded) **De Mysteriis**: for obvious reasons, Aarseth's parents didn't really want the bass parts of their son's murderer to be audible on the album, and the concurrent spate of church burnings across the country didn't help matters either. Nevertheless, they do say there's no such thing as bad publicity, and, sure enough, in 1994, the utter masterpiece finally emerged in all its glory: taking the blueprint only hinted at in the band's **Deathcrush** and **Pure Fucking Armageddon** demos, but painting it across a far more expansive canvas, it may have disturbed people, but it most certainly didn't disappoint.

Though crude compared to what would follow on later releases, **Freezing Moon**, **Funeral Fog**, **Pagan Fears** and **From the Dark Past** are in many ways far closer to the fans' vision of 'The True Mayhem': the one rogue element is admittedly Csihar's deep, bone-rattling vocal, which sounds more akin to someone intoning through a bone-trumpet than the 'bird shriek' archetypally associated with the genre, but everything else - the rumbling blastbeats, the chilling icy riffs and yes, even Grisnackh's squalling basslines (which, despite repeated claims that he would, drummer Hellhammer never removed or re-recorded) - is Black Metal Incarnate. As the 21st century dawned, the band would eventually forsake Satanism for a more pantheistic obsession with war, chaos, apocalypse and human frailty, re-shaping their sound into a far proggier, if still outwardly sinister, direction: but **De Mysteriis Dom Sathanas** - not just a great Satanic record, but one of the greatest Metal albums period - remains as viscerally powerful today as 25 years ago. Practically every subsequent 'extreme metal' band, whether Satanic or not, has attempted to rip it off in some way, and even Mayhem themselves have never recorded anything quite so vicious since.

SABBATH ASSEMBLY - Quaternity (2014)

Their second album **Ye Are Gods** may have all the catchiest melodies, but of the six releases thus far from this Anglo-American occult collective, this is undoubtedly the most in keeping with the theme of this book. For those not in the know, Sabbath Assembly are the modern-day musical prophets of the Process Church Of The Final Judgment, formed in London in 1962 (the Church, not the band) by excommunicated Scientologists Robert De Grimston and Mary-Ann MacLean: it would be too easy to refer to them as 'Christian Satanists', but in essence, that's precisely what they are, believing, as did noted psychologist-philosopher Carl Jung, that the souls of all humans are comprised equally of four elements known as Jehovah (strength) Lucifer (light) Satan (separation) and Christ (unification) Moreover, only by understanding of which of these is reflected most in the individual's personality may one progress in life.

It's irrelevant whether we believe any of it, merely that the members of Sabbath Assembly do. And, judging from the footage I've seen, they do: unlike many other 'occult rock' acts, their doctrines are 100 per cent sincere and not intended for sensationalist effect. For one thing, their music's far too subtle: despite occasionally plunging into heavier waters in a live setting, they are not a metal band, nor do they sound remotely like Black Sabbath (Comus crossed with Pearls Before Swine, Affinity and a touch of Linda Perhacs is closer to it) and for another, their knowledge of their Church and its history displays a near-meticulousness only ever found in persons fully devoted to their aims. Plus, their promotional videos (usually derived from Seventies films even I haven't bloody heard of, which is saying something) are sublime. Every track on

this album is astounding, but esotericists should pay particular attention to the final trilogy of **I Satan**, **Lucifer** and **The Four Horsemen**.

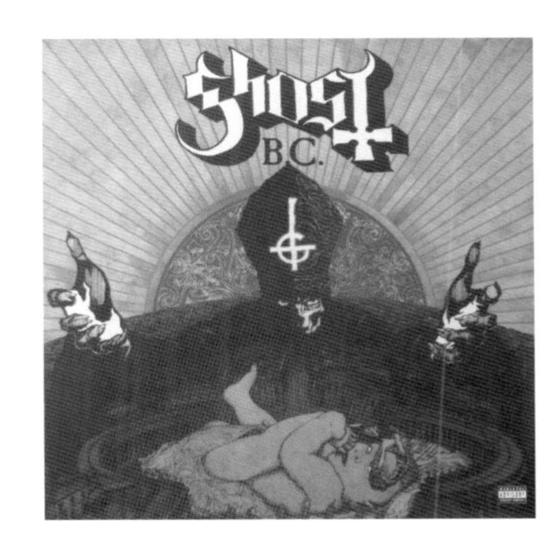

GHOST - Infestissumam (2015)

And so, finally, we reach the end - or is it? Are this Swedish shock-rock act, led by the mysterious Papa Emeritus, the genuine article, or a pack of camp old bollocks? Despite all their protestations towards being 'true devotees' of Thee Evil One, even to the point of dressing in alchemically-symbolic costumes deliberately designed to invert the principles of Catholicism towards Satanic worship, it's sometimes hard to take Ghost seriously: the fact that they also once claimed their frontman had been *"portrayed by a different vocalist on each release"* and refer to all other personnel as *"Nameless Ghouls"* does little to dissuade the more cynical rock listener from this assertion, especially when it's since been rumoured that one of them is Dave Grohl. Smoke and mirrors, dear boy, smoke and mirrors: surely, considering how long we've all been listening to Kiss, Alice Cooper, the Residents and even Slipknot, haven't we seen this *all* before?

On the other hand, they do make unbelievably fine records: underneath all the flim-flams and legedermain, the fact remains that Emeritus (since revealed, though unfortunately only due to a lawsuit, as plain old Tobias Forge) and his crew know how to craft instantly memorable pop-rock songs, and that, rather than any form of metal, is what they should truly be recognised for. Moreover, with each successive album relying less on chugging riffs and more on quirky keyboards, eerie melodies and Beatlesque harmonies, it looks like it's finally happening: the MIDI church organs, backing vocals and cod-Gregorian choruses are still there, but rather than being drenched in volume, they're part of a far more appealing and textured recipe.

Ultimately, whether they genuinely worship Satan or not is irrelevant: the simple fact remains that in this, the second decade of the 21st century, they have finally achieved what previous generations of bands found impossible and brought the occult and the Dark Arts fearlessly into the mainstream. True, it has provided them with more than a few headaches, particularly in the US bible belt, and they may yet, in the manner of their predecessors Simmons and Stanley, uncloak themselves to mass disappointment, but right now, their pallid masks are the most acceptable face Satanic rock has ever had. *And* they do Abba, Eurythmics, Bunnymen and even Roky Erickson covers. Raise thy horns aloft.

SATANIC SUPERSTARS

Carl Abrahamsson is a writer, filmmaker, musician and publisher specialising in material about the arts & entertainment, esoteric history and occulture.
www.patreon.com/vanessa23carl
www.carlabrahamsson.com
www.trapart.net

Sammm Agnew is a Freelance Special effects and Prosthetic Makeup Hair and Body Designer and Artist with 15 years working across Film,TV, Fashion, Music and Commercial fields.
She is a PGDip student of Humanistic Integrative Transpersonal Psychotherapy with a special interest in Existentialist philosophy, Jungian Alchemy and Archetypal theory. She is focused on the shared realms and frontiers of human experience.

Sarah Appleton is a writer/ producer at her production company Caprisar Productions Ltd. Follow her on Twitter @ sarahappleton_

Jason Atomic is a London based artist and curator with an obsession for cults and the occult. He is the founder of Satanic Mojo Comix & hosts regular life drawing sessions with his muse Manko & the Art Model Collective.
satanicmojo.blogspot.com/

Bruce Barnard is a father, writer and folklore enthusiast who lives on the same estate where the events in his article took place. He welcomes feedback on barnard. bruce@icloud.com

Gipsie Castiglione writes about perfume and lovely things. She can be found at instagram.com/spellboundlondon.

Billy Chainsaw leads a diverse life. Having spent countless but highly satisfying years as the Editor-in-Chief of porn mag **Club International** (US edition), and film editor of **Bizarre**, as well as writing for numerous publications including **Empire** and **Kerrang**), in 2012, he had an epiphany and 'chose art'.He has achieved acclaim for his Cut Up Pop Art, and experimental Cut Up movies… drawing on obsessions developed in his early teens, including American comic books, masks, the movies and magick; as well as cartoon surrealism, tattoos, Lucha Libre, and his metaphysical muse William S Burroughs.
www.koolkrakenincorporated.com

Simret Cheema-Innis is a film director, producer and model.
https://wickergirl.com/

The Church of Rational Satanism
http://www.churchofrationalsatanism.com/
https://www.facebook.com/CoRSmerch/

The Church of Satan
https://www.churchofsatan.com/
twitter.com/churchofsatan

Divine Interventions
www.divine-interventions.com

Darius Drewe divides his time between drinking real ale, collecting music and films, reviewing gigs, and writing about cinema and cult TV for very little money.

K.K. Eye
I can be dug up, creaky from rigor mortis, at my YouTube channel KK Eye. Come visit me there for videos on sigils, tarot, magick words, crystal balls and other techniques to manifest your desires. Also: jokes. My Instagram feed is kissesofthefemmefatale, so please go there to see photos of me wearing the fuck out of red lipstick and black vintage dresses. You will also have to read jokes about necrophilia.
See you soon!

Ilya Falchevsky is a Russian photographer and artist, now based in London.

David Flint is the editor and publisher of **The Reprobate** and related publications such as this. In a previous life, he brought you such delightful publications as **Sheer Filth**, **Headpress**, **Divinity** and **Sexadelic**, and was once a prolific writer for the sort of magazines where no one read the words.

A.D. Hitchin is a writer and editor whose work spans both the commercial and the counterculture. You can follow his continuing adventures here:
https://www.facebook.com/A.D.Hitchin
https://twitter.com/adhitchin
http://adhitchin.tumblr.com/

Daz Lawrence
Half a lifetime of writing about music has left him able to write in complete darkness, in pudles of a wide variety of beverages, surrounded by idiots. Wrote for the seminal **Here Be Monsters**'zine for ten years, then subsequently interfered on several publications and websites, sometimes after being asked. Staunchly left-handed. Blisteringly negative.

C.J. Lines has written two excellent books, a lot of fascinating articles, and several thousand pointless tweets. Follow him on Twitter (@cjlines) to learn more about all of these things.

Logospilgrim is a writer, a coconut atheist, and a gonzo maverick. She's genderqueer, asexual, bi-romantic. These days, she writes mostly about joyful secular living and being a happy introvert tomboy. She has a degree in Religious Studies and a large toy collection. She's learning to play the ukulele, and she can juggle. She loves the 70s, making macramé, and drinking Jack Daniel's. She's also known as the quiet professor. She's the author of **Rascal: A Manifesto,** among other fiendish titles.
www.logospilgrim.com

Lydia Lunch is a musician, performer, filmmaker and art-terrorist.If you are unfamiliar with her work, you are probably reading the wrong book.
https://www.facebook.com/LydiaLunch/
www.lydia-lunch.net

Groovie Mann is the founding member of My Life with the Thrill Kill Kult.
https://www.facebook.com/larrabee.reed
https://www.facebook.com/thrillkillkult//

David McGillivray's strange career has included everything from horror to panto. But sex and censorship has remained a constant, e.g. the book **Doing Rude Things**, the film **Trouser Bar**.
https://www.facebook.com/trouserbar/

Keri O'Shea runs and writes for the film and culture site **Warped Perspective** (http://warped-perspective.com/) whilst dividing the rest of her time between lurid cinema, scandalous history, heavy metal and good beer. You may follow her on Twitter: @Hellbound_Heart

The Partridge Family Temple
PFT! FREAKS UNITE
Who are you? Where are you?
How are you?
Send us your name and email address and we'll keep you un-informed
Official website:
http://www.thepartridgefamilytemple.org/albuquerque/
Facebook: https://www.facebook.com/ThePartridgeFamilyTempleScene/
Twitter: https://twitter.com/partridgetemple
Tumblr: https://thepartridgefamilytemple.tumblr.com
Wale Song Partridge
Inhstagram: whalesongpartridge
https://www.facebook.com/AnneFrankYogoStudio/

Boyd Rice is a musician, writer and all-round creative genius.
http://boydriceofficial.bigcartel.com/

The Satanic Temple
https://thesatanictemple.com/

Nikolas Schreck is a musician, singer-songwriter, author and film-maker based in Berlin.
www.nikolasschreck.eu Instagram: Nikolas Schreck (Official) Facebook: Nikolas Schreck (Official)

Tom Six is the man who brought you the **Human Centipede** films. His new project is **The Onania Club**, which he assures us will make grown men cry.
https://www.sixentertainmentcompany.com/tom-six

Ben Spurling is little more than a horror snob who does *not* believe bad horror is better than no horror. When he's not writing, he's reading everything from philosophy to theological analysis to the better horror and mainstream fiction. But his real spark comes from discovering forgotten words, discarded idioms, and original ways to repurpose commonly dulled vocabulary. If you're brave enough, he can currently be reached via the kind gentlemen at horrorpedia.com and reprobatemagazine.uk.

Nigel Wingrove is the managing director of Salvation Films, the creator of the Redemption Films label and the blog Scum Nation. His films include the long-banned **Visions of Ecstasy** and **Sacred Flesh**.
http://www.nigelwingrove.com/
https://www.salvation-films.com/

That's all Folks!
10¢
MAKES
2 QUARTS